IMAGES
of Rail

ELGIN, JOLIET AND EASTERN RAILWAY

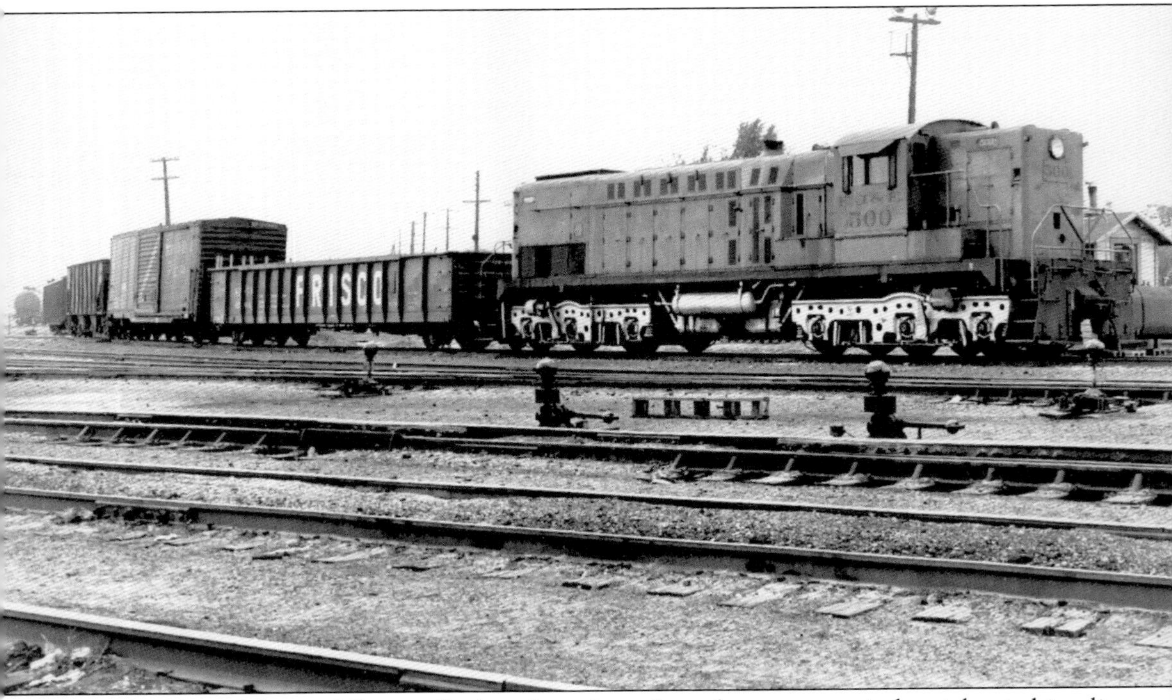

The Elgin, Joliet and Eastern Railway has always been known as an industrial switching line and a bridge carrier for freight traveling between railroads in the Chicago area. This was a typical scene of the duties it has performed for about the last 120 years: providing fast and efficient freight service for its industrial customers and other railroads. In June 1971, No. 500 was switching cars at the East Joliet yard. (Bill Raia collection.)

On the cover: In the spring of 1964, Elgin, Joliet and Eastern Railway train No. 43 had just completed its switching duties at the interchange with the Illinois Central in Matteson. It was preparing to resume its westbound journey between Gary (Kirk Yard) and East Joliet. (J-Milepost June 1964.)

IMAGES
of Rail

Elgin, Joliet and Eastern Railway

Paul W. Jaenicke and Ralph A. Eisenbrandt

ARCADIA PUBLISHING

ISBN 978-0-7385-5057-2

Published by Arcadia Publishing
Charleston, South Carolina

Printed in the United States of America

Library of Congress Catalog Card Number: 2007924179

For all general information contact Arcadia Publishing at:
Telephone 843-853-2070
Fax 843-853-0044
E-mail sales@arcadiapublishing.com
For customer service and orders:
Toll-Free 1-888-313-2665

Visit us on the Internet at www.arcadiapublishing.com

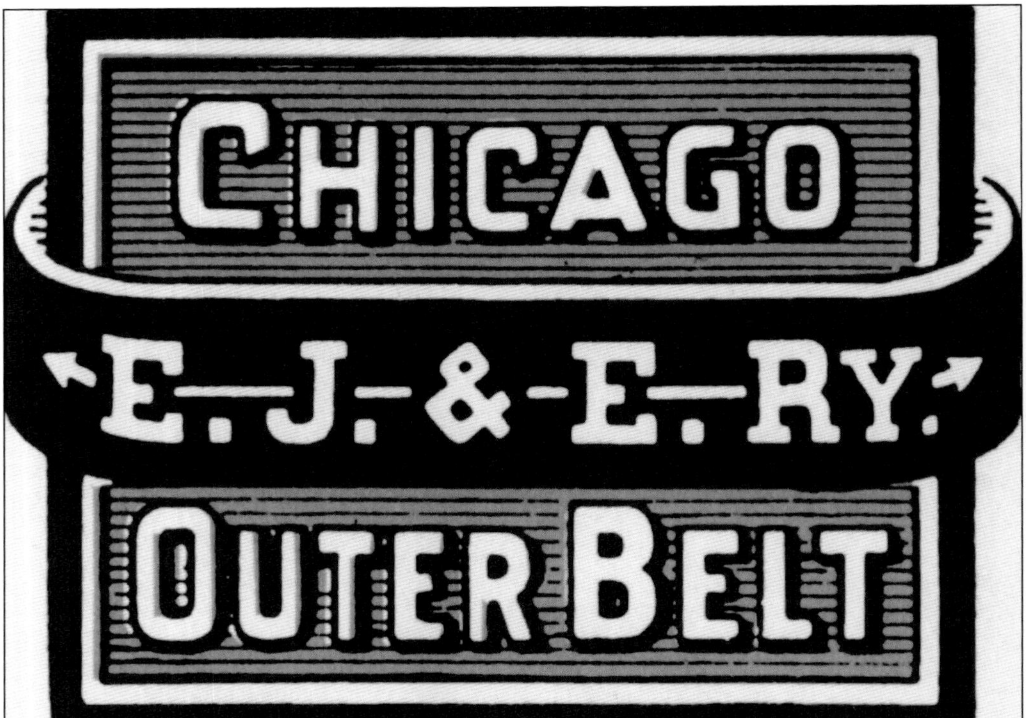

The EJ&E used the "Chicago Outer Belt Line" logo in various forms from around 1900 right up until the mid-1970s. It was an enduring symbol for a railroad that prided itself in expediting freight traffic around the Chicago area, along with serving the steel industry to the south of the city. Over the years, the railroad boasted of connecting with more than 30 different railroads entering the Chicago area.

Contents

ACKNOWLEDGMENTS

The following people have provided photographs and/or information about the Elgin, Joliet and Eastern Railway (EJ&E), also known as the "J", which made this book possible: EJ&E people Willard "Buzz" Carey, Gerald "Barney" Craig, Robert Hamma, Gordon Holmquist, and Robert K. Miller, and the late R. J. Shiek, R. J. Benson, Norma Benson, and Howard Lenhardt. Also noted railroad photographers Paul Meyer and Bill Raia, and railroader Mark Stanek have proven invaluable.

The following are also acknowledged for their excellent records and information about the EJ&E: the J-Milepost, Diesel Era Magazine, Chicago Heights Public Library, Frankfort Public Library, Joliet Area Historical Society, Joliet Public Library, Plainfield Historical Society, and the EJ&E archives Web site.

Appreciation is also expressed to AnnKaryn Bettenhausen for her assistance in the preparation of the text.

Introduction

The Joliet and Northern Indiana Railroad was conceived by Joliet businessmen as a way to avoid the congestion and delay of transferring freight via Chicago. Upon its completion, the Michigan Central Railroad leased the Joliet and Northern Indiana Railroad and service was implemented in July 1855. The line quickly became known as the Joliet Cut-Off Railroad.

In 1873, Jacob Henry and friends of Joliet proposed the building of the Joliet and Valparaiso Railway. Their idea was to add another route to the east by connecting with the Pittsburgh, Fort Wayne, and Chicago Railroad at Valparaiso, Indiana. The company was capitalized at $1 million, and by 1876, some portions of the right-of-way had been secured. The project was never finished, quite likely because the capital would have been insufficient to build its 54-mile line across the difficult terrain of Lake and Porter Counties in Indiana.

The Joliet, Aurora, and Northern Railroad was chartered in 1886. At that time, Aurora businessmen were driving wagon teams to Joliet so they could ship their products to eastern markets on the Joliet Cut-Off Railroad, thus avoiding the congestion and delays in Chicago. Also, the Joliet Cut-Off Railroad offered the same rates from Joliet as other railroads did via Chicago. Strangely there was opposition to the building of the railroad by the teamsters of Plainfield, who felt their jobs were threatened. The Joliet, Aurora, and Northern Railroad started operations on August 15, 1886.

What then led to the organizing of the EJ&E Railway? By 1880, the Michigan Central; the Chicago and Alton; the Chicago, Rock Island, and Pacific; and the Santa Fe Railroads were all saturated with traffic, generated both locally and long distance. With the building of new mills, it became apparent that another railroad would be a great advantage.

In April 1888, the Joliet, Aurora, and Northern Railroad line was sold to a newly formed EJ&E Railway, which intended to build a line from Valparaiso to Joliet, then on to the Milwaukee Railroad near Elgin. Officially EJ&E operations began on January 1, 1889. The EJ&E soon acquired two more important links, the Gardner, Coal City, and Northern Railroad (the portion remaining today is known as the "Illinois River line") from Coster to Walker, near Plainfield and the Waukegan and Southwestern Railroad, which had been under construction from Waukegan toward Elgin.

The EJ&E never reached Valparaiso but instead terminated its eastern end at Porter, Indiana, in 1893. Two more line segments along the Lake Michigan lakefront were built in 1896–1897 as the Calumet and Blue Island, and the Chicago, Lake Shore, and Eastern Railroad. The Griffith and Northern was a separate segment started in 1899 connecting the then main line with the Lake Michigan lakefront at what would become Gary. A final acquisition in 1905 was the Rockdale, Joliet, and Lockport Railway.

When all acquisitions and connections were complete, the EJ&E operated the following subdivisions and branches: The west end of the EJ&E main line was the single-track western subdivision, and it extended from Waukegan to Joliet. The Aurora Branch ran 9.55 miles from Normantown to Aurora; the double track from Joliet to Kirk Yard was the eastern subdivision; the single-track line from Griffith to Porter was the 20.50-miles-long Porter Branch. The single track Rockdale Branch ran 6.46 miles from Rockdale Junction (western subdivision milepost J3.46) to Rockdale; and the single track Gardner, Coal City and Northern (GCC&N) ran south for about 30 miles from Walker (western subdivision milepost J9.90) to South Wilmington. By 1965, this line had been cut back to branch milepost 19.56. The line from Kirk Yard to South Chicago was 12.37 miles of double track. The EJ&E also operated numerous other industrial lines or branches. The Aurora and the Porter branches have been abandoned and removed. Service on the Rockdale line has also been abandoned.

The EJ&E claims several firsts in railroading. It was one of the first to install continuous butt-welded rail in main line service, and, for a time, had the longest installation anywhere in the world, between Joliet and Plainfield. The EJ&E track structure and maintenance has always been first class. The EJ&E was one of the first class 1 railroads (at that time) to be completely dieselized (1949). It was the first to install a wheel-truing machine that could be used, without removing the wheels, to recontour locomotive or car wheels.

Kirk Yard in Gary became, in 1952, the first automatic, electrically operated car retarder yard in the world. In 1963, the EJ&E was the first railroad to install a mechanized car repair billing system. It was also the first line haul railroad in its class to earn, by 1963, the Railroad Employees National Safety Award three years in a row.

This book is a look at the EJ&E through the years. It is not meant to be an in-depth corporate history, nor is it meant to be a book filled with rosters, photographs of every single locomotive, or a chronological covering of every event that ever happened along the railroad. It is a view of the EJ&E as an outstanding example of railroading, its facilities and equipment, and last but not least, the employees and their families.

One

The Early Days

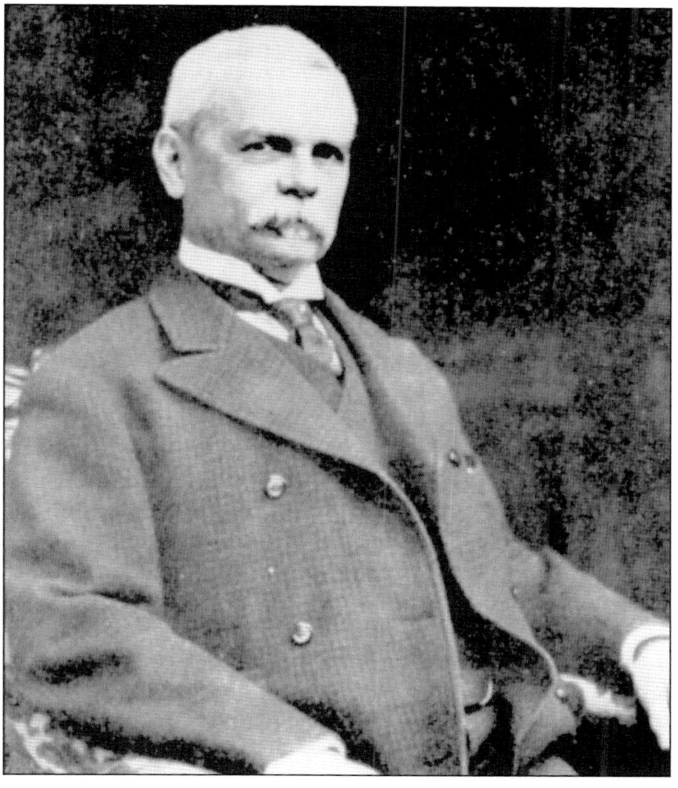

Samuel Spencer, a Georgian born in 1844 and former Confederate army soldier, is considered the first president of the Elgin, Joliet and Eastern Railway (EJ&E), also nicknamed the "J". His service lasted from 1889 to 1899. His major accomplishments appear to be guiding the company in its formative years and managing early financial dealings and preparing to bring the various predecessor lines into the EJ&E. His office was in New York City, where he also served as the president of the Southern Railway. The early town of Spencer, in New Lenox Township, was not named for him. The small village was platted as a way station on the Joliet Cut-Off Railroad in 1855 by Nelson D. Elwood and Sherman W. Bowen of Joliet.

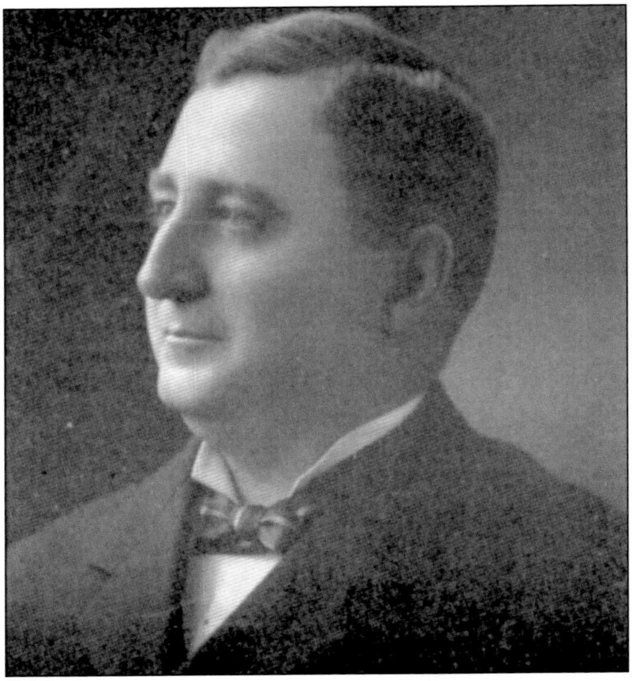

Charles Ackert was listed as president of the railroad from 1899 to 1901. He was general manager for 10 years and succeeded Samuel Spencer. His efforts resulted in bringing to the EJ&E many of the early, leading management people of the railroad. Ackert established the first *J-Picnic* in 1898.

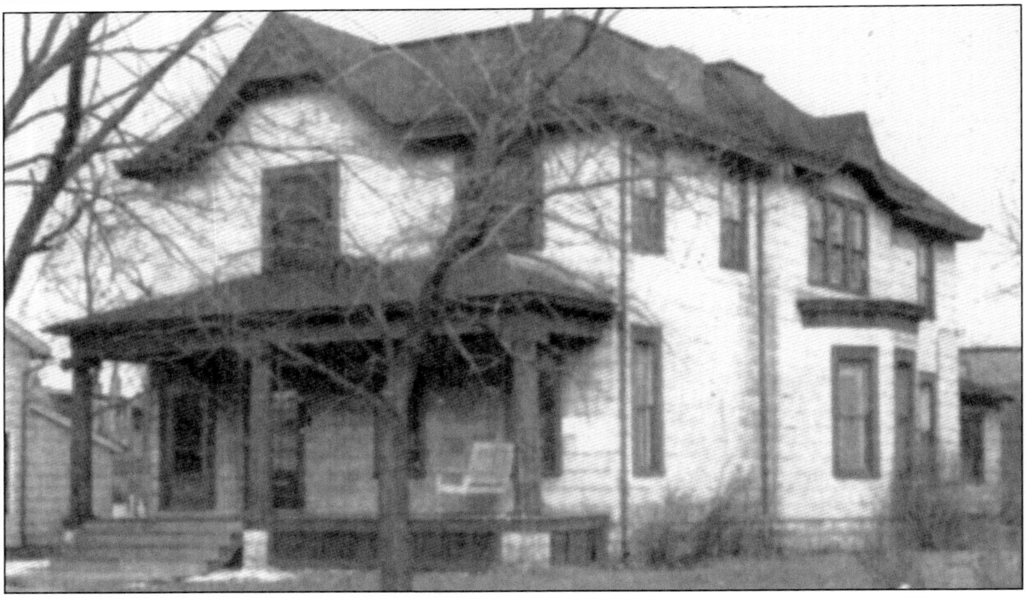

EJ&E predecessor Joliet, Aurora, and Northern Railway was organized in this house at 108 Eastern Avenue, Joliet, on March 22, 1884. The railway company filed incorporation papers on April 30, 1884. The company was capitalized at $2 million. The intention was to build the railroad west from the Indiana/Illinois state line westward across Illinois to the east bank of the Mississippi River opposite Dubuque. Only the line between Joliet and Aurora was actually constructed. All property of the Joliet, Aurora, and Northern Railway was sold in 1888 to a new company, the EJ&E. The EJ&E then put together a line from Spaulding, near Elgin, through Joliet, eventually reaching Porter and Gary, Indiana.

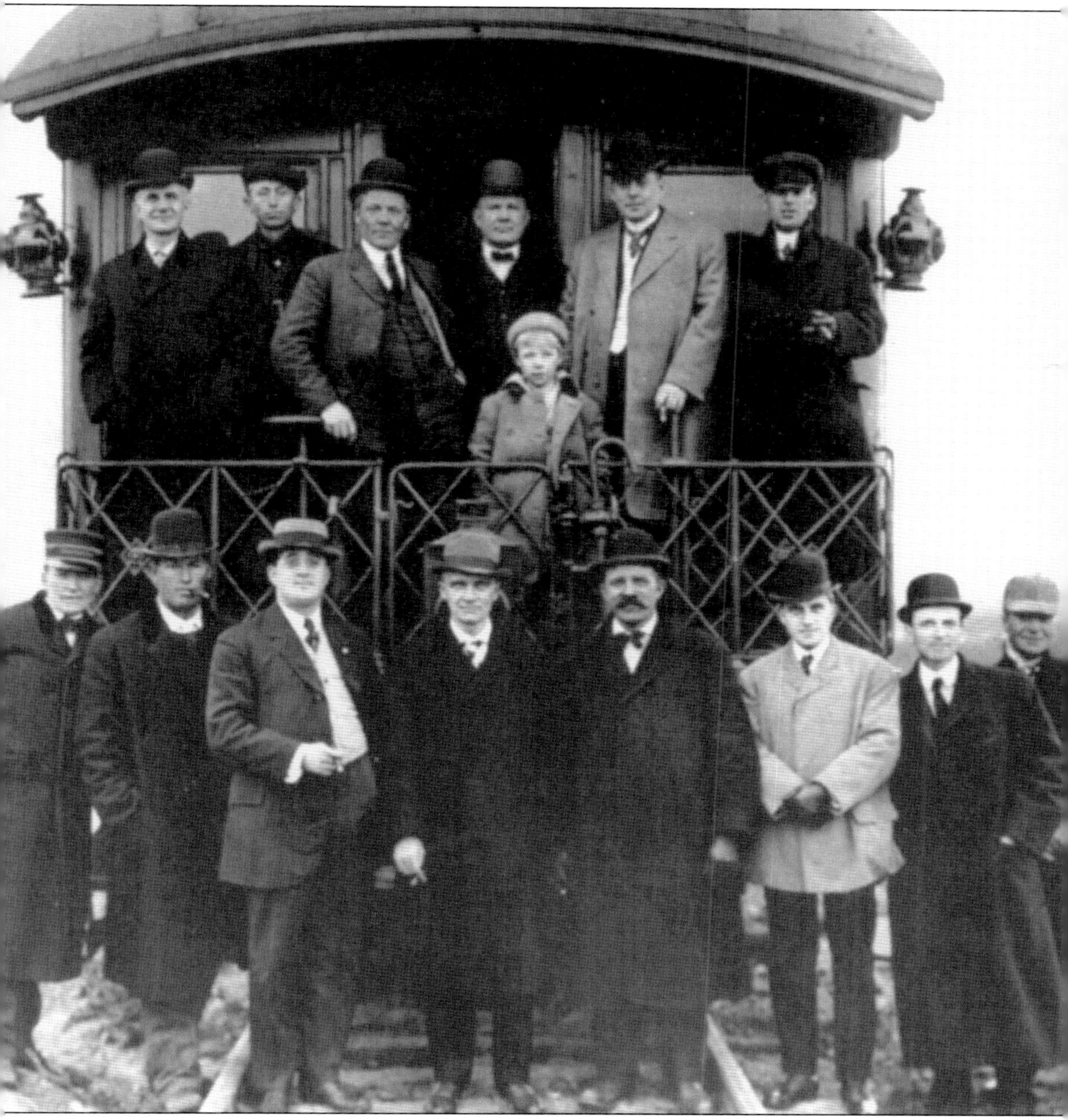

It was a cold November 15, 1908, when these men gathered to ride the inspection car *Buffington* between Griffith and Kirk Yard. The EJ&E had just completed a new elevation to carry its tracks over the busy lines of the Pennsylvania, the Wabash, the Baltimore and Ohio, and the New York Central Railroads and a couple of highways. The young boy pictured is Jack Kirk Jr., son of John Kirk, for whom Kirk Yard was named.

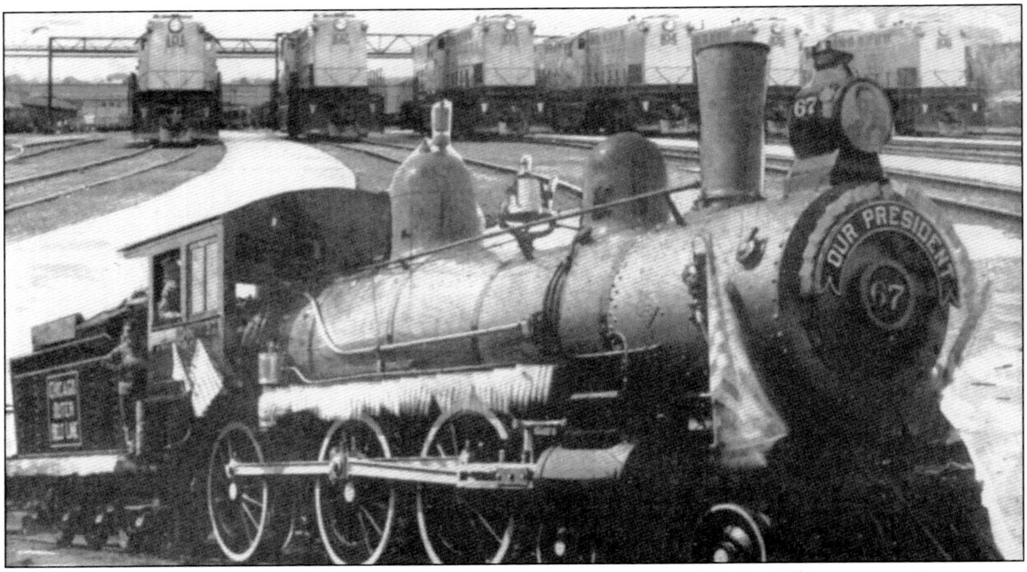

A montage shows a proud lineup of new diesel locomotives at the top. The new engines soon helped the "J" end its dependence on steam locomotives. Pres. Theodore Roosevelt's special train ran from Aurora to Joliet in 1903 covering 22 miles in 22 minutes, but the true story was rarely told. Departure from Aurora was delayed because Jolietian Col. John Lambert wanted his private car added to the train. President Roosevelt ordered the car off the train. The engineer ran at 60 miles per hour and reached downtown Joliet a few minutes past 3:00 p.m. The special left Joliet on the Chicago and Alton Railroad en route to Bloomington.

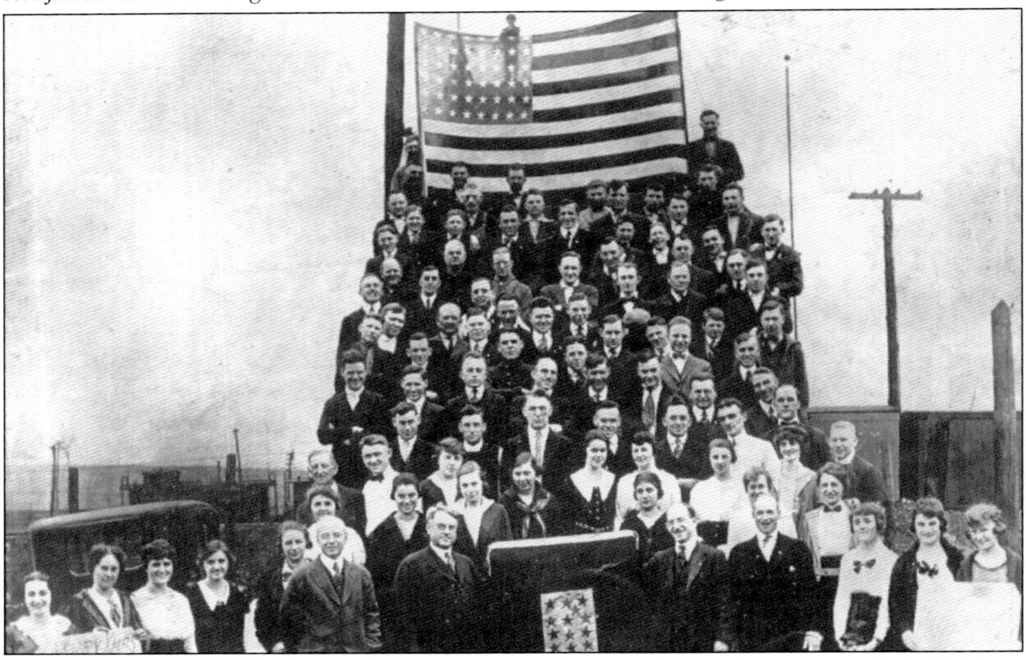

The East Joliet Agents Office and Freight Transfer House workers gathered in the fall of 1917 for a patriotic display of the flag. The message held by the two women at the lower left reads, "Merry Xmas to our boys," and "EJ&E Happy Family."

ELGIN, JOLIET & EASTERN RAILWAY. 471

C. H. ACKERT, President and General Manager, Chicago, Ill.
R. A. DUGAN, Assistant General Manager, Joliet, Ill.
A. F. BANKS, Traffic Manager, Chicago, Ill.
F. E. LEARNED, Assistant Traffic Manager, "
F. D. RAYMOND, Secretary and Treasurer, "
K. K. KNAPP, General Counsel, 130 La Salle Street, "

W. D. HAYNIE, Attorney, Chicago, Ill.
F. W. SUTTON, Auditor, "
C. S. McMANUS, General Superintendent, Joliet, Ill.
C. C. HILL, Chief Engineer, "
JOHN HORRIGAN, Master Mechanic,
General Offices—"The Rookery," Chicago, Ill.

20	14	22	12	18	Mls	*January* 8, 1899.	Mls	7	11	17	19	21
	P M		A M			LVE.] *Central time.* [ARR.		P M	P M	P M		
	*3 00		†7 00		0	**Waukegan**	130	5 30	8 30	10 15		
	5 00		8 20		8	**Rondout**	122	6 00	8 00	9 55		
	5 20		8 40		13	**Leithton**	117	4 20	7 25	9 30		
	6 10		9 50		20	Lake Zurich	110	3 50	6 55	9 05		
	6 30		10 10		24	**Barrington**	106	3 15	6 30	8 45		
	7 00		10 40		29	Clark's	101	2 40	5 40	8 05		
	7 45		11 05		35	arr. **Spaulding** lve.	95	2 15	5 15	7 45		
	7 45		12 25		35	lve. **Spaulding** arr.	95	1 15	4 05	7 00		
	8 05		12 45		39	Wayne	91	12 45	3 45	6 30		
	8 15		1 10		42	**Ingalton**	88	12 01	3 30	6 10		
	8 25		1 45		44	**West Chicago**	86	11 30	3 20	6 00		
	8 45		2 05		48	Warrenhurst	82	10 55	3 00	5 35		
	9 10		2 30		54	Frontenac	76	10 25	2 30	5 05		
	9 30		3 30		60	**Normantown**	70	9 45	2 00	4 44		
	9 40		4 20		63	**Walker**	67	9 18	1 30	4 20		
	9 45		4 25		64	Plainfield	66	8 40	1 25	4 15		
	10 05		4 45		68	Coynes	62	8 25	1 00	4 00		
A M	10 30	P M	5 00	A M	73	arr. **East Joliet** lve.	57	†8 00	*12 30	3 45	P M	P M
†8 00	P M	†4 30	P M	*2 00	73	lve. **East Joliet** arr.	57	A M	Noon	1 00	4 00	7 45
8 40		5 10		2 40	81	**Brisbane**	49			12 30	3 20	7 15
9 05		5 30		3 05	87	**Frankfort**	43			12 15	3 00	6 55
9 35		5 50		3 25	94	**Matteson**	36			11 50	2 40	6 30
9 45		6 05		3 50	98	**Chicago Heights**	32			11 40	†2 15	†6 15
A M		P M		4 45	104	**Dyer**	26			11 00	P M	P M
				5 05	107	**Hartsdale**	23			10 35		
				5 40	109	**Griffith**	21	*		10 15		
				6 35	119	**Hobart**	11			9 15		
				7 05	125	**McCool**	5			8 25		
4	2			7 10	127	**Crocker**	3	1		8 05	3	
P M	A M			7 20	130	arr. **Porter** lve.	0	A M		*7 50	P M	
†4 20	†7 10			A M	0	lve. **Aurora** arr.	24	10 00		A M	7 10	
4 25	7 15				2	East Aurora	22	9 55			7 05	
4 35	7 24				7	Wolf's	17	9 40			6 52	
4 44	7 32				10	**Normantown**	14	9 32			6 42	
4 50	7 40				12	**Walker**	12	9 18			6 35	
4 53	7 42				13	Plainfield	11	9 15			6 30	
5 10	8 00				23	East Joliet	1	8 35			5 55	
5 25	8 10				24	**Joliet**	0	†8 20			†5 40	
P M	A M					ARRIVE] [LEAVE		A M			P M	

☞ This is a belt road for the transfer of through freight, and does passenger business between the stations indicated.

	Mls	STATIONS.	Mls
No passenger service.		LEAVE] [ARRIVE	
	0	**Walker**	32
	1	Plainfield	31
	4	Caton Farm	28
	12	**Minooka**	20
	18	Divine	14
	21	Dell Abbey	11
	24	Carbon Hill	8
	26	**Coal City**	6
	27	Centerville	5
	30	**Mazonia**	2
	32	arr. **Coster** lve.	0

* Daily; † daily, except Sunday.

CONNECTIONS.

Aurora—With Chicago, Burlington & Quincy R.R.
Barrington—With Chicago & North-western Ry.
Brisbane—With Wabash R.R.
Chicago Heights—With Chicago & Eastern Illinois R.R.
Coal City—With Atchison, Topeka & Santa Fe Ry.
Coster—With Cleveland, Cincinnati, Chic. & St. Louis Ry.
Crocker—With Wabash R.R.
Dyer—With Chicago, Indianapolis & Louisville Ry.
Griffith—With Grand Trunk Ry. and Erie R.R.
Hartsdale—With Pittsburg, Cincin. Chic. & St. Louis Ry.
Hobart—With Pittsburg, Ft. Wayne & Chicago Ry. (Penna. Co.) and New York, Chicago & St. Louis R.R.
Ingalton—With Chicago Great Western Ry.
Joliet—With Chicago & Alton and Chicago, Rock Island & Pacific Rys.; A. T. & Santa Fe Ry. and Mich. Cent. R.R.
Leithton—With Wisconsin Central Ry.
Matteson—With Illinois Central R.R.
Mazonia—With Chicago & Alton Ry.
Minooka—With Chicago, Rock Island & Pacific Ry.
McCool—With Baltimore & Ohio R.R.
Porter—With Lake Shore & Michigan Southern Ry.
Rondout—With Chicago, Milwaukee & St. Paul Ry.
Spaulding—With Chicago, Milwaukee & St. Paul Ry.
Waukegan—With Chicago & North-western Ry.
West Chicago—With Chicago & North-western Ry.

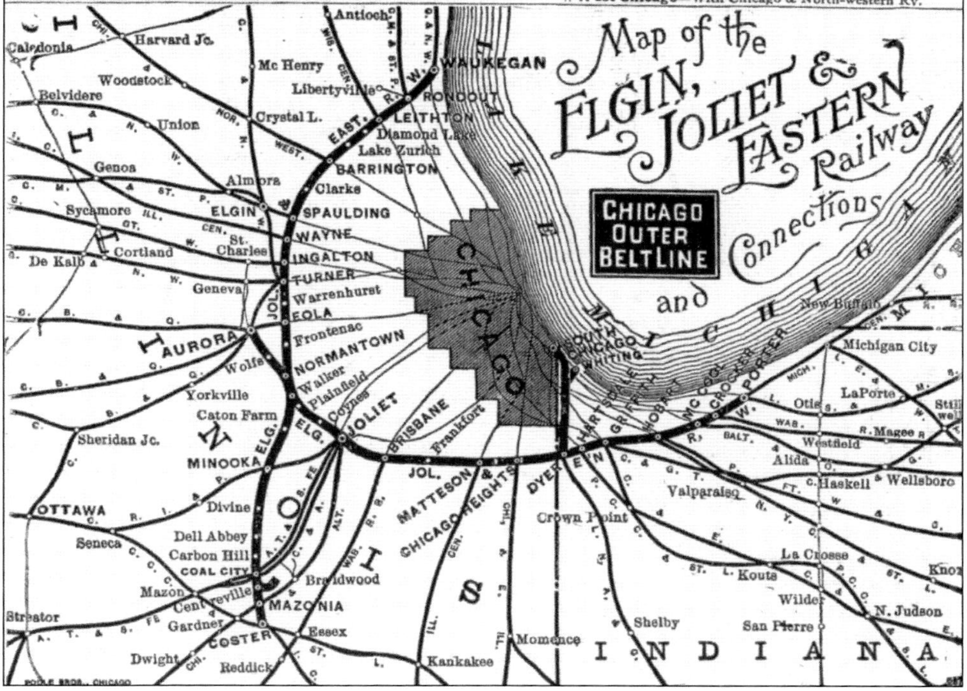

Up until 1907, the EJ&E offered regular passenger train service over its Waukegan to Porter main line. The Official Railway Guide for March 1909 shows how extensive the passenger service was. It took approximately six and a half hours to travel the 47 miles between East Joliet and Porter. One interesting note that appears in the middle of the page indicates, "This is a belt road for the transfer of through freight, and does passenger business between the stations indicated."

ELGIN, JOLIET & EASTERN RAILWAY.

695

A. F. BANKS, President, Chicago, Ill.
S. M. ROGERS, Vice-President, "
F. E. LEARNED, Traffic Manager, "
W. K. ALLEN, Secretary and Treasurer, "
F. L. KOONTZ, Assistant Secretary and Treasurer, "
C. H. KENZEL, Assistant Purchasing Agent, "
H. M. DE GETTE, Freight Claim Agent, "
F. W. SUTTON, Auditor, "
K. K. KNAPP, General Counsel, "
R. W. CAMPBELL, Attorney. "

P. F. McMANUS, Superintendent, Joliet, Ill.
J. KIRK, Superintendent Terminals, Gary, Ind.
C. H. DORLEY, Assistant Supt. Terminals, South Chicago, Ill.
GEO. S. ATTERBURY, General Agent, Com'l Nat'l Bank Bldg, Chicago, Ill.
G. A. COMSTOCK, Traveling Freight Agent, " "
W. J. DIBBLE, Traveling Freight Agent, " "
A. MONTZHEIMER, Chief Engineer, Joliet, Ill.
JOHN HORRIGAN, Superintendent of Motive Power, "
G. C. McNALLY, Superintendent of Car Service, "
General Offices– Commercial Nat'l Bank Bldg, Chicago, Ill.

JOLIET DIVISION.

Freight Service Only.

Extra trains will be run as volume of traffic demands.

12	10	6	4	Mls	*June 1, 1909.*	5	11	15	9
P M	P M	A M	A M		LEAVE] [ARRIVE	P M	P M	A M	
*6 00	*2 00	*7 00	*4 00	0	**Waukegan** ♁	7 15	11 50	4 00	
8 15	2 15	7 15	4 15	3.63	North Chicago	6 50	11 25	3 25	
8 25	2 25	8 15	4 25	6.00	Upton	6 40	11 10	3 10	
10 30	4 00	9 20	6 30	7.51	**Rondout** ♁	6 30	11 00	3 00	
10 50	4 25	9 45	6 55	12.82	**Leithton** ♁	5 50	10 10	2 10	
11 00	4 35	9 55	7 05	14.29	Diamond Lake	5 35	9 50	1 55	
11 10	4 50	10 05	7 15	16.24	Gilmer ♁	5 27	9 42	1 45	
11 30	5 15	10 20	7 30	19.88	Lake Zurich ♁	5 15	9 30	1 35	
11 50	5 30	10 45	7 45	23.80	**Barrington** ♁	4 45	9 10	1 20	
12 10	5 50	10 55	8 05	29.35	Sutton ♁	4 15	8 40	12 45	A M
12 45	6 25	1 25	8 35	35.47	**Spaulding** ♁	3 55	8 15	12 25	7 45
12 55	6 35	1 35	8 45	37.95	Munger	2 40	7 05	11 20	7 35
1 10	6 50	11 45	8 55	39.38	**Wayne** ♁	2 30	6 50	11 10	7 25
1 30	7 05	11 50	9 00	42.14	**Ingalton** ♁	2 20	6 35	11 00	7 15
1 55	7 30	12 15	9 20	43.87	**West Chicago** ♁	1 40	5 20	10 05	6 35
2 20	7 45	12 25	9 32	48.46	Warrenhurst ♁	1 25	4 55	9 45	6 15
— —	— —	— —	— —	50.43	Electric Junction	— —	— —	— —	— —
2 35	8 05	12 45	9 50	54.35	Frontenac ♁	1 00	4 35	9 25	5 55
2 55	8 25	1 00	10 10	60.23	**Normantown** ♁	12 15	4 10	9 00	5 25
3 05	8 40	1 10	10 20	63.13	**Walker** ♁	11 55	3 50	8 40	5 00
3 07	8 42	1 12	10 22	63.66	Plainfield ♁	11 45	3 40	8 15	4 30
3 20	9 00	1 25	10 35	66.09	Coynes ♁	11 30	3 25	8 00	4 15
3 25	9 05	1 30	10 40	69.71	**Rockdale Junc.** ♁	11 20	3 20	7 55	4 05
				73.31	**Rockdale**				
6 30	12 15	6 00	3 00	73.09	**East Joliet** ♁	11 00	5 00	7 50	3 45
7 05	12 40	6 25	3 55	81.31	**Brisbane** ♁	6 35	11 35	3 30	2 00
7 30	1 10	6 55	4 15	87.12	**Frankfort** ♁	6 15	11 15	3 10	1 40
7 40	1 20	7 05	4 23	91.51	Learned ♁	6 00	11 00	2 45	1 20
7 50	1 30	7 15	4 30	94.65	**Matteson** ♁	5 45	10 45	2 30	1 05
8 05	1 40	7 35	4 40	98.23	**Chicago Heights** ♁	5 30	10 30	2 10	12 45
8 40	2 25	8 15	5 15	104.37	**Dyer** ♁	5 00	10 00	1 40	12 10
9 00	2 45	8 40	5 35	106.89	**Hartsdale** ♁	4 50	9 50	1 20	11 45
9 30	3 35	9 15	6 15	109.31	**Griffith** ♁	4 40	9 30	12 50	11 15
10 20	4 45	10 15	7 16	118.46	**Hobart** ♁	*4 10	8 50	*11 50	10 15
A M	5 15	10 40	7 35	125.19	**McCool** ♁	A M	8 25	A M	9 50
	5 35	10 50	7 45	126.58	**Crocker** ♁		8 00		9 15
	6 00	11 10	8 00	129.80	**Porter** ♁		*7 30		*8 45
	A M	P M	P M		ARRIVE] [LEAVE		A M		P M

GARY DIVISION.

				Mls.	*June 1, 1909.*				
				0	lv. **South Chicago** ar.				
				1.10	100th Street Yard				
				4.13	Whiting (Lake Front)				
				7.33	**Indiana Harbor**				
	Freight			9.01	**Buffington**		Freight		
				10.04	Stockton				
	Service			10.89	Kirk Yard		Service		
	only.			13.78	**Gary**		only.		
				0	**South Chicago**				
				10.89	Kirk Yard				
				10.99	Pine				
				12.39	Clarke				
				12.75	**Curtis**				
				13.48	arr. **Cavanaugh** lve.				

CONNECTIONS.

A. E. & C. Ry ....At Electric Junction and Wayne, Ill.
A. T. & S. F. Ry............At Joliet, Ill.
B. & O. R.R............At McCool and Curtis, Ind.
Belt Ry............At South Chicago, Ill., and 98th Street.
C. C. & L. R.R............At Griffith, Ind.
C. & A. R.R............At Joliet, Ill.
C. & E. I. R.R............At Chicago Heights, Ill.
C. B. & Q. R.R............At Aurora, Ill.
C. & N. W. Ry............At West Chicago, Barrington, Upton and Waukegan, Ill.
C. G. W. Ry............At Ingalton, Ill.
C. I. & L. Ry............At Dyer, Ind.
C. M. & St. P. Ry............At Spaulding and Rondout, Ill.
C. M. & G. Ry............At Joliet and Aurora, Ill.
C. R. I. & P. Ry............At Joliet and Minooka, Ill.
C. T. T. Ry............At Whiting and Hammond, Ind.
C. C. C. & St. L. Ry............At Coster, Ill.
Erie R.R............At Griffith, Ind.
Grand Trunk Ry. System ..At Griffith, Ind.
Illinois Central R.R............At Matteson and Munger, Ill.
Indiana Harbor R.R............At Hammond and Indiana Harbor, Ind.
L. S. & M. S. Ry............At Porter and Pine, Ind.
M. C. R.R............At Hartsdale, Ind., and Joliet, Ill.
M. St. P. & Slt. Ste. M. Ry..At Leithton, Ill.
N. Y. C. & St. L. Ry....... At Hobart, Ind.
P. Ft. W. & C. Ry............At Hobart and Clarke, Ind.
P. C. C. & St. L. Ry............At Hartsdale, Ind.
P. M. R.R ....At Porter, Ind.
Wabash R.R............At Crocker, Ind., and Brisbane, Ill.

JOLIET DIVISION.

AURORA AND JOLIET.

Fht.	54	50	Mls.	*June 1, 1909*	Fht.	55	57
	P M	A M		LEAVE] [ARRIVE		P M	P M
	†3 00	†7 45	0	**Aurora** ♁		1 25	7 40
P M	3 05	7 50	.94	Aurora Junction ♁	A M	1 20	7 35
*4 00	3 10	8 15	1.72	East Aurora ♁	10 25	1 00	7 15
4 30	3 25	8 30	6.42	Wolfs ♁	10 05	12 35	6 55
4 45	3 35	8 45	0.63	Normantown ♁	9 45	12 25	6 40
8 30	4 25	9 45		**East Joliet** ♁	*8 00	†11 10	†5 25
P M	P M	A M		ARRIVE] [LEAVE	A M	A M	P M

Extra trains will be run as volume of traffic demands.

WALKER AND SOUTH WILMINGTON.—Freight Service Only.

72	70	Mls.	*June 1, 1909.*	71	73
P M	A M		LEAVE] [ARRIVE	P M	P M
*8 25	¶5 30	0	**Walker** ♁	2 00	10 50
8 35	5 50	4.27	Caton Farm ♁	1 45	10 35
8 50	6 15	11.64	Minooka ♁	1 20	10 00
9 05	6 40	17.81	Divine ♁	12 20	9 05
9 15	6 50	21.47	Dell Abbey	12 05	8 45
9 25	7 00	23.92	Carbon Hill	11 55	8 35
9 30	7 15	24.02	Coal City ♁	11 50	†8 30
P M	A M	26.72	Centerville	11 45	P M
		30.39	Mazonia ♁	11 20	
		31.41	Coster ♁	*11 15	
		32.72	**South Wilmington** ♁	A M	
			ARRIVE] [LEAVE		

GRIFFITH AND SOUTH CHICAGO.—Freight Service Only.

14	2	Mls.	*June 1, 1909.*	7	13
P M	A M		LEAVE] [ARRIVE	A M	A M
†11 55	*8 00	0	**Griffith** ♁	4 20	11 00
12 05	8 10	1.51	Ridge	4 10	10 50
12 10	8 15	3.51	Van Loon	4 00	10 40
12 15	8 20	4.50	Sand Pit ♁	3 55	10 35
12 20	8 25	5.51	Ivanhoe	3 50	10 30
12 25	8 30	6.61	Cavanaugh ♁	3 45	10 25
12 35	8 35	8.57	**Shearson** ♁	¶3 30	10 20
Night	8 50	11.88	**Hammond** ♁	A M	10 10
	9 00	13.10	State Line ♁		*10 00
	A M	19.28	ar. **Ninety-eighth St.** ♁ lv. (*South Chicago.*)		A M

SHEARSON AND WHITING.—Freight Service Only

14	Mls.	*June 1, 1909.*	7
Night		LEAVE] [ARRIVE	A M
†12 35	0	**Shearson** ♁	3 30
1 00	3.32	**Whiting** ♁	¶12 45
A M		ARRIVE] [LEAVE	A M

Trains marked * run daily; † daily, except Sunday; ¶ daily, except Monday. ♁ Telegraph stations.

THIS LINE performs a general interchange of carload traffic between all Eastern, Western, Northern and Southern roads and Fast Freight lines operating via Chicago.

Traffic routed via the E. J. & E. Ry. will avoid the congested terminals in the city of Chicago. Our fast train service assures quick handling. Icing facilities are maintained at Joliet.

This Company owns good dock facilities on Lake Michigan at South Chicago and Waukegan, Ill.

This line offers exceptionally good locations for factories and warehouses, offering cheap land, abundant fuel and water supply.

Labor conditions are good at all points, and good homes for employees.

Direct rail connections to all points in the United States via all lines entering Chicago. Chicago rates apply.

Further information upon application.

In the Official Railway Guide for September 1910, passenger service was only offered between Aurora and Joliet. Service to the east was abandoned the previous year due to the building of the Joliet and Southern Interurban Traction electrified line that paralleled the EJ&E between Joliet and Chicago Heights. A little-known fact was that the EJ&E did continue to carry passengers in its cabooses until the mid-1960s.

Two

A Well-Engineered and Well-Equipped Railroad

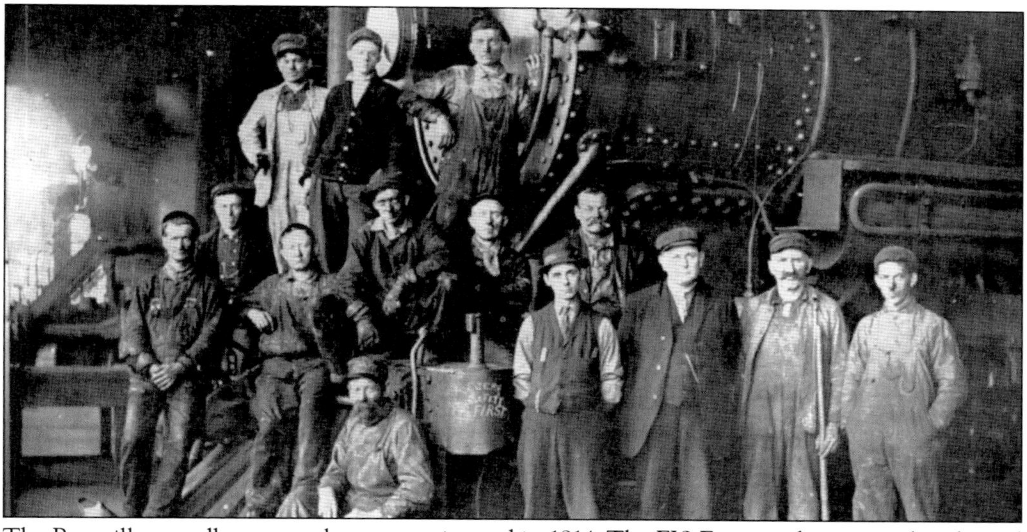

The Rossville roundhouse employees are pictured in 1914. The EJ&E, its predecessor railroads, and several affiliated railway lines came under the control of a group of steel companies, which in turn became the United States Steel Corporation. Thus the corporate history of the great EJ&E is too complicated to cover here. To understand it, one needs to consult a book like the *Poor's Manual of Railroads*. One such line was the Calumet and Blue Island Railroad (C&BI), which was organized in 1889. On March 31, 1893, the Chicago and Eastern Illinois Railroad (C&EI) granted trackage rights to the C&BI from Chicago Heights to the Danville soft coal fields and limestone quarries. The C&BI was absorbed by the Chicago, Lake Shore and Eastern Railway (CLS&E) and in turn was later consolidated with the EJ&E. About 79 miles south of Chicago Heights in Rossville, Vermillion County, was a well-equipped CLS&E terminal. It consisted of a 10-stall (originally a 5-stall) roundhouse and turntable, yard office, coaling tower, sand tower, water tower, YMCA building, and other structures. South of Rossville, trains were run south to coal mines and limestone quarries on branch lines leading to Sidell and Little Vermillion and also to Jackson, Indiana. Eventually the mines shut down, and the trains hauling coal from this area ceased in April 1947.

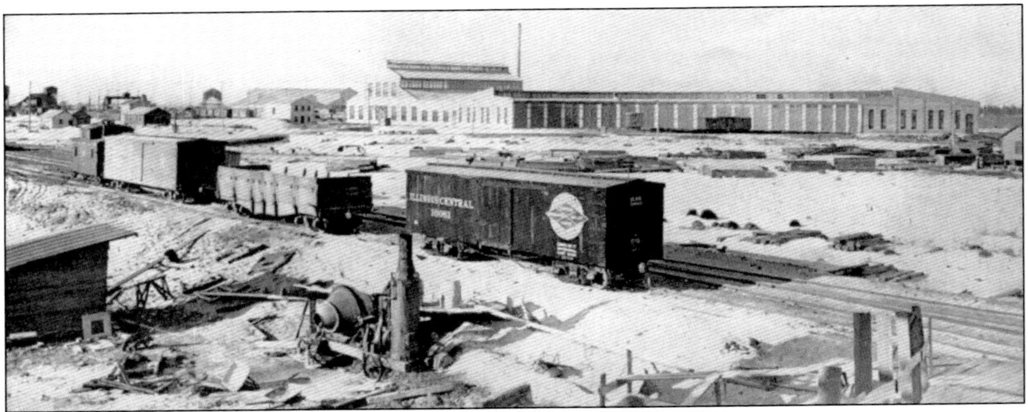

The new Kirk Yard in Gary, Indiana, is seen here, when it was under construction. Note the 20-stall roundhouse. To the left of the roundhouse are other buildings still under construction or just completed. The yard was named for John Kirk, a railroad official.

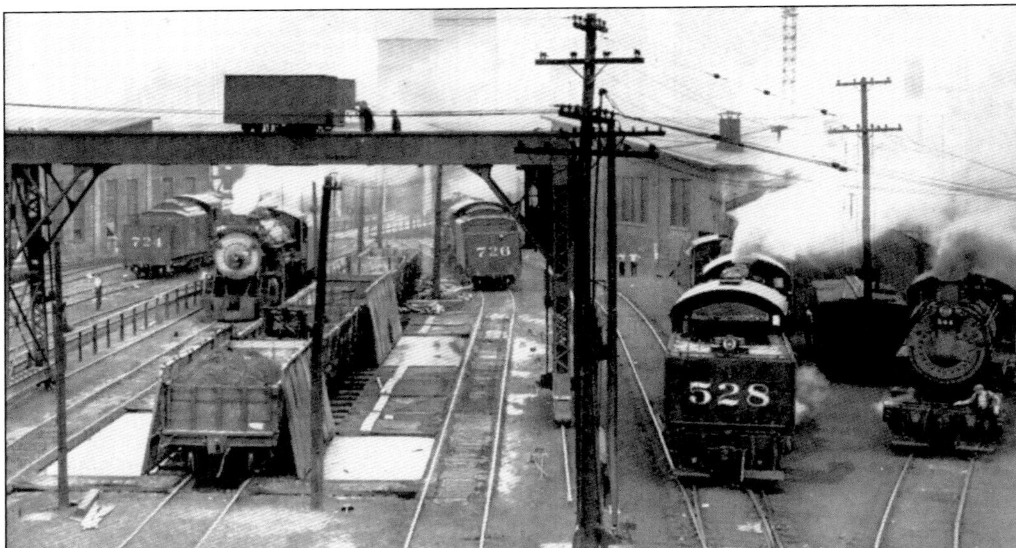

Steam locomotive maintenance was labor intensive for railroads. This was the cinder pit area at the East Joliet roundhouse. The cinders were dumped from the locomotive firebox into a pit under the tracks. The cinders were then lifted up and out by the overhead clamshell crane, straddling the tracks. The crane dumped the cinders into gondola cars. The cinders were then shipped to various locations to be used as fill, roadbed, driveways, and other things.

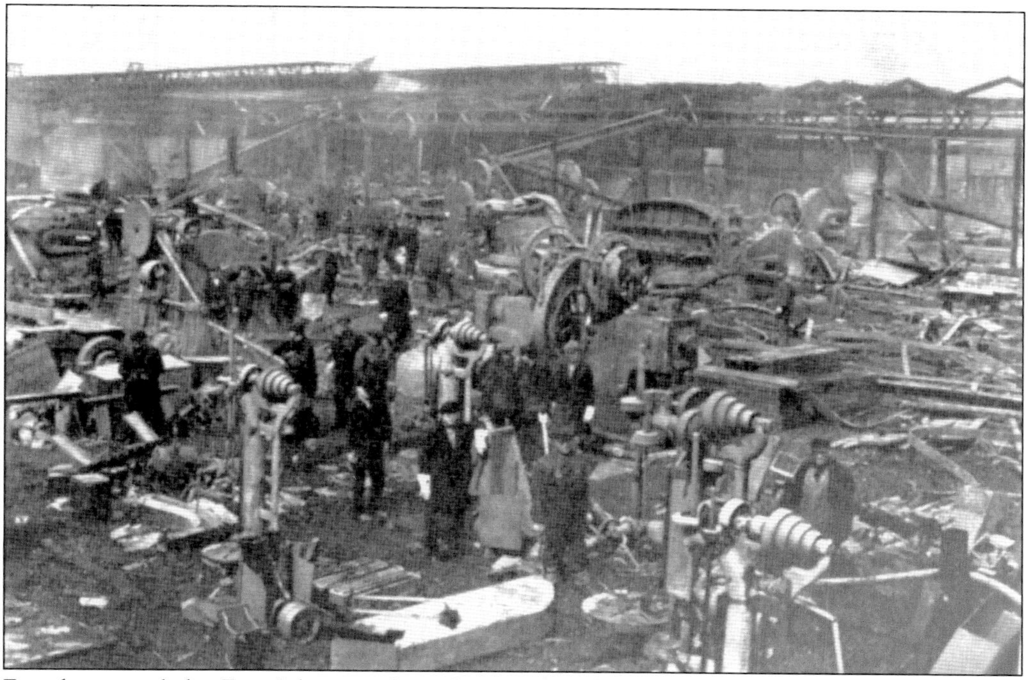

Fire devastated the East Joliet car shops late in the afternoon of March 28, 1923. Afterward machines, freight cars, parts, and the building lay in ruins. The shop complex was rebuilt and went on to serve many more decades. The EJ&E did extensive car and locomotive rebuilding at the East Joliet shops.

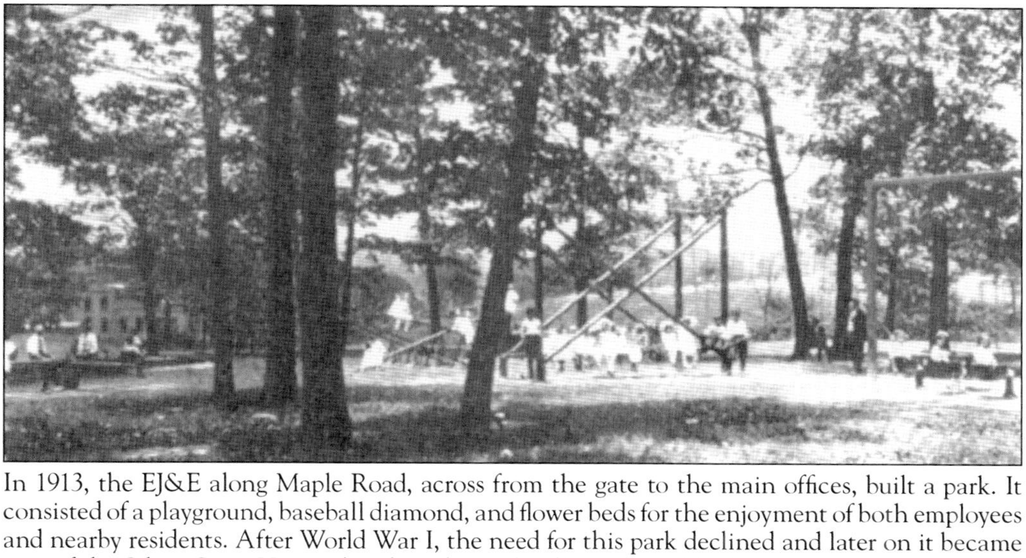

In 1913, the EJ&E along Maple Road, across from the gate to the main offices, built a park. It consisted of a playground, baseball diamond, and flower beds for the enjoyment of both employees and nearby residents. After World War I, the need for this park declined and later on it became part of the Silver Cross Hospital parking lot and radio station WJOL.

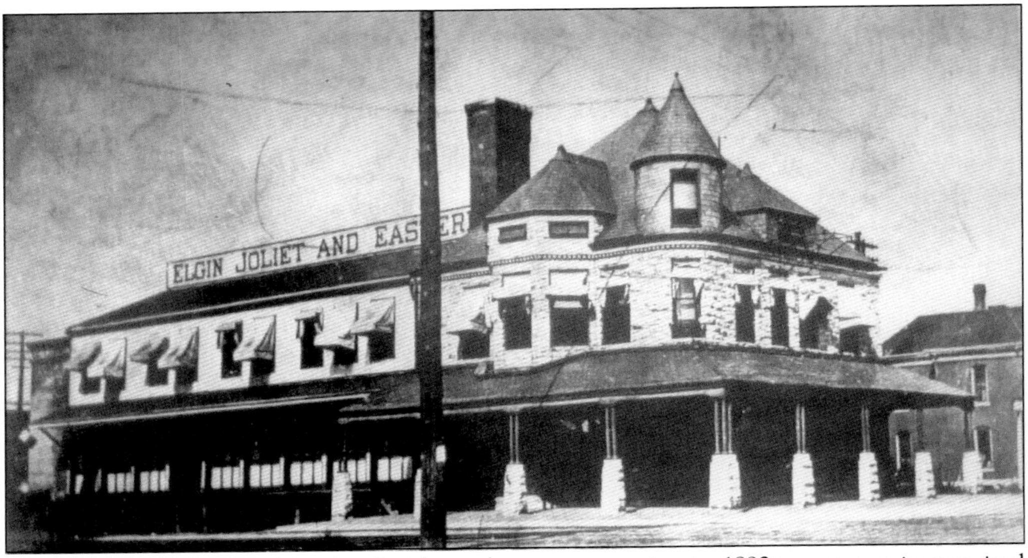

The EJ&E built this combination freight and passenger station in 1892 to serve as its terminal in downtown Joliet. The Joliet and Eastern Traction line acquired it after the EJ&E abandoned passenger service. It was occupied by the Fitzgerald Furniture store for many years and is now the headquarters station of the Joliet Fire Department. Silver Cross Stadium, home to the Joliet Jackhammers minor-league baseball team, is now across the street.

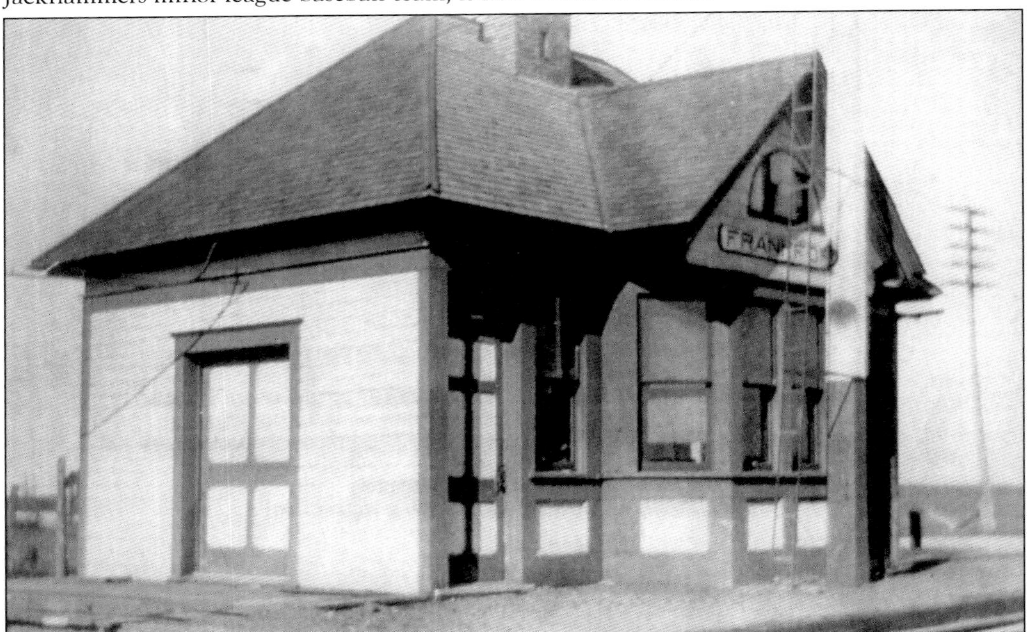

The EJ&E station in Frankfort was built around 1890. It served passenger and freight customers of the railroad and was conveniently located between the Oak Street and Center Road crossings. J. L. Green was the agent there when the railroad started service in 1889. Later John Staff represented the railroad. It was closed by August 1947. Local farmer Henry Hossbach purchased the structure for $100 and demolished it. The lumber was used on his nearby farm.

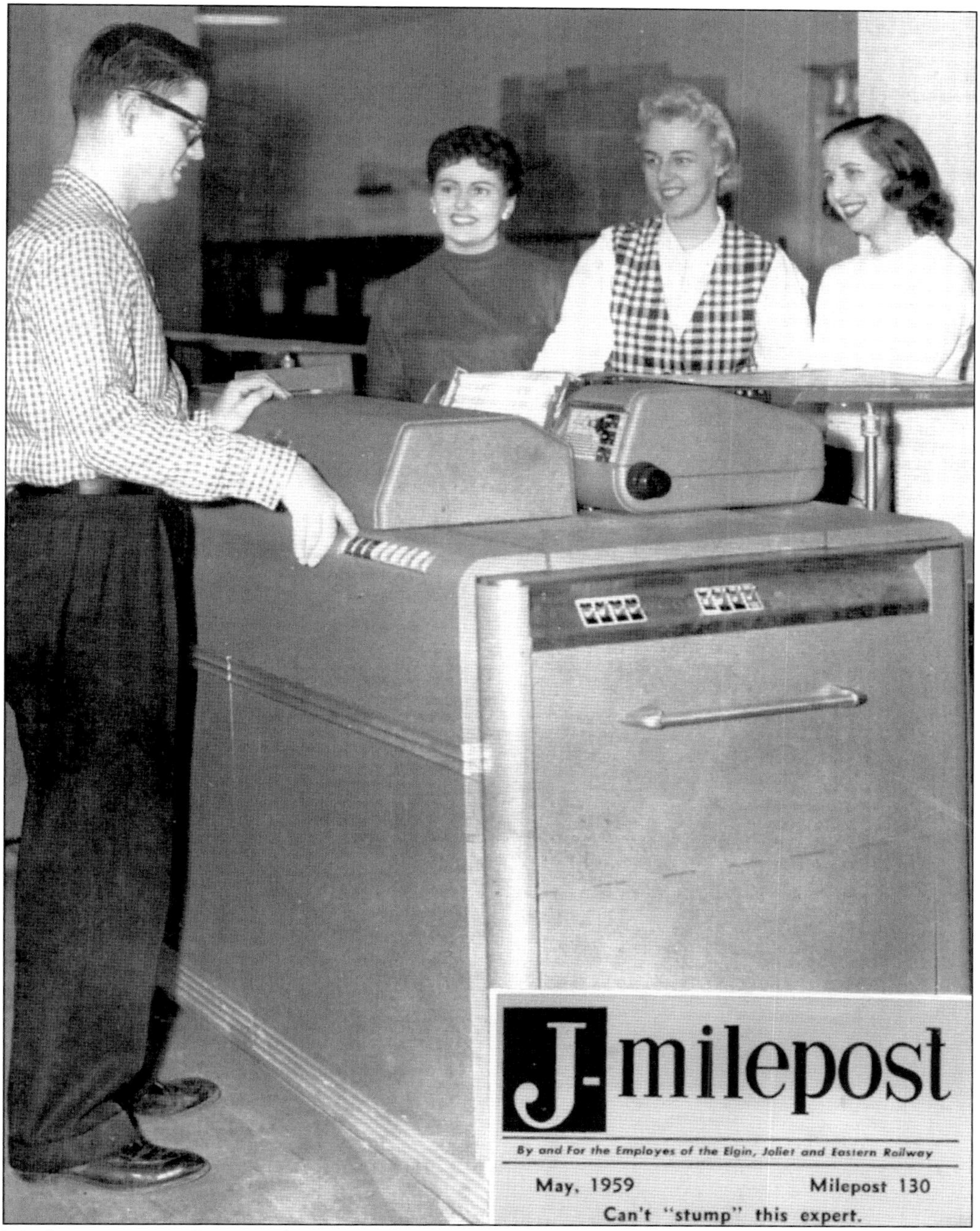

Machine operator Raymond Muenzing operates the IBM 407 accounting machine in early 1959 as (from left to right) Arlene Lawson, Patricia McDonald, and Cecelia O'Daniels watch. The EJ&E started using punch cards in 1937 for payroll accounting and was a railroad leader in mechanizing clerical tasks.

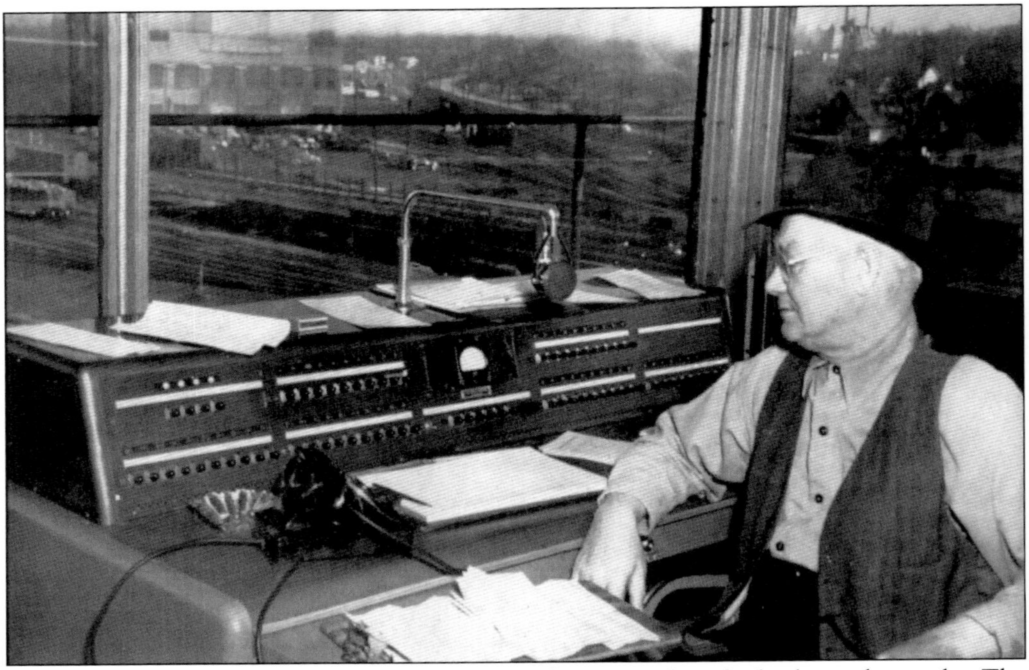

East Joliet yardmaster Tom McLaughlin surveys the action from high above the tracks. The EJ&E had a high steel tower, on the north side of the Jackson Street highway bridge, from which the yardmasters had a commanding view of operations in both directions. The console on the desk controls talkback and paging loudspeakers located alongside the tracks below. There was another similar yardmaster's tower at the north end of the East Joliet yard. *J-Milepost* consulting editor Bob Benson had a great photographer's eye for the dramatic railroad photograph, as evidenced by this shot.

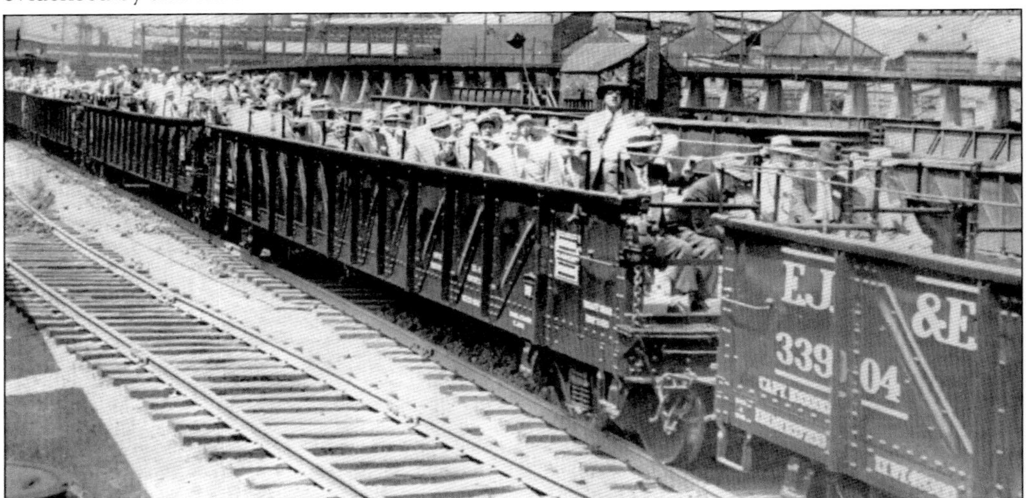

The American Association of Railroad Superintendents held their 54th annual meeting in Chicago on June 6–8, 1950. The EJ&E treated over 200 visitors to a tour of operations at South Chicago and Gary. The shiny, very clean gondola cars were outfitted with seats for the trip. Special trains like this were an excellent way for the railroad to showcase its excellent facilities.

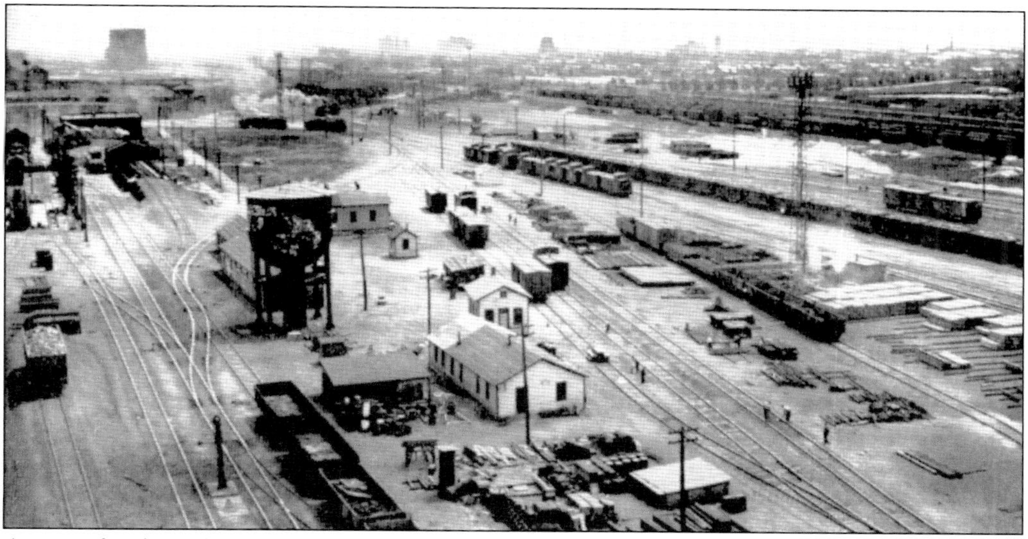

A view of Kirk Yard in 1927 shows part of the engine servicing area. On the right, the ever-present maintenance of way workers attend to track repairs. Construction of the new Kirk Yard was completed in 1908. It was built west of the United States Steel Gary Works, which started steel production the following year. The yard required extensive grading to raise the tracks out of the swampy areas. The yard was named after John Kirk, who was the first Gary superintendent of the CLS&E, a predecessor of the EJ&E.

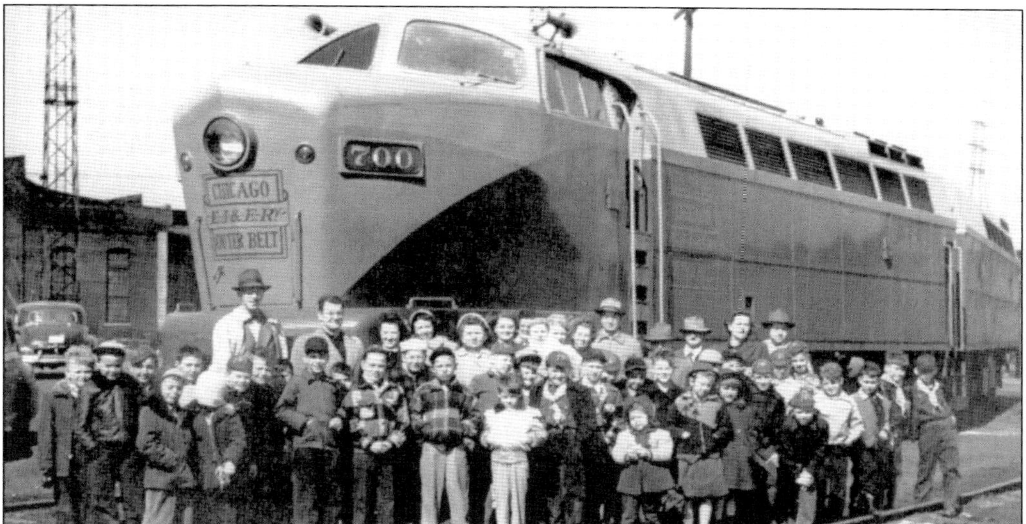

Cub Scout Pack 290 of Chesterton, Indiana, was on a field trip to Kirk Yard on Sunday, April 22, 1951. The boys were likely studying for their railroading merit badge. No doubt they were enthralled by the big, shiny, brand-new diesel locomotive. Ralph Carpenter, Kirk Yard switchman, arranged the visit. Engine No. 700 was a model DR-4-4-1500 road freight cab (A) unit and booster (B) unit built by the Baldwin Locomotive Company. Operated as an A-B-B-A set, the locomotives generated a total of 6,000 horsepower.

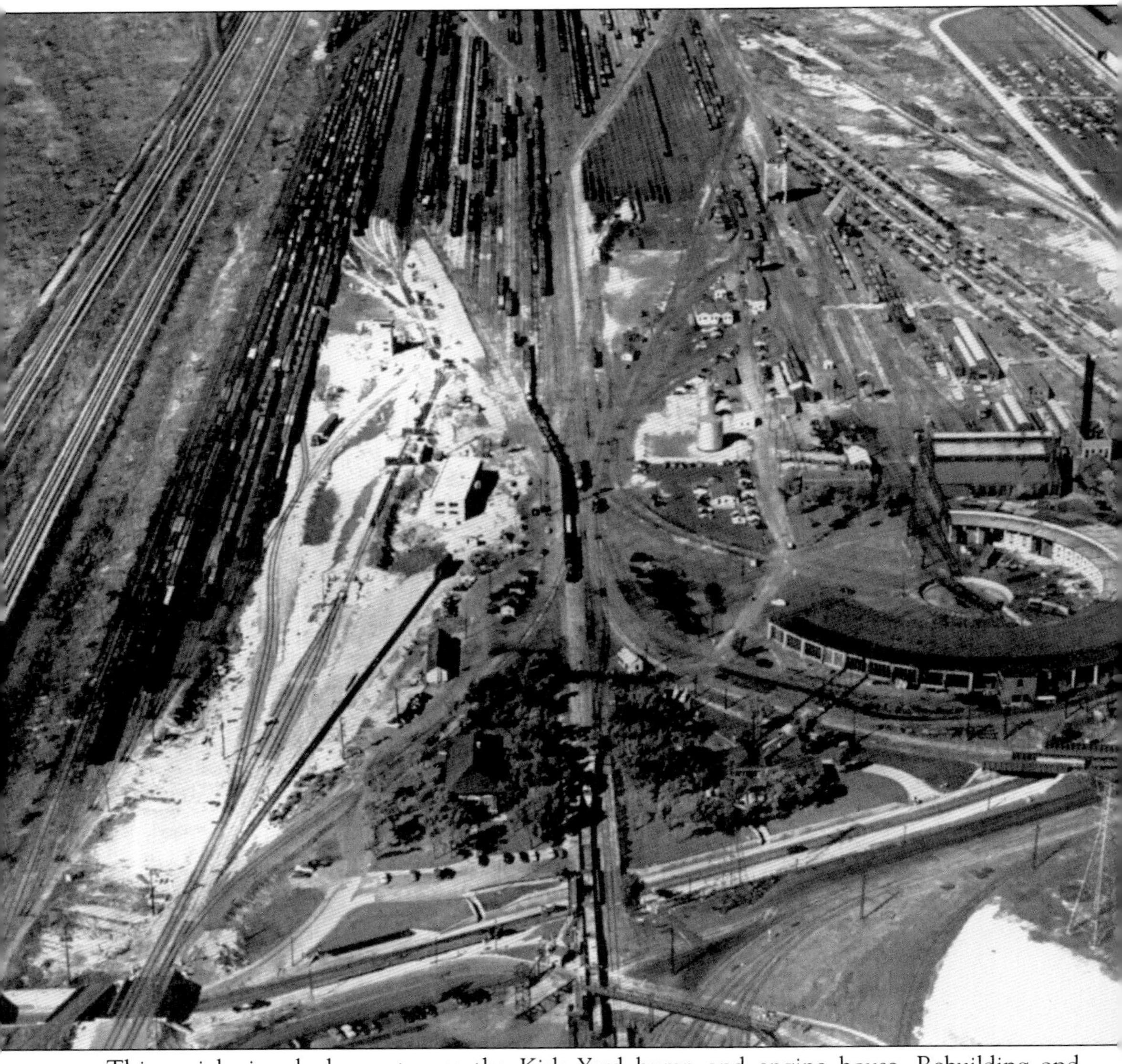

This aerial view looks west over the Kirk Yard hump and engine house. Rebuilding and modernizing was a massive undertaking by the EJ&E in the 1950s. When completed, there were 58 tracks in the classification yard having a capacity of 4,560 freight cars. There were two receiving yards totaling 21 tracks with a capacity of over 2,000 cars. Two storage yards would hold 1,200 cars. A new, modern interlocking plant operated from a tower controlled access to the west end of the yard. Today much has been changed, but Kirk Yard continues to be a vital facility in the efficient handling of freight traffic.

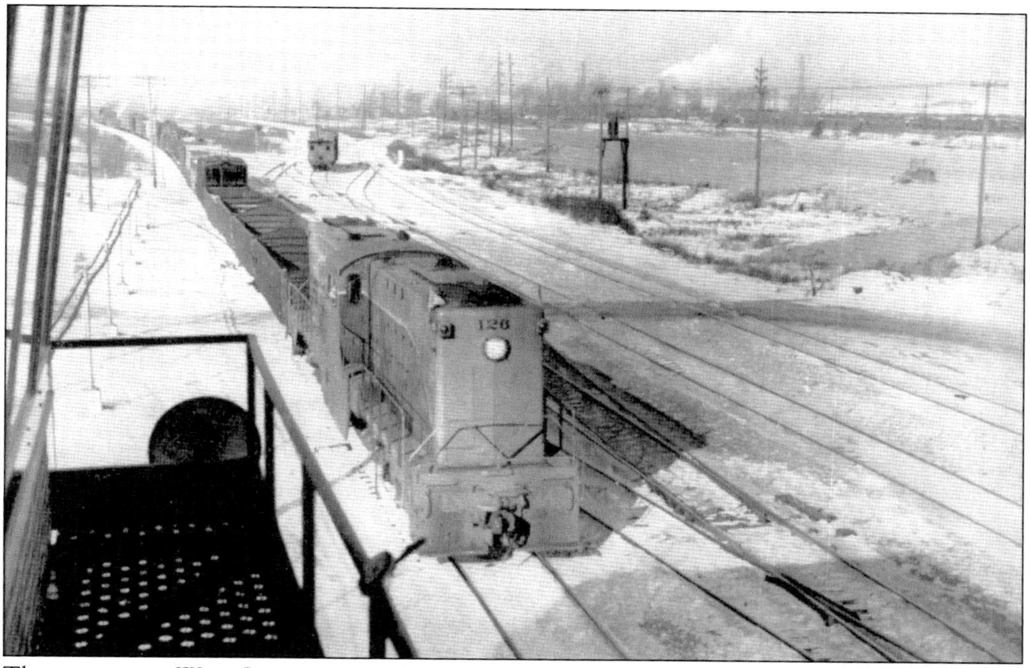

The operator at West Gate tower, Kirk Yard, had this view of Extra 126 East as it pulled into the receiving yard on a cold winter day. The train, with conductor Herb Secor and engineer Howard Wilkins, left East Joliet a few hours earlier.

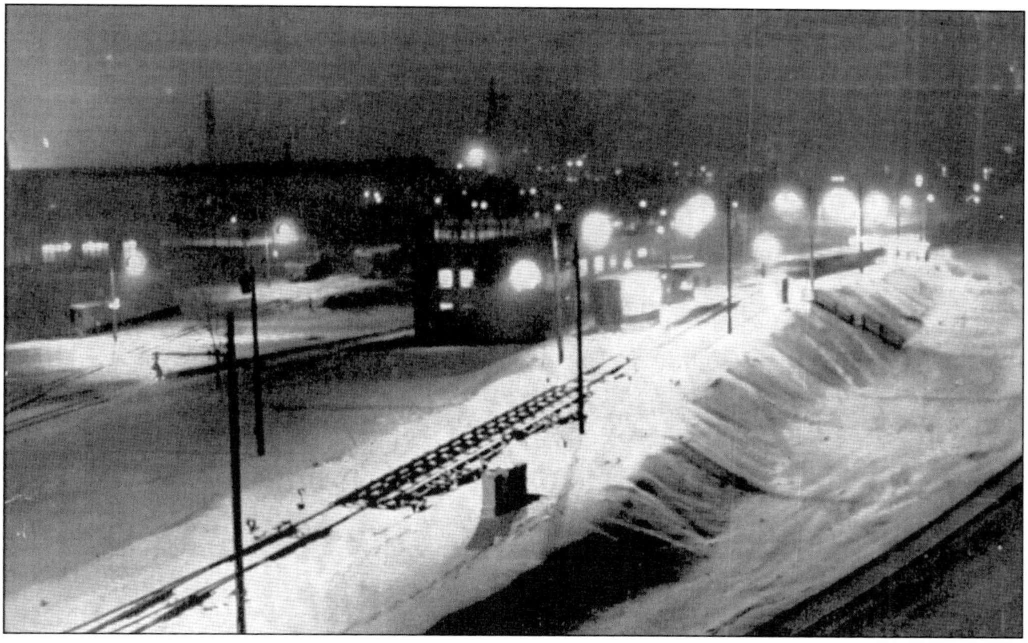

Gary clerk John Donaval took this photograph at the Kirk Yard hump looking northeast. Railroad employees have always, and continue, to work under the most severe of weather conditions. As cars start down the hump, they first encounter the master retarder in the center of the picture. There are additional retarders farther along the tracks.

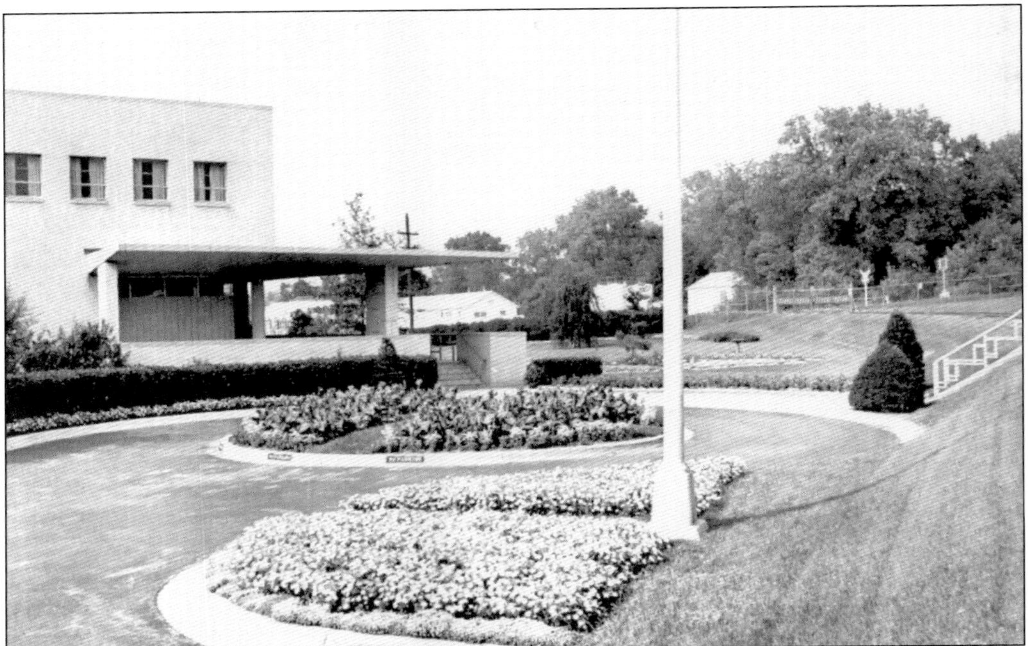

In the early 1950s, the EJ&E built a new office and operations building adjacent to the East Joliet yard. The new structure brought together staff people of several departments. Great pride was also taken by the railroad in maintaining a beautiful flower garden in front of the building. The EJ&E reached its high point in employment in 1951, with 5,900 employees.

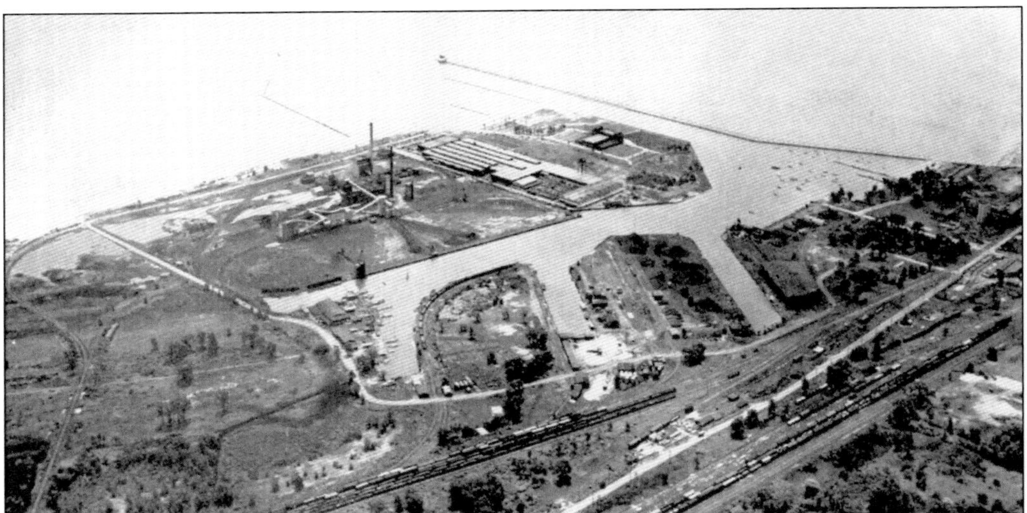

This is an aerial view of the Waukegan waterfront in 1947. The Larsen Marine Service can be seen on the left bank of Slip No. 3, the inner slip. Slip No. 2, the center slip, shows Baker's Fishing Boats docked on the right bank. Slip No. 1, at the right, shows the Northwest Hanna Coal company on the left bank and the Hussey Coal Company on the right bank. Left of the Johnson Motor plant, on the outer peninsula, was the old North Shore Coke and Chemical plant. The EJ&E tracks are shown cutting through the open country to the left, extending east to the shore, and then south along it.

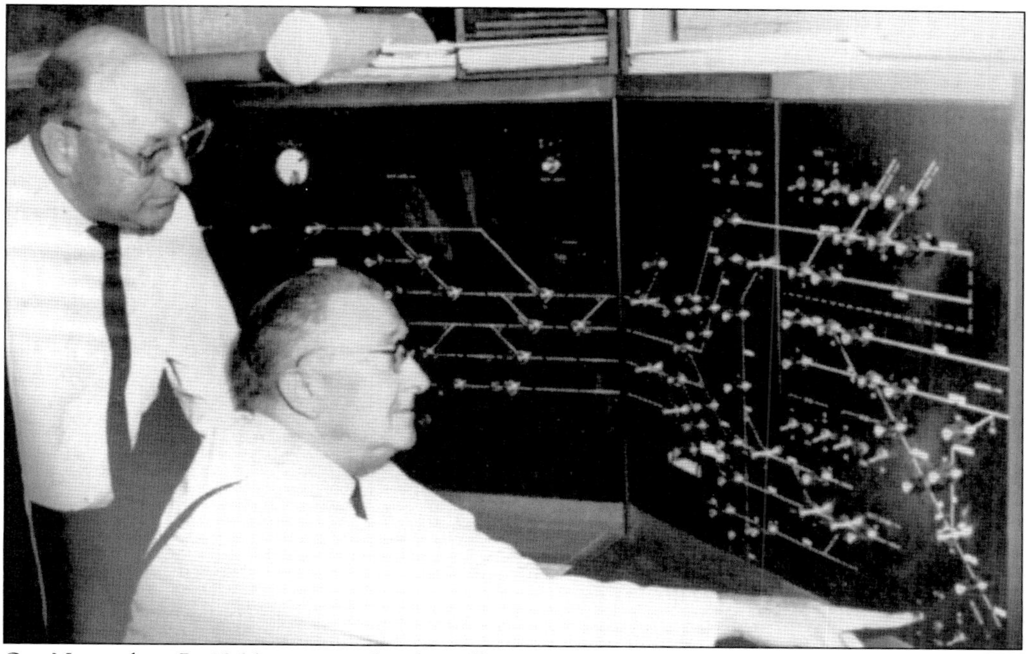

On November 7, 1966, a centralized traffic control system, including remotely controlled electrically operated switches, was installed at Kirk Yard Junction Tower. The system controlled the double-track main line between Cavanaugh and Kirk Yard Junction. Operator Larry Walker is shown at the control board, and standing is signal supervisor Edward Gawenda.

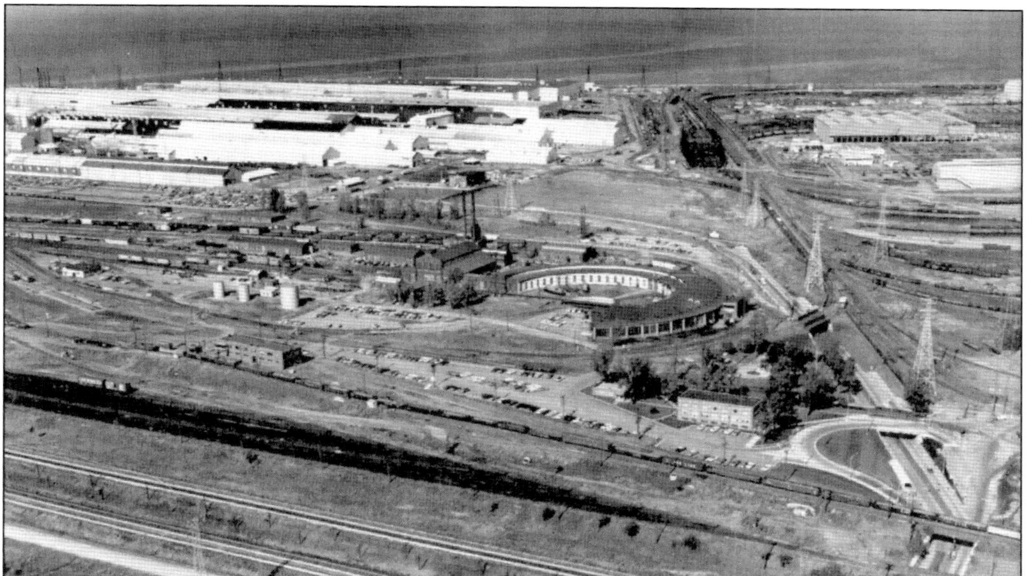

This aerial view of Kirk Yard was taken in June 1969. Looking north and visible to the upper left was the sheet and tin operations of United States Steel Corporation's Gary Works. In the upper right is the Merchant Mill. The car department offices, labor dormitory, shops, roundhouse facilities, hump yard office, main office, and annex building are all pictured in the photograph. The street in the lower right corner is Buchanan Street.

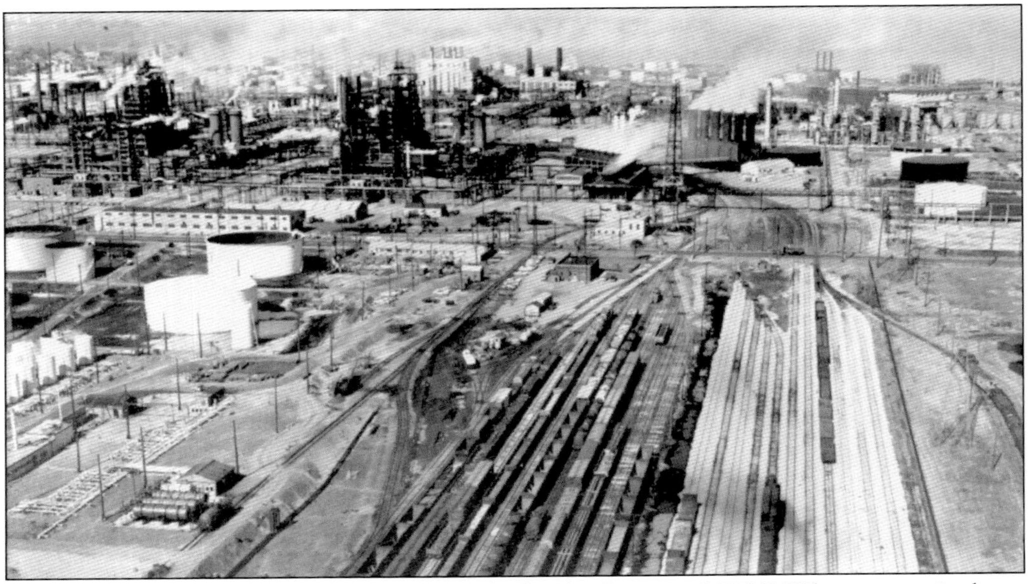

This aerial view, looking north, of the Standard Oil refinery and EJ&E Whiting terminal was taken in the summer of 1969. The EJ&E yard office can be seen to the left of the yard and south of 129th Street. Across the street was the engine house. The refinery got its start in 1889 and eventually grew to occupy 1,700 acres of land and employ 2,500 workers. Gasoline, jet fuel, kerosene, heating oil, industrial fuel, and lubricating oil were just some of the products produced at the plant. In addition, a research laboratory was located on the premises.

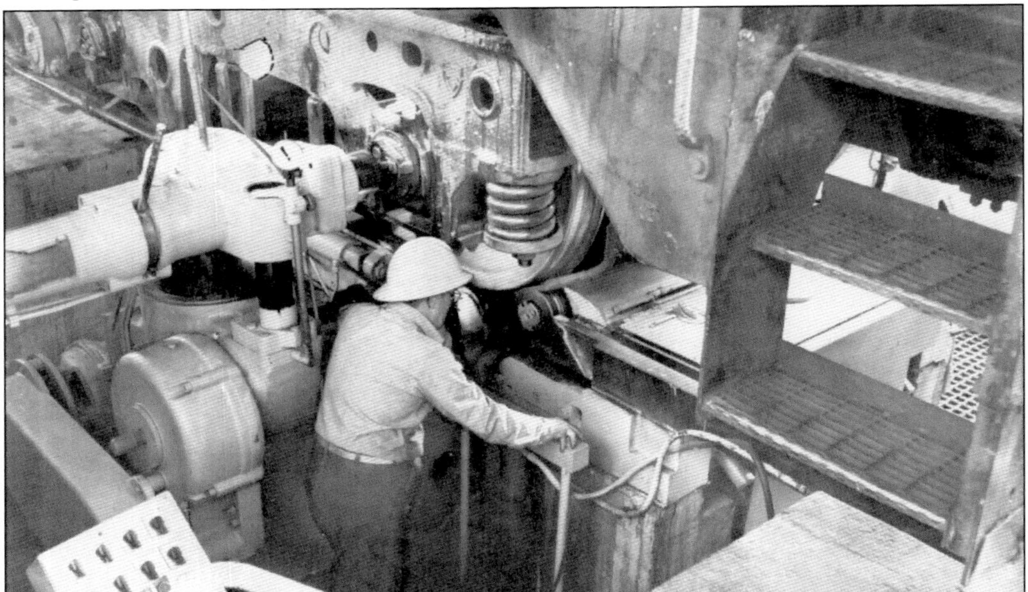

In 1950, the EJ&E was the first railroad in the world to install a wheel-truing machine. The special lathe did not require the removal of the wheels from the locomotive or car. Wheels could easily be restored to a perfect contour. It was located at the Joliet locomotive shop. Machinist Richard Criche is shown working on a reengined Baldwin DT-6-6-2000 center cab locomotive in June 1965.

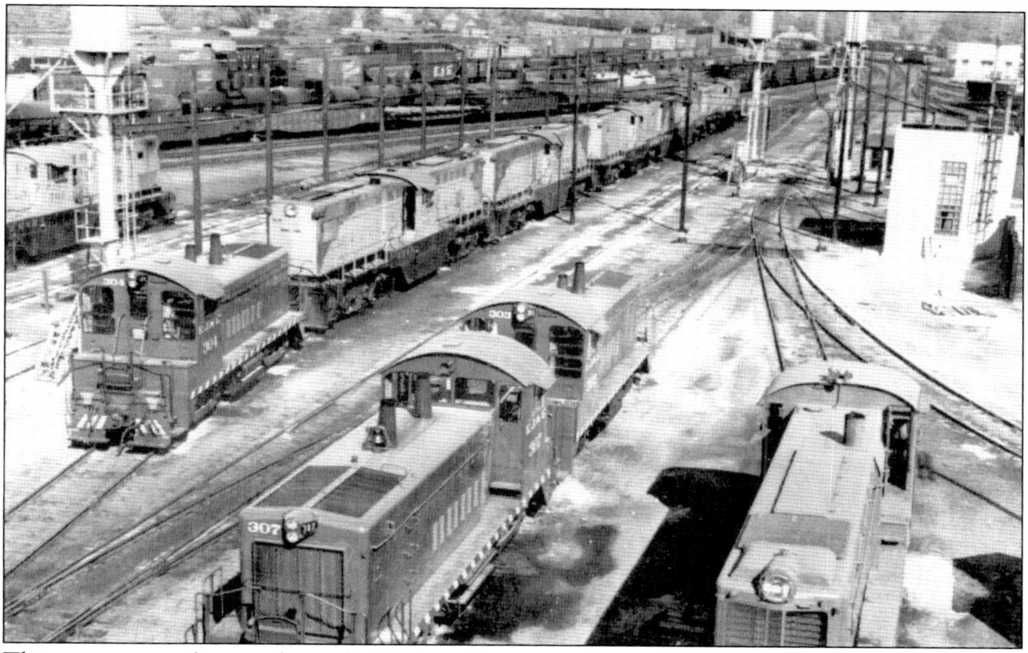

This scene was taken in the early 1960s at the engine house in Joliet. The EJ&E had a total of 130 diesels on its roster during this time. Shown here are 11 diesels including Baldwin DT-6-6-2000 road transfer units, Baldwin VO1000 switchers, and Electro-Motive Division (EMD) of General Motors SW1200 switchers.

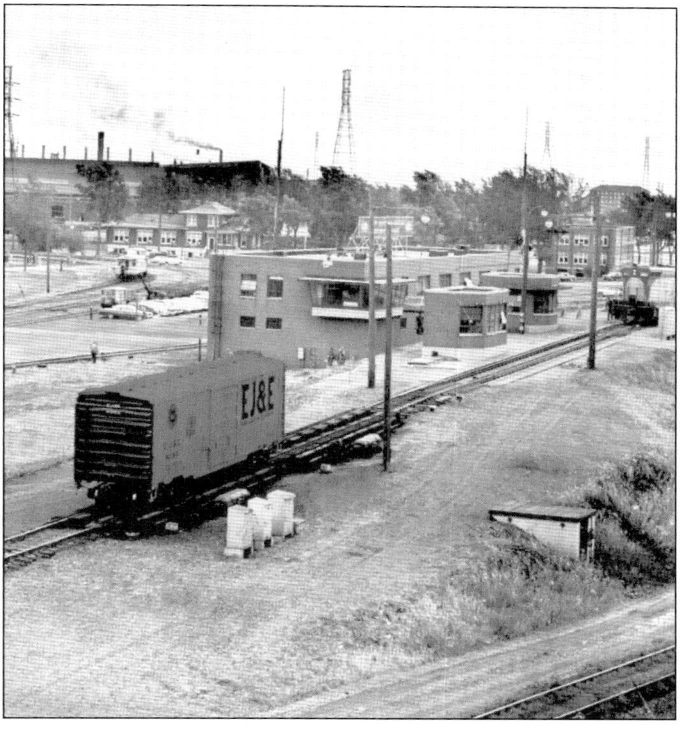

The new electronic car retarders installed at Kirk Yard in 1952 were the first in the world. In 1964, an EJ&E boxcar is shown moving down the crest through the electronic retarders, which slowed the movement of the car. The retarder operator, in a tower, watched the operation and could manually override the electronic function of the retarders and manually control the speed and spacing of the cars. In 1964, 4,200 cars were moving in and out of Kirk Yard each day. Over 1,500 were being classified over the hump in a 24-hour period.

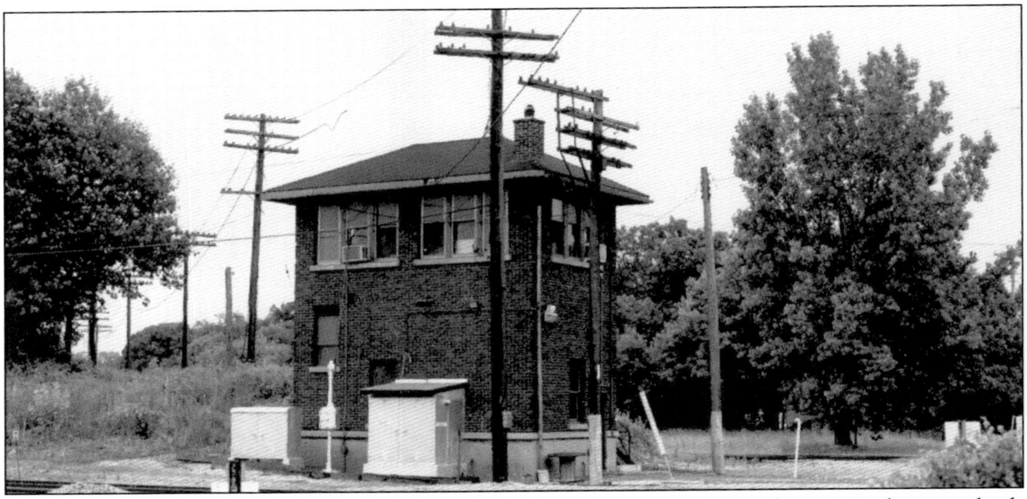

The EJ&E constructed the second Griffith tower in 1924 to replace the original one, which was destroyed by fire. Griffith tower protected the crossings and interchange connections of the EJ&E, the Michigan Central, the Erie, the Chesapeake and Ohio, and the Grand Trunk Western railroads. In 1947, a fire broke out in the tower, which caused the death of the operator on duty. At one time, the tower men handled up to 180 trains a day, and Griffith was by far the busiest tower on the EJ&E system. It was closed in December 1999, and due to a notable preservation effort, the tower was preserved by the Griffith Historical Society and moved across tracks to a new location in July 2000. Only the EJ&E and Grand Trunk Western railroads remain today, and their train dispatchers now control the signals from Joliet and Troy, Michigan.

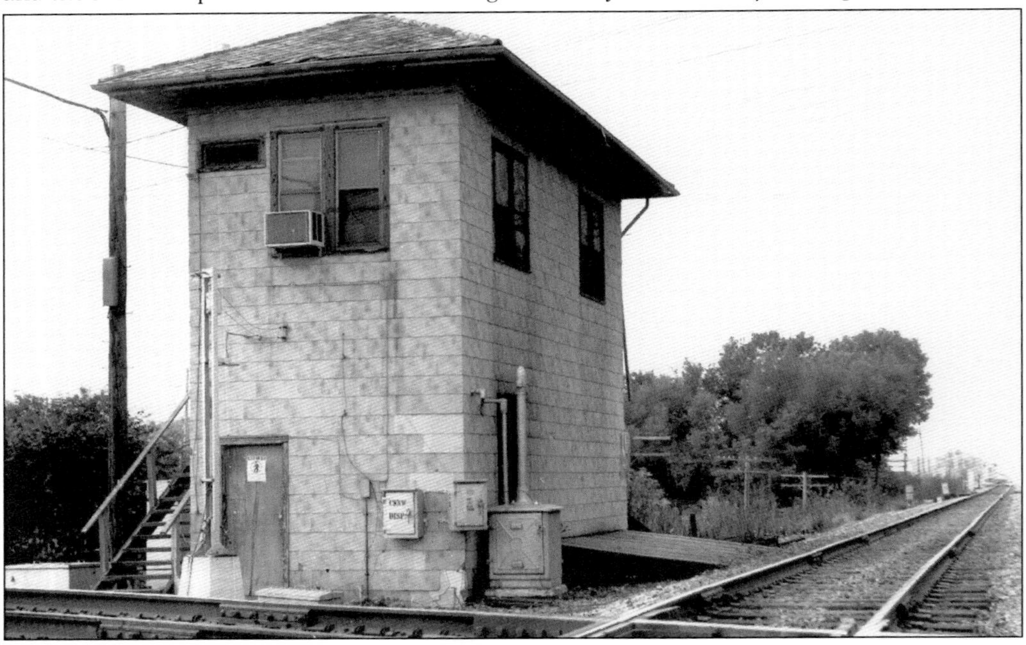

Barrington tower had protected the crossing and interchange of the EJ&E with the Chicago and Northwestern Railway Northwest line. This picture shows it in its twilight years in September 1995. The tower was closed in May 2006 and demolished in August the same year. The EJ&E train dispatcher in Joliet now controls the crossing. (Bill Raia collection.)

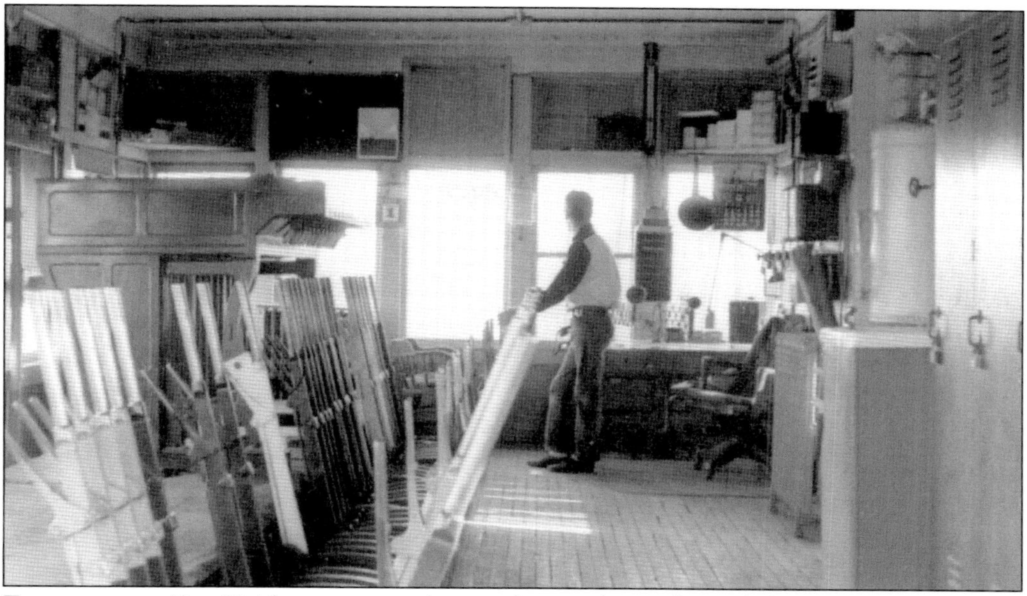

Tower operator Don Heisler prepares to line up the switches and signals for an approaching train at the Rock Island tower in 1958. The former Rock Island (now Metra) tracks crossed the EJ&E on the north side of the tower; the Michigan Central Railroad tracks crossed the EJ&E on the south side, south of Hickory Creek. The levers were connected to track switches and derails by a pipeline alongside the tracks. The EJ&E is now a single track and the Metra train dispatcher in Chicago controls the signals. (R. A. Eisenbrandt.)

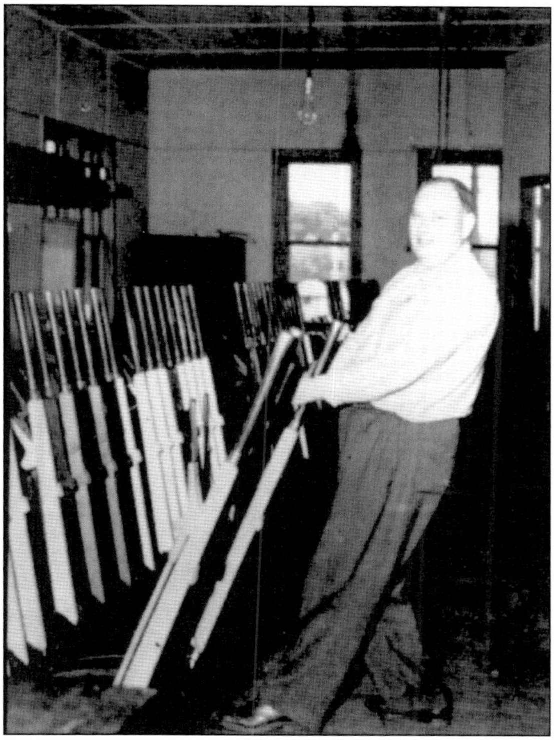

In 1964, the EJ&E converted the 1888-built mechanical interlocking plant at McCool, into an all-relay-type system. The tower had protected the crossing of the EJ&E and the Baltimore and Ohio Railroad and was demolished shortly after. Control of this crossing was then given to the Baltimore and Ohio Railroad centralized traffic control dispatcher in Akron, which was 310 miles to the east. The EJ&E tracks between Griffith and Porter were later abandoned in 1985.

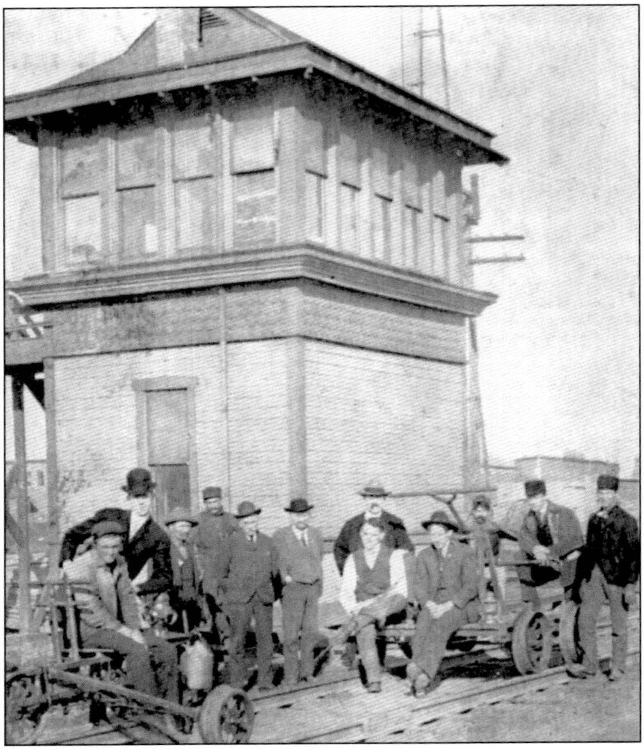

This was the tower at Chicago Heights on a November day in 1904. The tower had 24 levers and controlled the crossing of the single-track EJ&E and the double-tracked C&EI. Gathered around for the photograph are day towerman George Bigelow; night towerman Fritz Wenberg; lampman Herman Palmer; lamp inspector Dana Bigelow; section foreman George Martin; section men John Toman and Joe Francisco; agent A. L. Palmer; office cashier George Clark; and surveyors Fred Sabin and William Pomeroy.

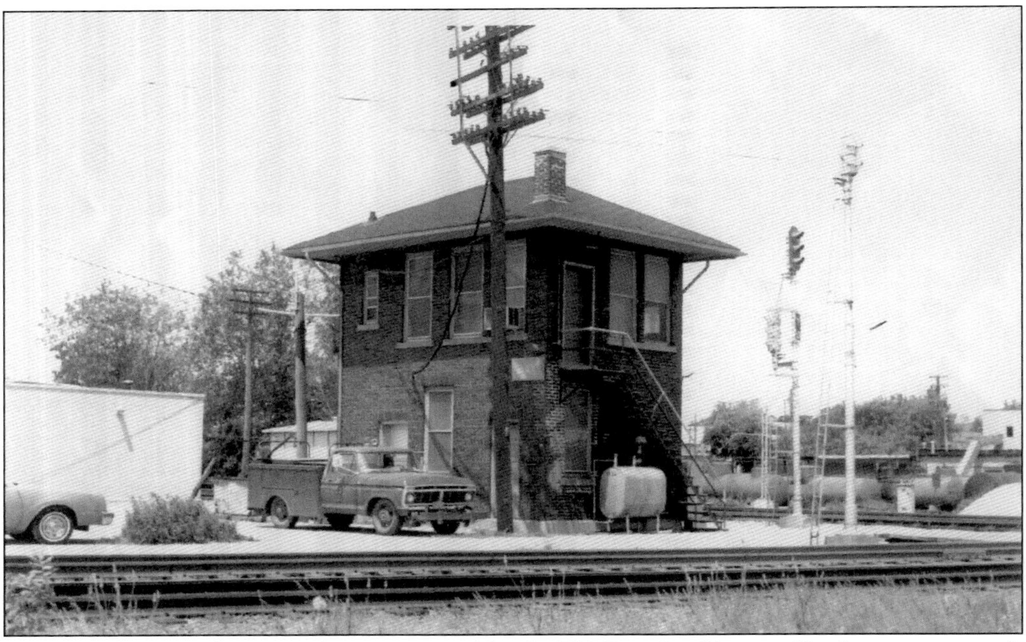

This was the second tower to be constructed by the EJ&E at the Chicago Heights crossing with the C&EI, shown here in June 1981. The operations at the brick tower were closed in 1993, but the building was still standing. The EJ&E train dispatcher in Joliet now controls the crossing. (Bill Raia collection.)

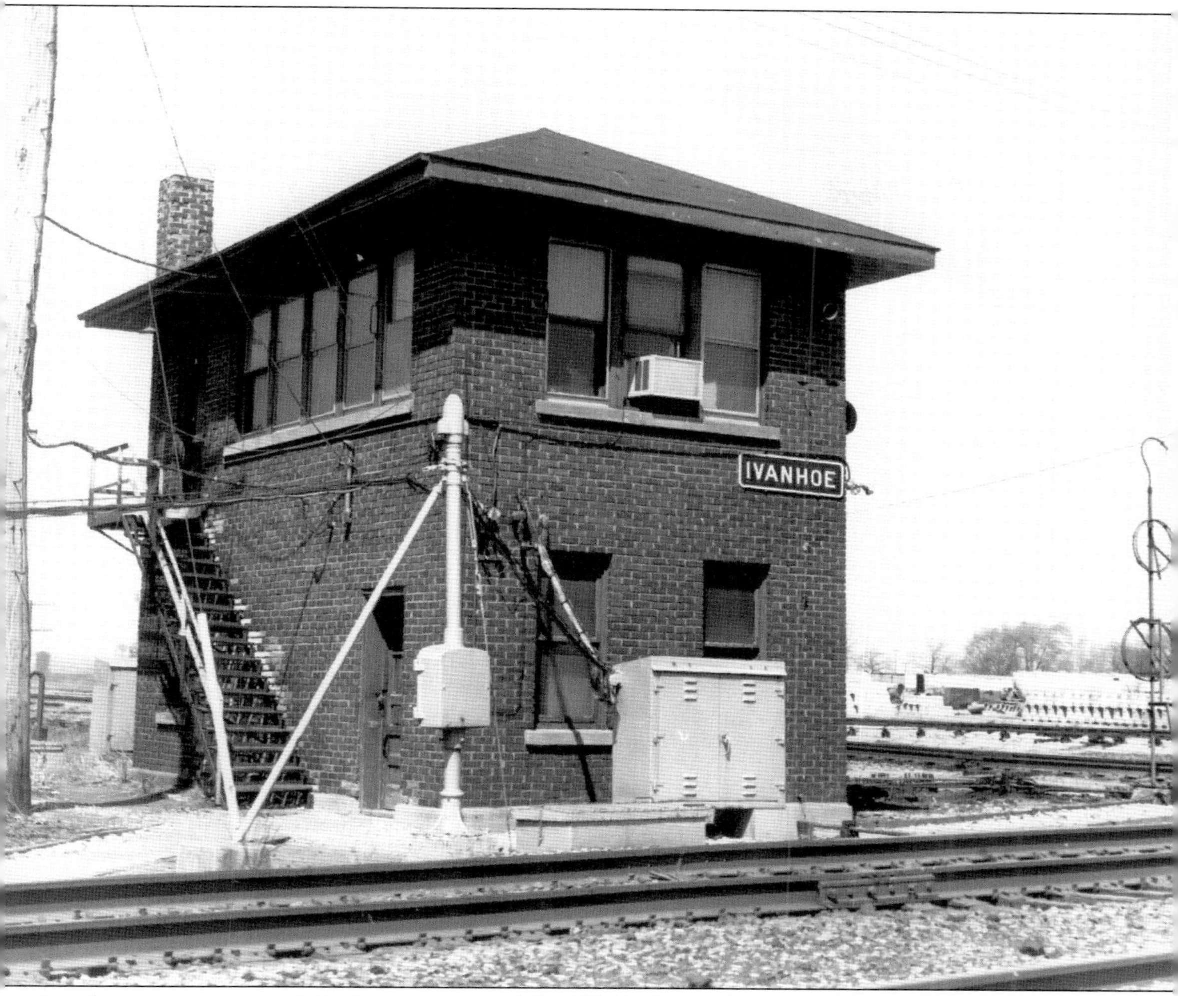

Ivanhoe tower protected the busy crossing of the EJ&E, the Michigan Central, and the Indiana Harbor Belt's Gary and Western branch. The famous Hagenbeck and Wallace circus train wreck happened near here on the Michigan Central on June 22, 1918. The tower was converted from manual control to remote control from the dispatchers office in Joliet in June 1994. (Bill Raia collection.)

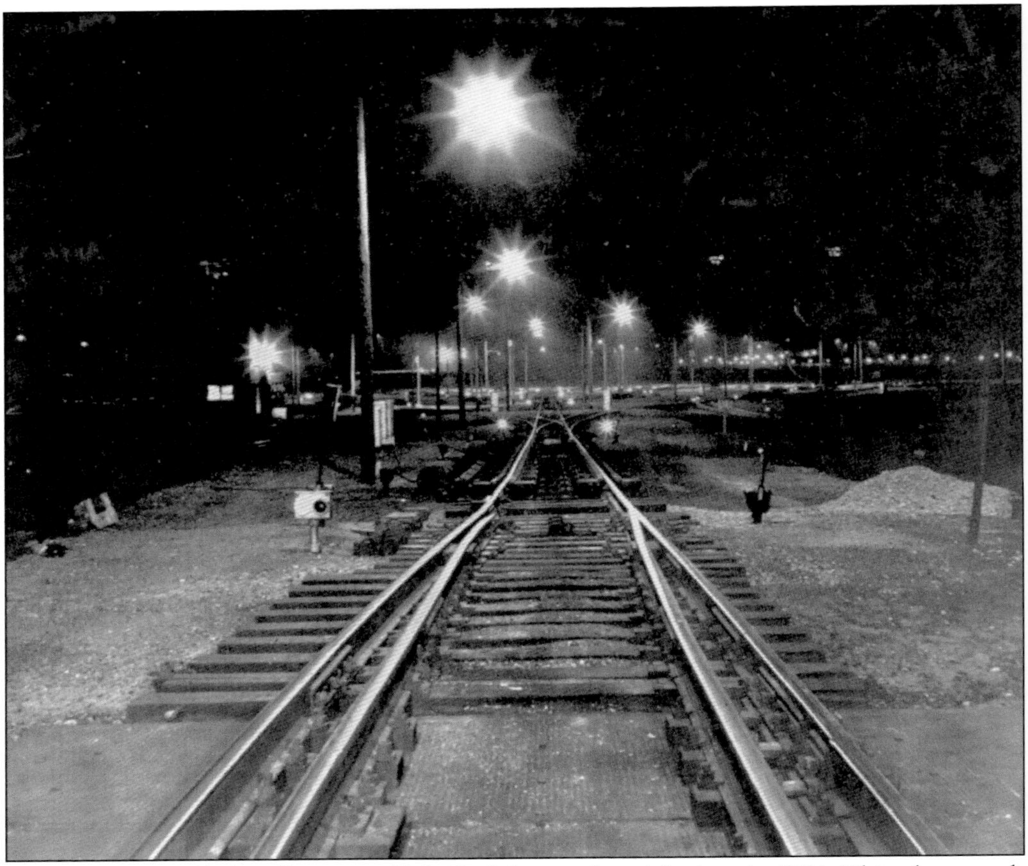

A myriad of floodlights illuminate Kirk Yard during the nighttime in 1954. This photograph shows the view looking down the hump toward the classification yard. Good lighting in yards was, and still is, a vital safety feature of good railroading.

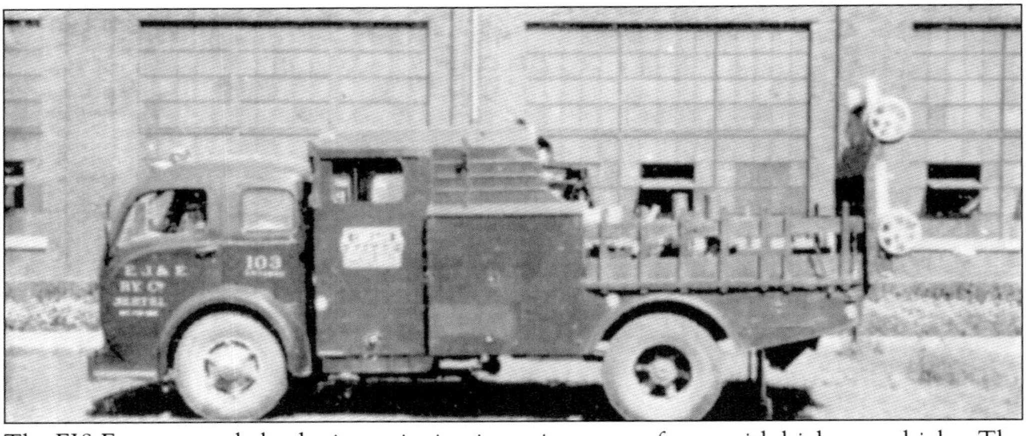

The EJ&E was an early leader in equipping its maintenance forces with highway vehicles. The White motor truck shown here had an extra cab to seat additional men, and both covered and open areas for tools and equipment. Many trucks had power-lift tailgates, cranes, winches, and other features.

Three

How the EJ&E Ran the Trains

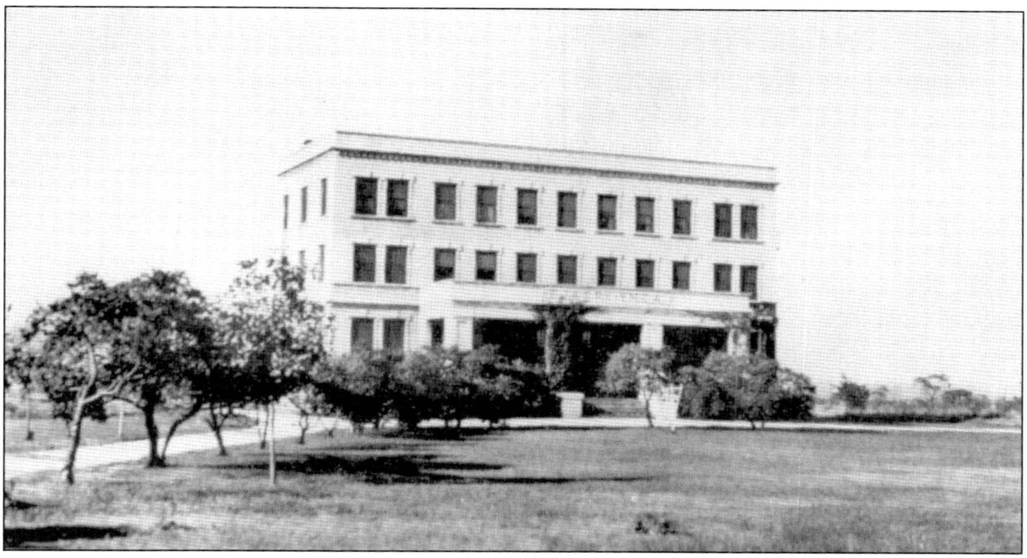

The EJ&E constructed the YMCA at Rossville in 1914 to serve as a home away from home for train crews coming down from the Chicago area. It was located south of the village of Rossville and has since been demolished. The line to Rossville was at its busiest during the pre-Depression years of the 1920s. From August 1923 to July 1924, 1,160 northbound loaded trains had left this area with nearly 54,000 carloads.

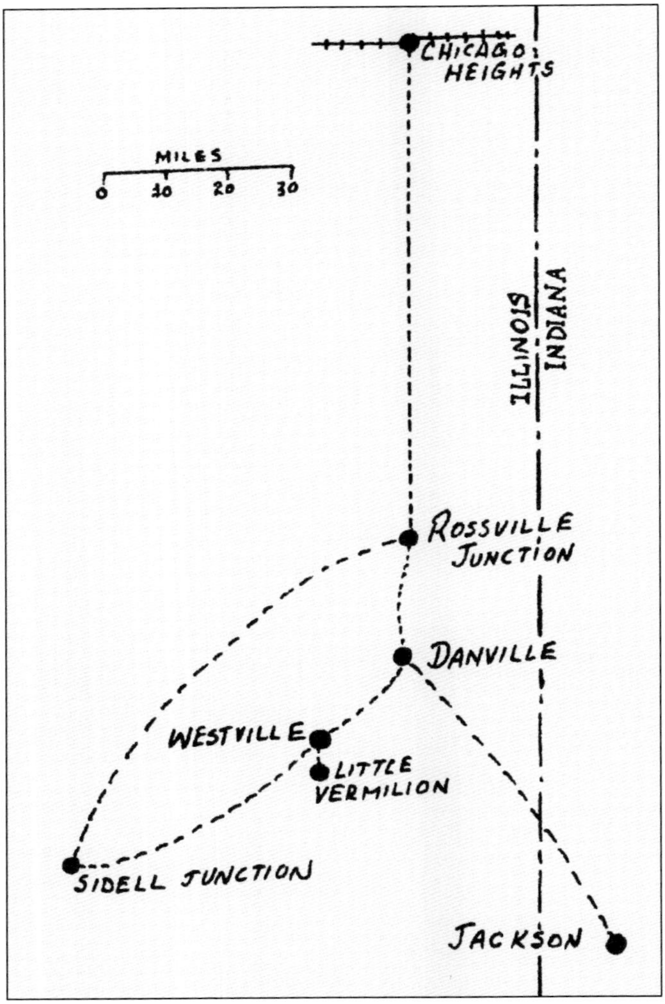

This map shows the area served by the EJ&E around Rossville, much of this on C&EI trackage rights. Due to the depletion of the mines and the decreasing demand of coal for industrial purposes, the service to the area was abandoned on April 30, 1947. The last train was dispatched northbound to Kirk Yard with only two loads.

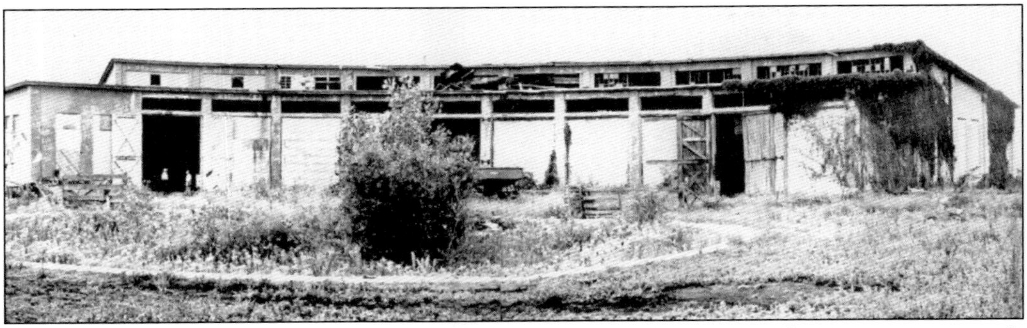

In 1893, a predecessor railroad of the EJ&E Railway, the CLS&E, made an agreement with the C&EI to have trackage rights over its line between Chicago Heights and Rossville located near Danville. This was to tap into the abundant soft coal reserves that the railroad needed for the growing demand of the Chicago-area steel mills. This picture shows the later 10-stall roundhouse built in 1913 at Rossville Junction as it looked years after the trackage rights were cancelled in 1947.

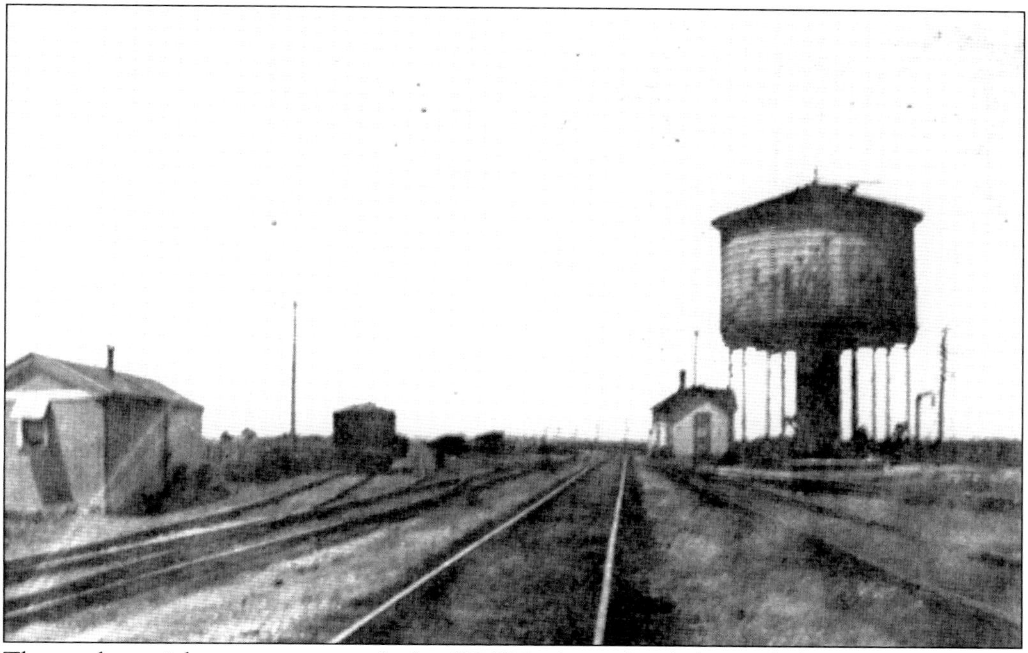

The trackage rights agreement with the C&EI had stipulated that only loaded coal cars and limestone deposits could be transported northbound and empties southbound. This photograph shows Rossville Junction before the roundhouse was built. Switch runs took empty cars to coal mines owned by United States Steel Corporation and brought loaded cars back to the Rossville yard. During the building of the Panama Canal (1910–1913), loaded limestone was carried by the EJ&E to Buffington to be converted into cement that was used in the construction of the canal.

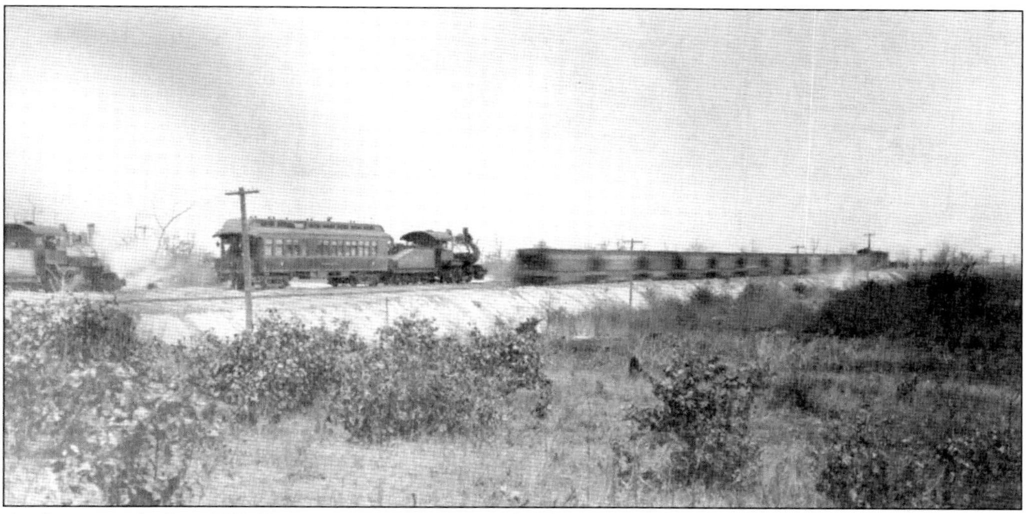

A glimpse of what EJ&E passenger equipment looked like can be seen in this scene taken on November 15, 1908. The train was a special passenger train consisting of the car *Buffington*, commemorating the first train crossing the new embankment leading to the Clark Road Bridge (No. 744), which was located west of Kirk Yard. This location was known as the high line and was near the bridge over the Wabash Railway.

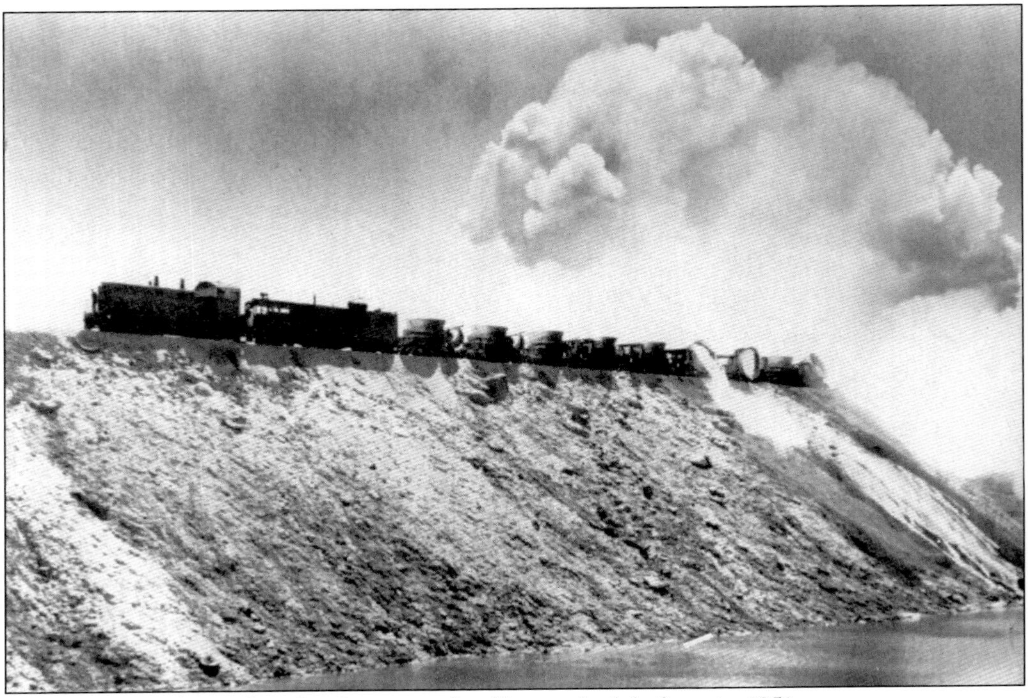

An EJ&E crew dumps hot slag from a steel mill near the lakefront in 1951.

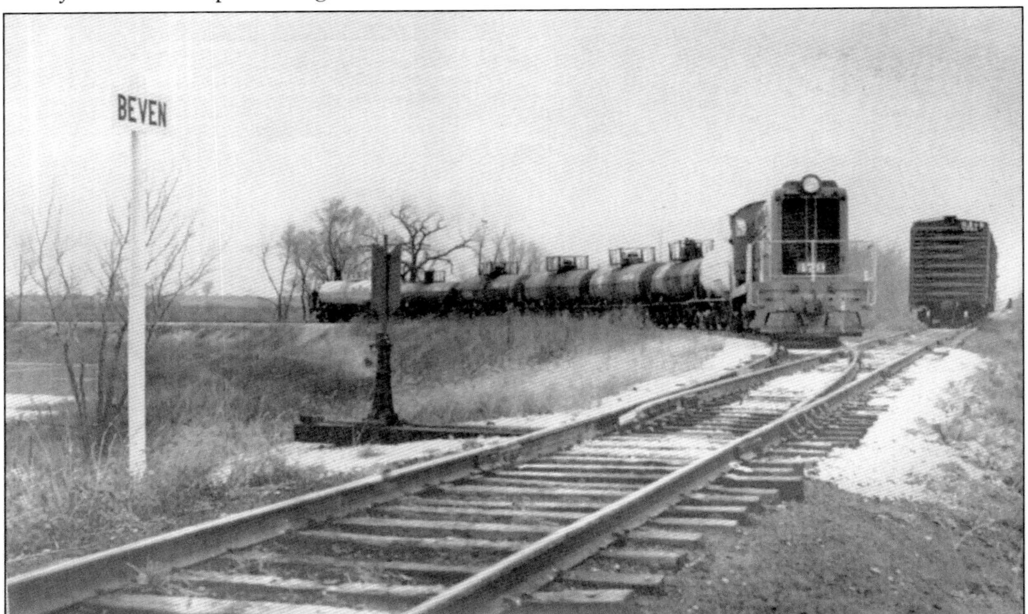

In 1963, a new station was named after retiring president Thomas Beven. It was located on the branch to Coal City, about one-half mile north of the Illinois River. A new spur was built west of there to serve industries that were located on the north bank of the river. The engine shown switching the spur was the No. 479, a Baldwin VO1000 that was built in 1944 and retired in 1975. The tank cars shown are carrying sulphuric acid to the Des Plaines Chemical Company.

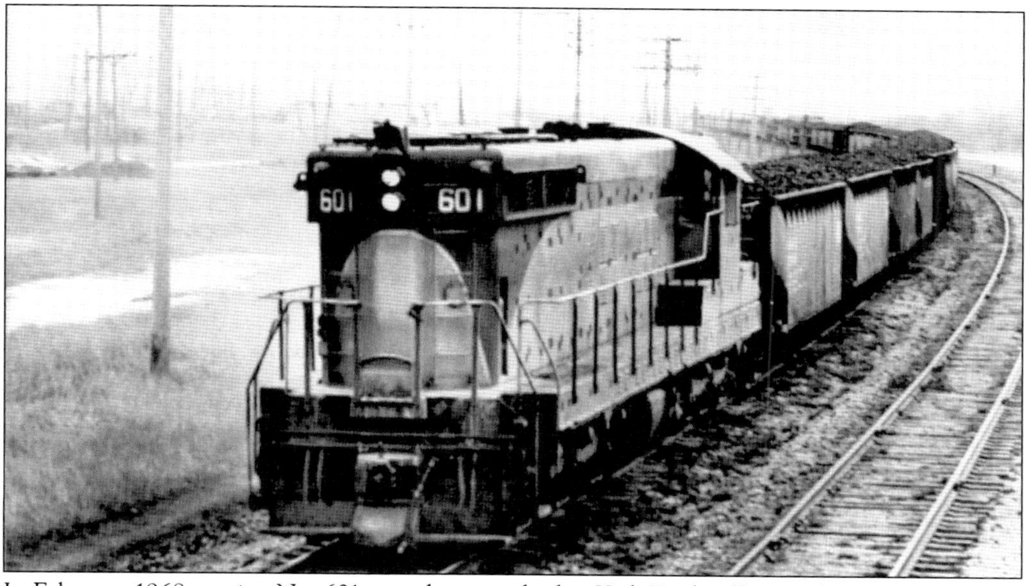

In February 1968, engine No. 601 was photographed at Kirk Yard pulling 83 hoppers of coke for the blast furnaces in south Chicago. The Norfolk and Western Railway delivered the train to the EJ&E at Van Loon. The engine was an SD9 built by EMD in March 1957 and was later sold to Montana Rail Link.

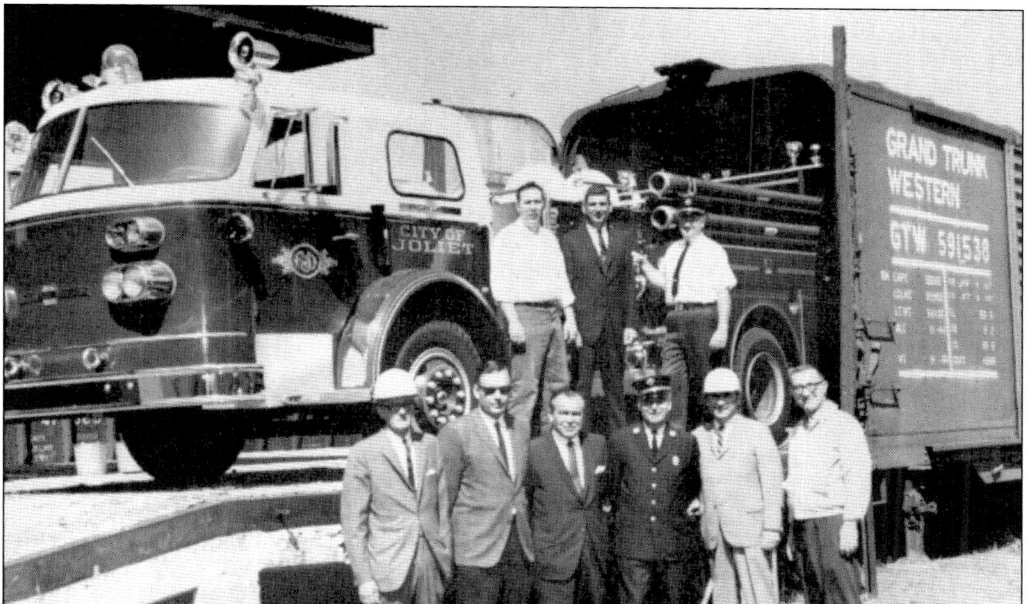

Delivering fire engines to on-line municipalities was a tradition on the EJ&E. In the summer of 1969, city officials from Joliet were on hand to receive this new piece of equipment. On the platform are, from left to right, fire department engineer Len Hohisel and assistant chiefs Ed Peters and Dan Russell. Standing below the platform are Joliet city officials (from left to right) comptroller Bob Frazer, councilmen Bob Hacker and George Tapella, Fire Chief Harold Rasmussen, city manager Bob Broucek, and councilman Dick Curran.

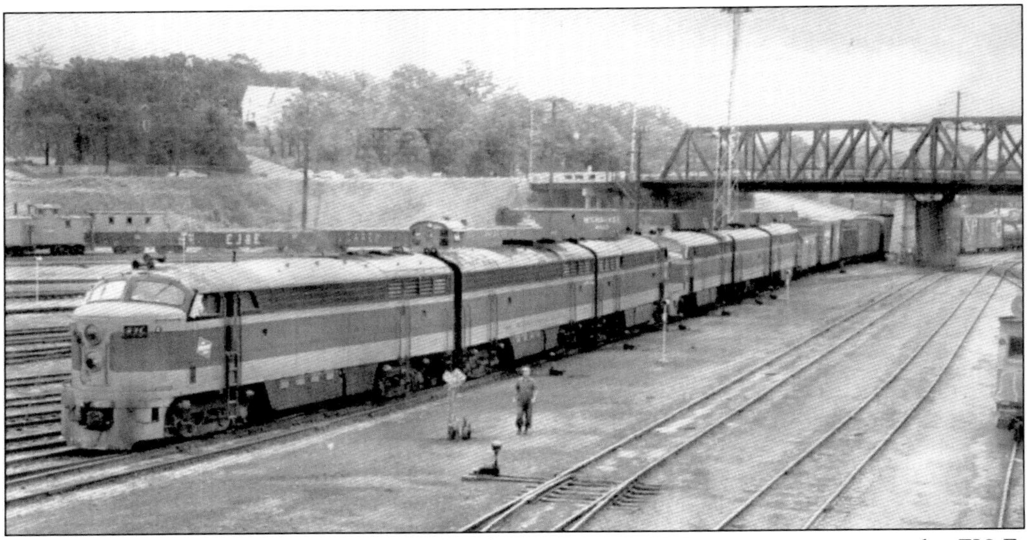

Detours of freight trains from other railroads were not a common occurrence on the EJ&E, but in June 1964, EJ&E came to the aid of the Milwaukee Road when the Baltimore and Ohio Chicago Terminal-Indiana Harbor Belt bridge over the Sanitary and Ship Canal at McCook collapsed. Milwaukee Road had rerouted its trains at Spaulding to the EJ&E tracks, which it used to reach East Joliet. At Washington Street, it connected to its own rails and proceeded south to Terre Haute, Indiana. This arrangement lasted until a temporary bridge at McCook was opened on July 6. A total of 55 Milwaukee Road trains had used the EJ&E detour during this period. The EJ&E in turn had detour agreements whereby it could run over other railroads. The Michigan Central Railroad was once used between Joliet and Hartsdale when a wreck blocked the EJ&E at Brisbane.

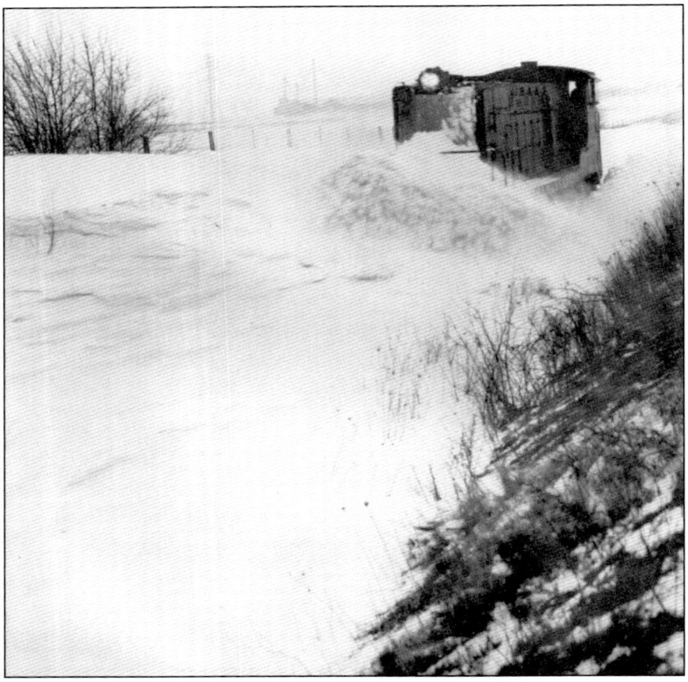

On January 26, 1967, 23 inches of snow fell in the Chicago area. It was during this time that the run to Aurora had encountered eight-foot snowdrifts. Each time a snowdrift was encountered, the engine was detached from the train and moved forward into the snow at 10 miles per hour to clear the track. The snowstorm was no obstacle for the dedicated EJ&E railroaders that kept operations from coming to a halt.

In the spring of 1967, the EJ&E became involved in grade crossing safety by participating in the Near Miss Program, which was a predecessor to Operation Lifesaver. Train crews were instructed to report any close encounters with school buses, vehicles transporting passengers for hire, or any vehicles carrying flammable or explosives. The report would be turned over to the Safety Department, which would write a letter to the offender; a personal visit would be made by a EJ&E special agent and the local authorities.

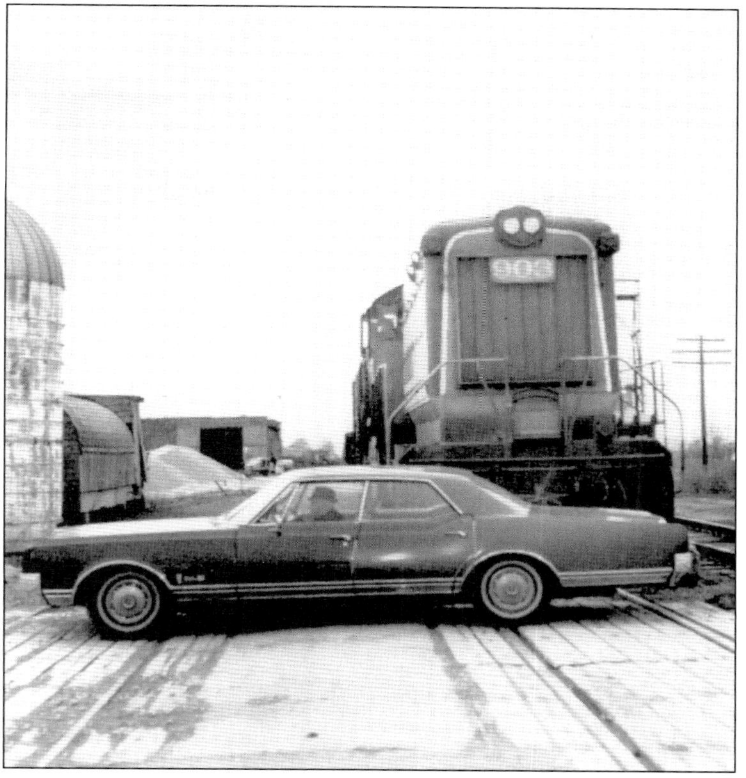

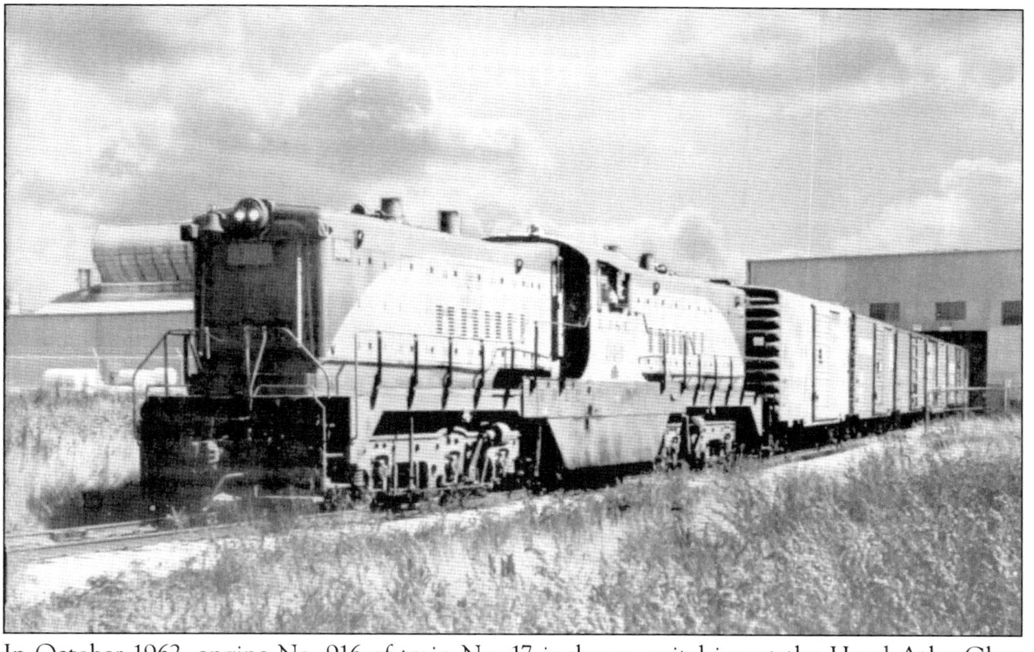

In October 1962, engine No. 916 of train No. 17 is shown switching at the Hazel Atlas Glass Division of Continental Can Company in Plainfield. Both the pickup and delivery of cars were handled daily at the plant.

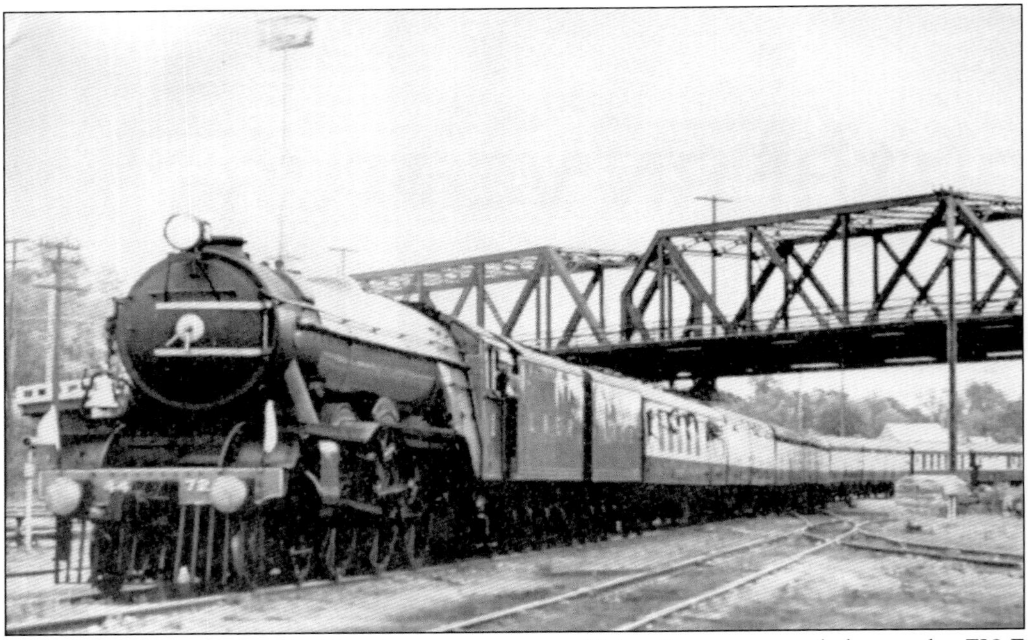

In the summer of 1971, the British passenger train *Flying Scotsman* traveled over the EJ&E between Hobart, Indiana, and Eola. The train was on a coast-to-coast goodwill trip destined for Fisherman's Wharf in San Francisco. The Norfolk and Western Railroad delivered the train to the EJ&E at Hobart and handed it over to the Burlington Northern Railroad at Eola. The *Flying Scotsman* held steam locomotive records for nonstop running and speed in Great Britain. Winston Churchill and Dwight Eisenhower used two of the cars during World War II.

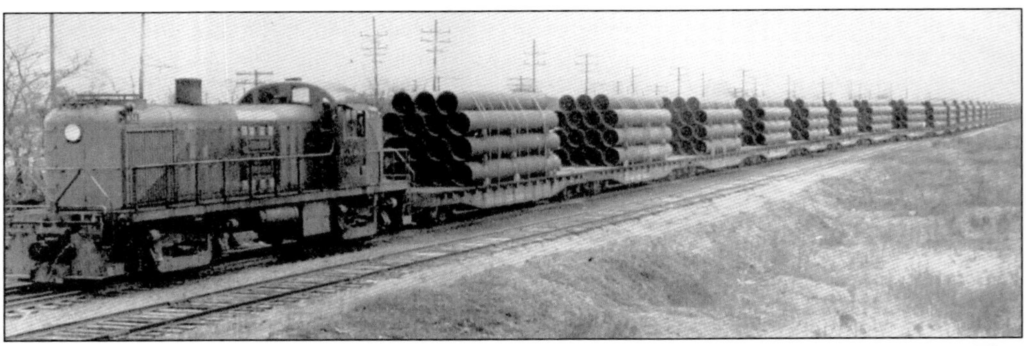

The EJ&E often handled special moves, and this one on April 11, 1950, was no exception. This trainload of pipe was received from the Santa Fe at Joliet and delivered to an eastern connection just a few hours later. Participating in the move were 13 different railroads.

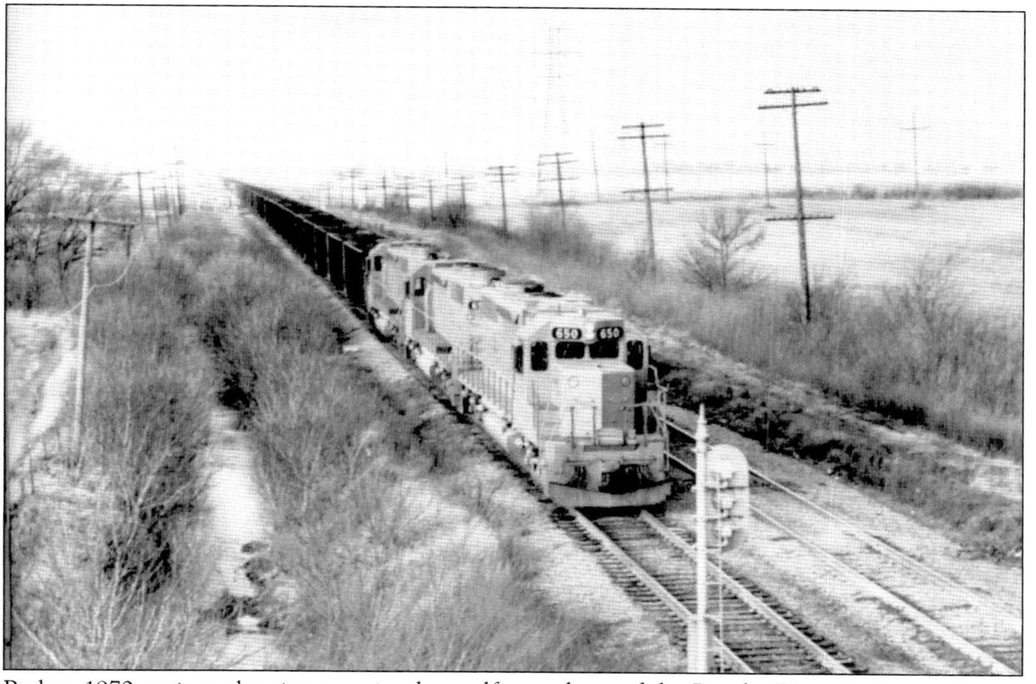

By late 1970, unit coal trains carrying low-sulfur coal out of the Powder River Basin area began running to Midwest power-generating stations. This was due to the newly passed Clean Air Act, which favored this coal with its lower sulfur dioxide content. This train originated at Colstrip, Montana, on the Burlington Northern Railroad and was headed for the Commonwealth Edison's State Line generating station. At Eola, the train made the switch from Burlington Northern Railroad to the EJ&E, where locomotives were also exchanged. This photograph was taken of the eastbound run at Brisbane.

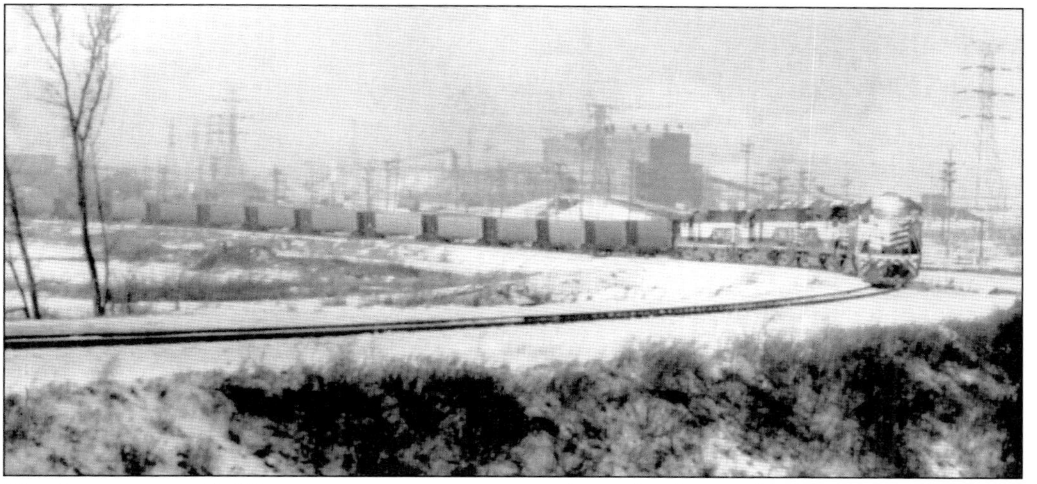

The Commonwealth Edison unit train is seen just after unloading at the State Line generating station and moving off the Lake Front line onto the CLS&E wye, en route back to East Joliet and the connection with the Gulf, Mobil and Ohio (GM&O) in December 1966. The high-sulfur coal was brought up from downstate Percy on the GM&O. The coal contract lasted until 1974, when low-sulfur coal from Montana and Wyoming became more desirable to burn.

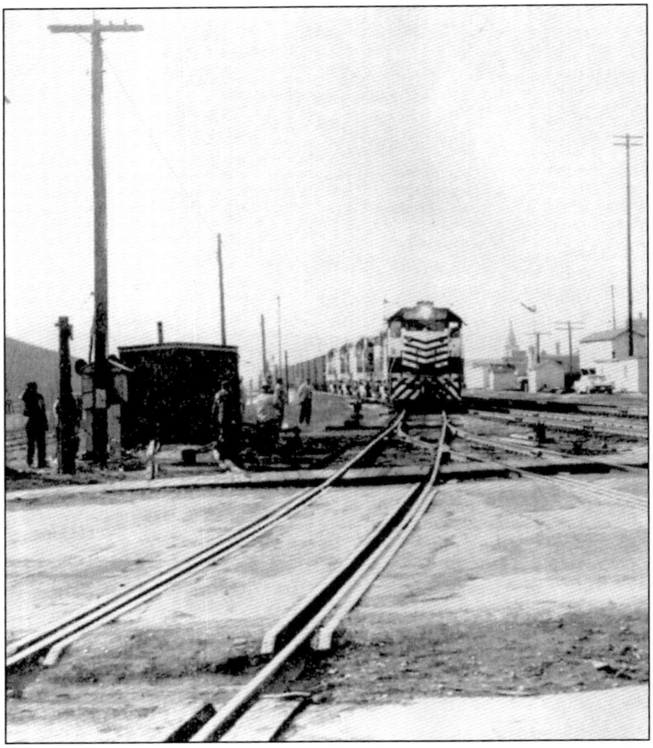

In the spring of 1966, Extra 607 North, the Commonwealth Edison unit train was ready to swing off the GM&O at Jackson Street in Joliet onto the EJ&E and become Extra GM&O 607 East to the EJ&E train dispatcher. Normal consist of this train was five GM&O GP35s pulling 102 cars with a capacity of 100 tons of coal per car. The train had taken a total of three hours to run from Joliet to the State Line generating station (Hammond, Indiana). Coal trains could also be sent to the generating station in Waukegan.

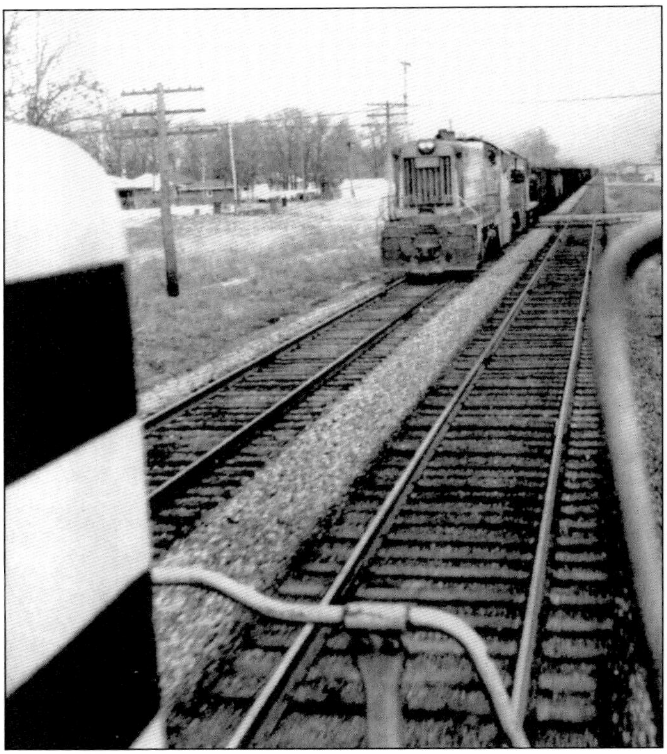

The Commonwealth Edison unit train was heading north where it met Extra 906-300, the Hartsdale turnout of Gary in the spring of 1966. Diesels, cars, or cabooses were never changed in the round-trip run from Percy to the State Line generating station. The train had a fast turnaround time that allowed the cars to be reloaded every other day, compared to conventional service, which would have taken the minimum of nine days to complete the turnaround.

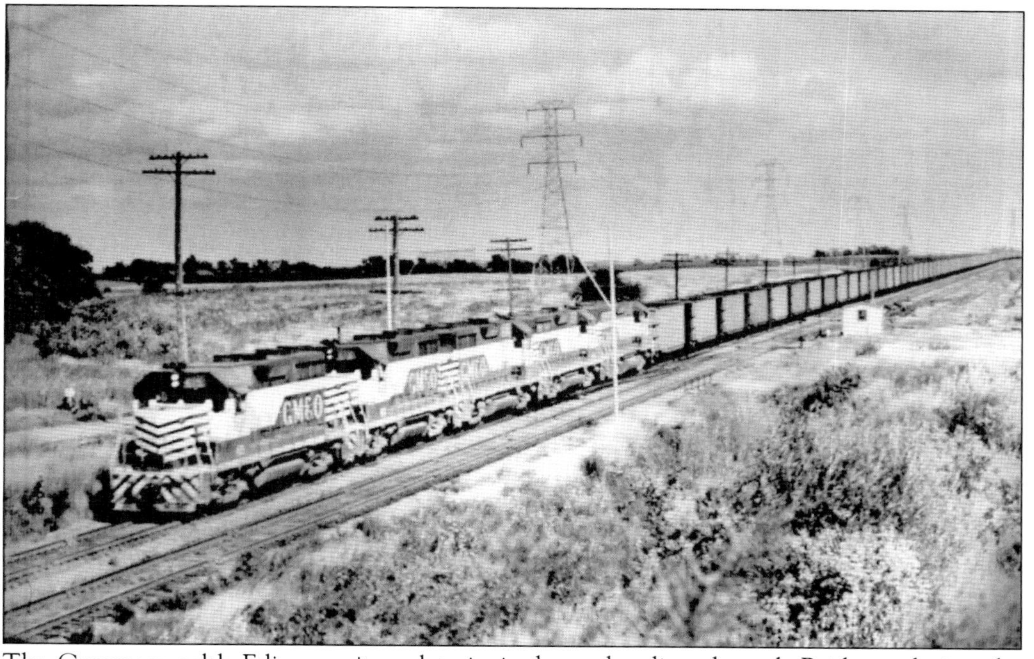

The Commonwealth Edison unit coal train is shown heading through Brisbane during the summer of 1966, on its way back to the mine in southern Illinois. The train completed the 700-mile round trip between the State Line generating station and Percy every other day. GM&O engines pulled the unit train for the total distance.

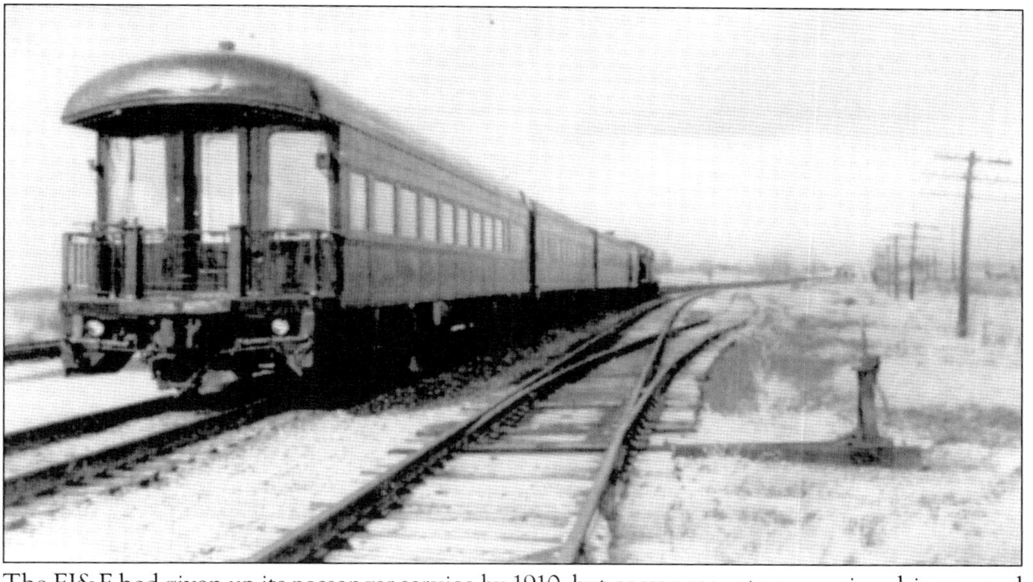

The EJ&E had given up its passenger service by 1910, but passenger extras carrying shippers and executives were run every so often. In October 1966, a three-car extra was run for prominent Chicago-area real estate executives to make them aware of industrial sites along the EJ&E right-of-way. The train run originated in South Chicago and made stops at Kirk Yard, East Joliet, Plainfield, and Spaulding yard (near Elgin) and ended in Waukegan, where awaiting automobiles took them back to Chicago.

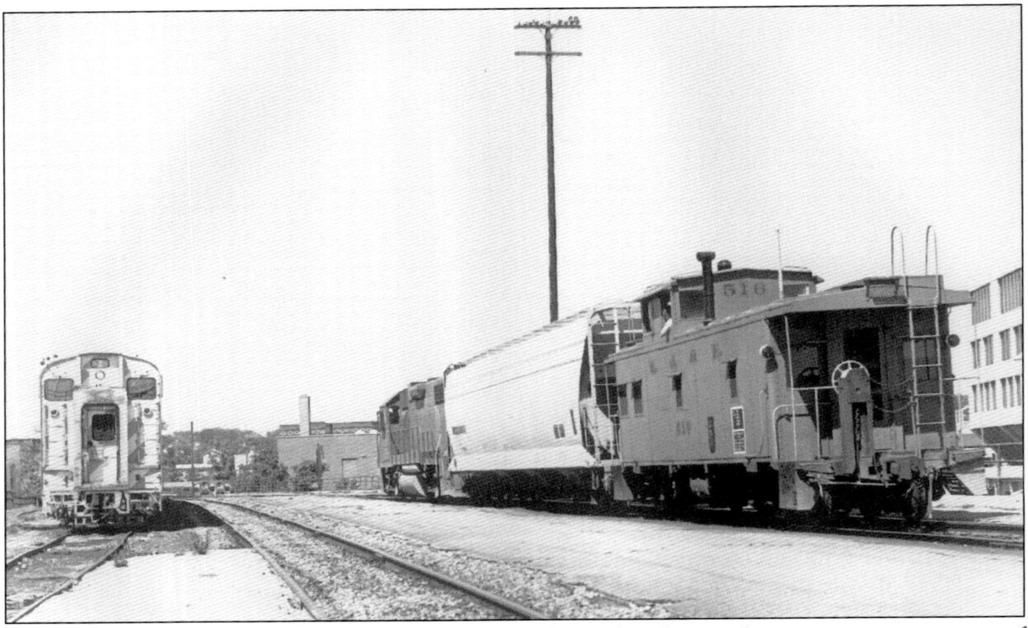

Shortly after the Chicago, Rock Island, and Pacific Railroad ceased operation on account of bankruptcy in March 1980, the EJ&E became the directed service carrier by the Interstate Commerce Commission on March 28, 1980, between East Joliet and Peoria. Usual motive power was GP38-2s and SW1200s. The EJ&E provided service on this line until May 31, 1980, when it was decided by the management that the price tag set by the bankruptcy court was more than what they wanted to pay. That spring, a Peoria-bound freight on Rock Island trackage was just outside the Joliet Union Station. (Bill Raia collection.)

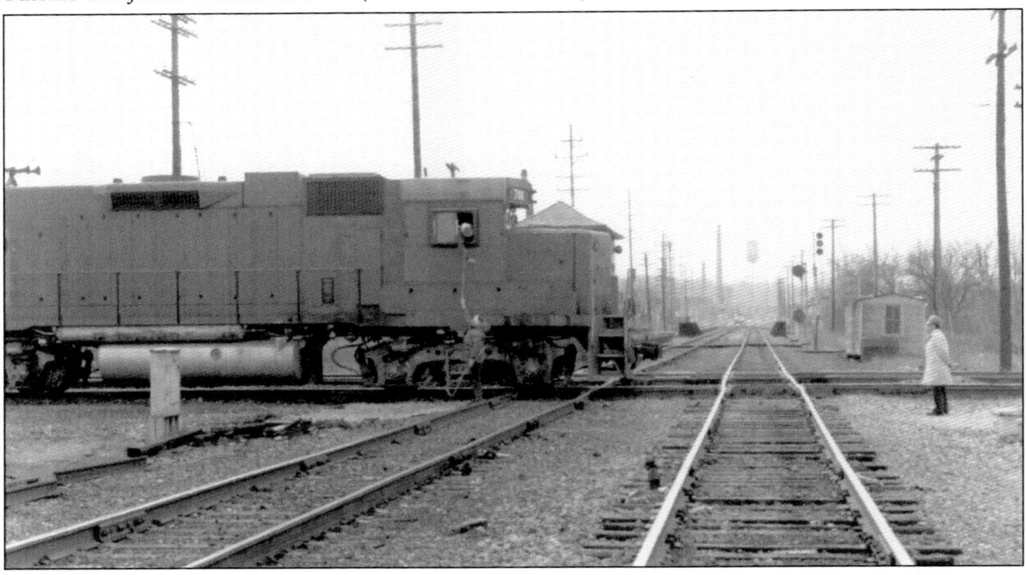

A westbound EJ&E freight train is to the north of the Rock Island tower in Joliet, catching train orders from the operator for the run to Peoria in the spring of 1980. The EJ&E was interested in this line because of the steel it could haul to the many Caterpillar plants in the Peoria area, in addition to the grain and chemical traffic that traversed this trackage. (Bill Raia collection.)

Four

The Employees that Made the Railroad What It Is Today

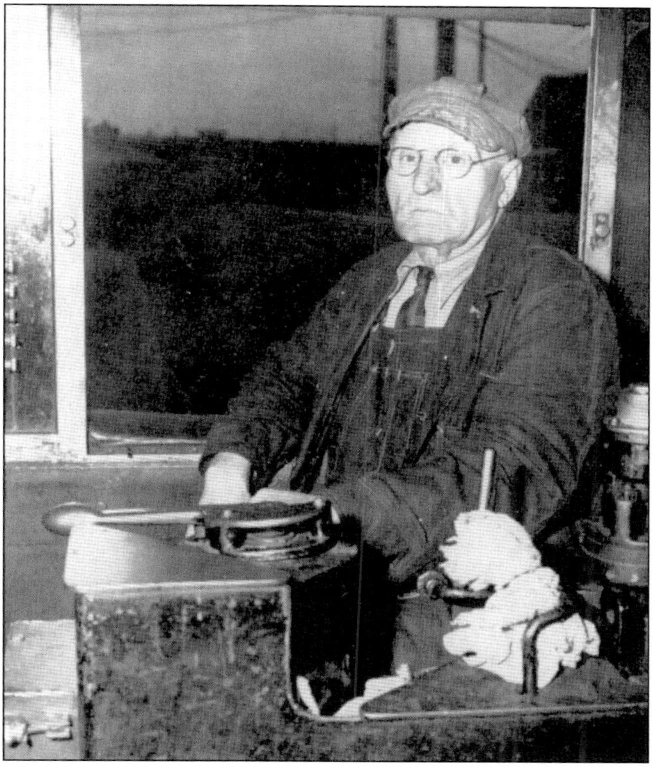

The EJ&E honored Otto Loeffler by naming him Mr. Jay of 1950. He completed 60 years of safety-starred service. Loeffler entered railroad service as a helper in 1890 and progressed to locomotive engineer. The EJ&E was and still is one of the most safety conscious railroads in the world.

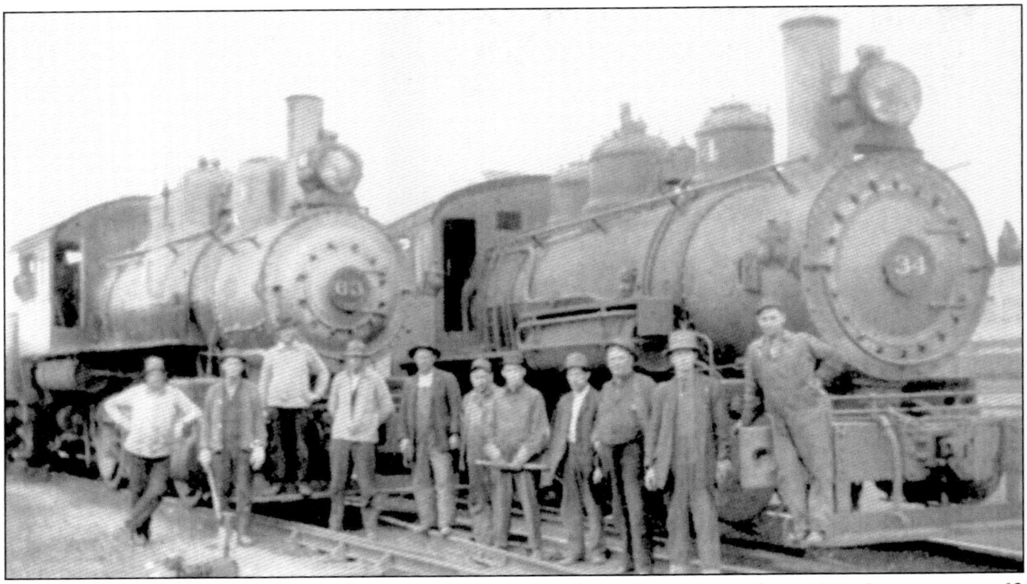

Locomotive 34 was built by Baldwin in 1903 as the 21 and was retired in 1941. Locomotive 63 was built by Alco Pittsburgh in 1907 as the 31 and was retired in 1940. Both locomotives were 0-6-0 switchers. The location of this photograph is not known, but it is dated 1920. Pictured are yardmaster Thomas Tracy (third from right) and two of his yard crews. Note the two switchmen holding brake clubs.

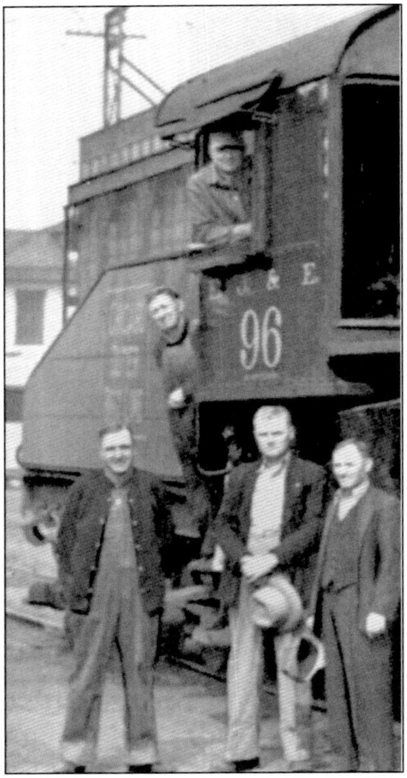

In 1939, an East Joliet switch crew took time out to pose for a photograph with trainmaster Al J. Fitzgerald (middle bottom). Switchman W. J. Carlson (bottom left) and foreman J. Engstrom (bottom right) worked with engineer B. Clow (in the engine cab window) and fireman S. Carlson (on engine steps). Fitzgerald was the "top kick" trainmaster-in-charge of the whole East Joliet yard. Engstrom was dressed rather well for someone working in a railroad yard switching freight cars.

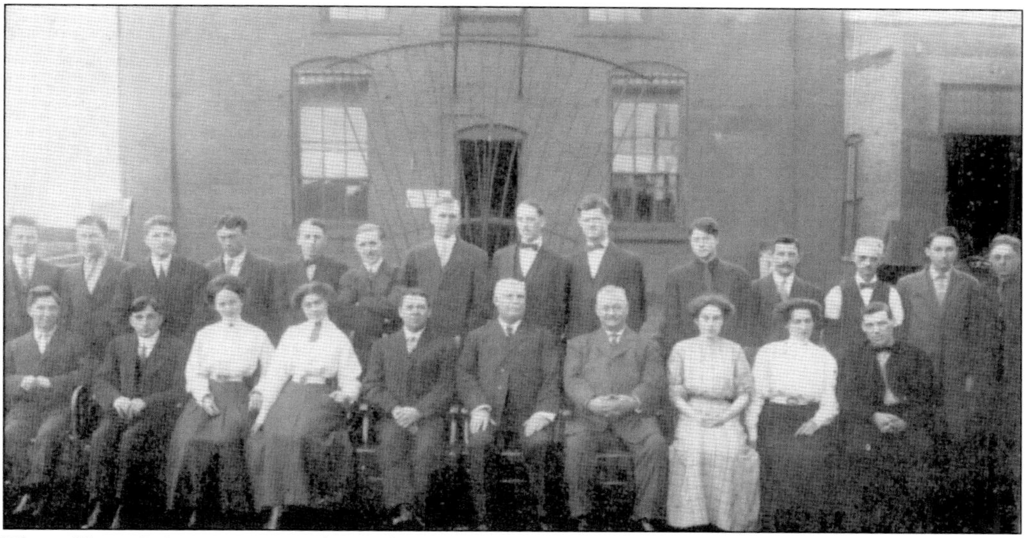

The office of the superintendent of motive power also had charge of the system storehouses in 1912. George S. Wright, fourth from right, was believed to be the topmost official in this photograph.

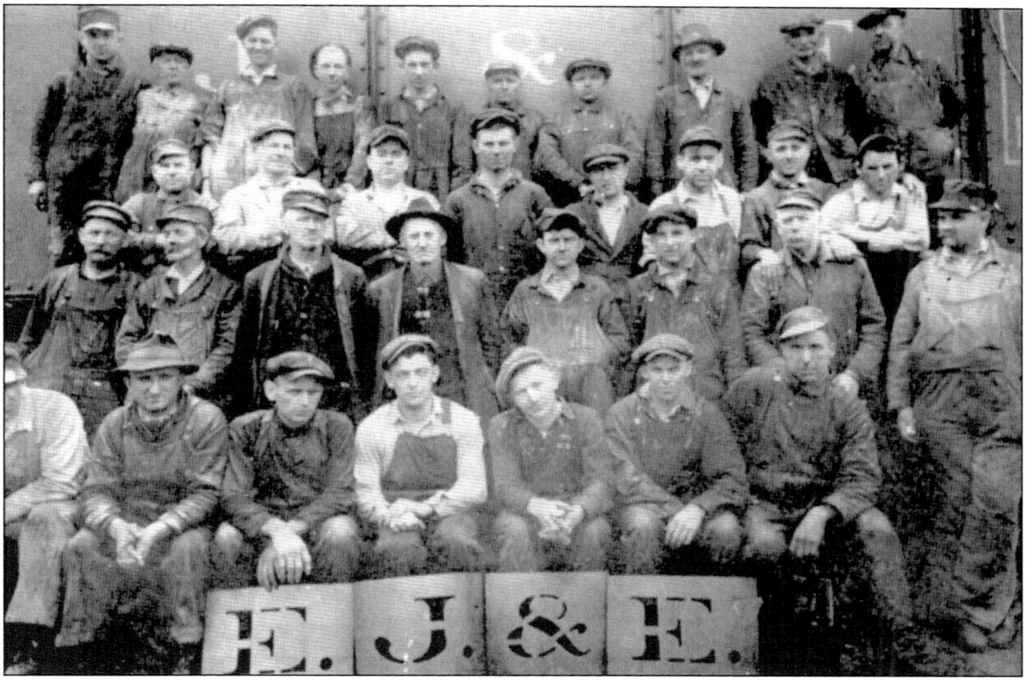

Here are just some of the EJ&E men who in 1923 repaired and maintained freight cars. Second row, fourth from the left is foreman Eric Erickson. Over the years, the EJ&E provided its employees, especially those in the shops, with better and better tools and equipment. Because the freight cars received very hard use hauling steel and other commodities, repair and even extensive rebuilding was frequently necessary.

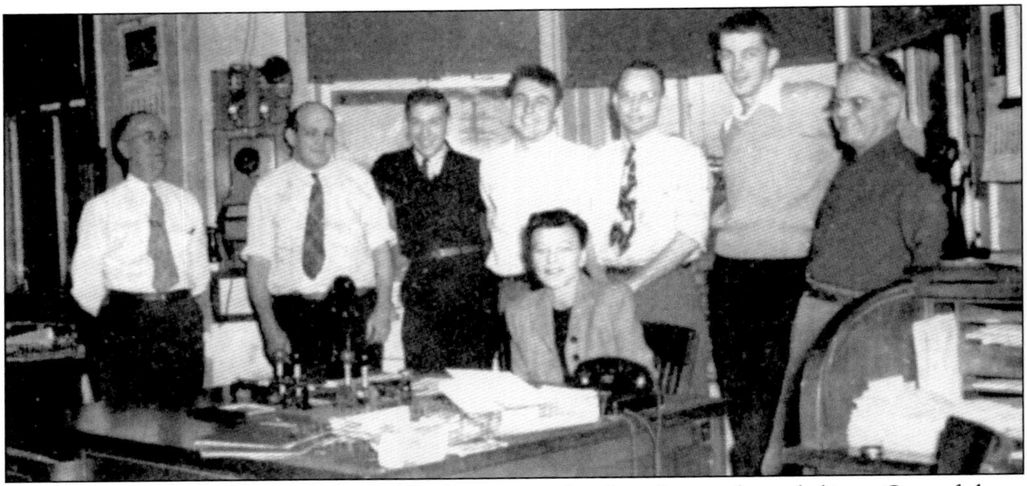

Because the EJ&E served hundreds of industries, it developed some branch lines. One of those was in Hammond where an agent's office was located at Hohman Avenue just south of Michigan Street. All of these employees were necessary to keep track of the business along the line. Agent Bill O'Neal was absent the day this photograph was taken. Seated is Esther Jacobs and standing are, from left to right, Paul Gaffney, Ted Kammer, Chuck Cahl, Bill Anderson, Fred Grimmer, Ed Zumbahlen, and Dewey Snyder.

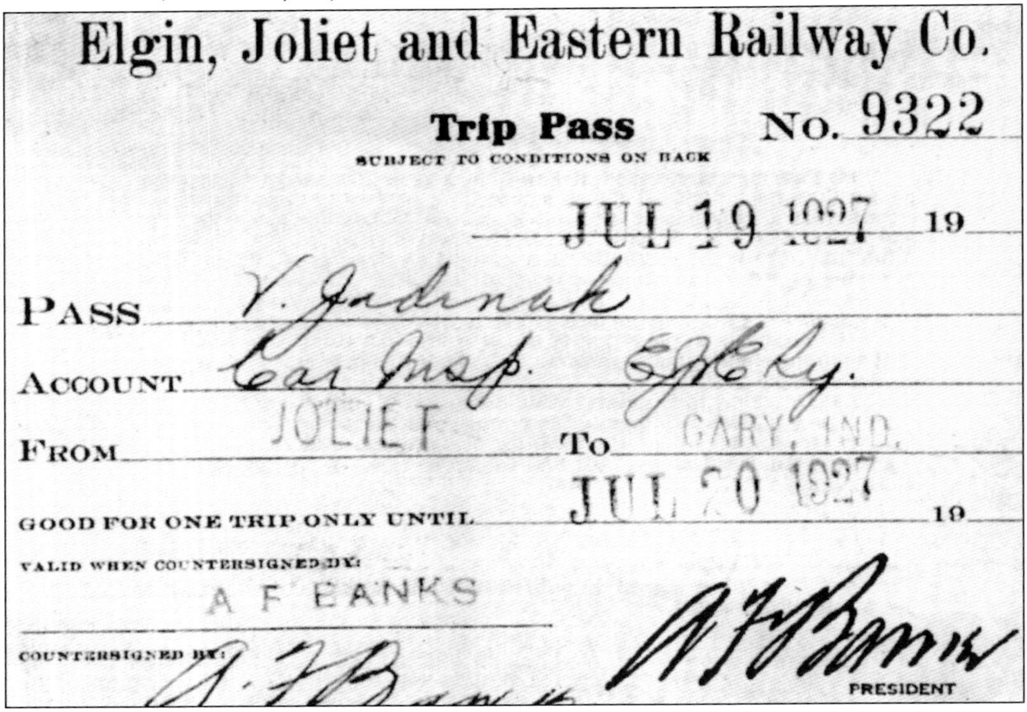

Elgin, Joliet and Eastern Railway Co.

Trip Pass No. 9322

SUBJECT TO CONDITIONS ON BACK

JUL 19 1927 19

PASS V. Jadrnak

ACCOUNT Car Insp. EJ&E Ry.

FROM JOLIET TO GARY, IND.

GOOD FOR ONE TRIP ONLY UNTIL JUL 20 1927 19

VALID WHEN COUNTERSIGNED BY:

A F BANKS

COUNTERSIGNED BY: A. F. Banks

A F Banks

PRESIDENT

Annual employee picnics were held at different locations like Dellwood Park in Lockport, Electric Park in Plainfield, or Highland Park in Joliet. Trip passes were issued to employees so they could ride special picnic trains. This particular pass was dated July 19, 1927, and was issued to Gary car man Victor Jadrnak. The first annual employee picnic was held on July 31, 1898, with over 600 employees and their families being taken to Lake Zurich.

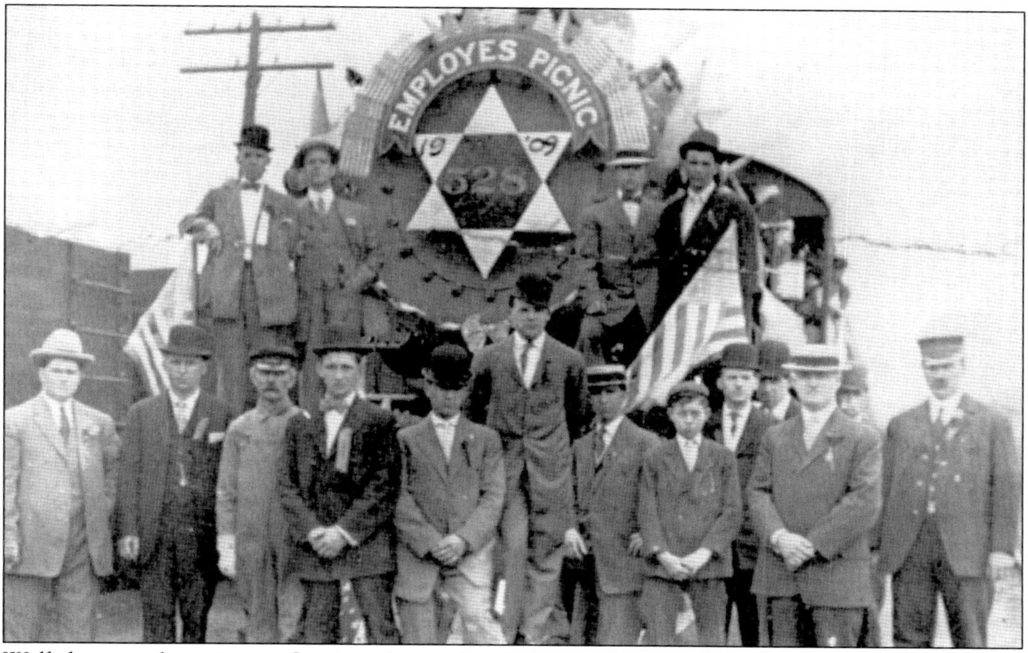

Well-decorated engines reflecting the pride of the employees of the EJ&E always pulled the picnic trains. Engine No. 528 was honored on June 21, 1909. Some members of the picnic committee posed here with the train crew for the photographer. Note the conductor in complete, brass-buttoned uniform on the right. Unfortunately, the names of everyone in the photograph were not recorded.

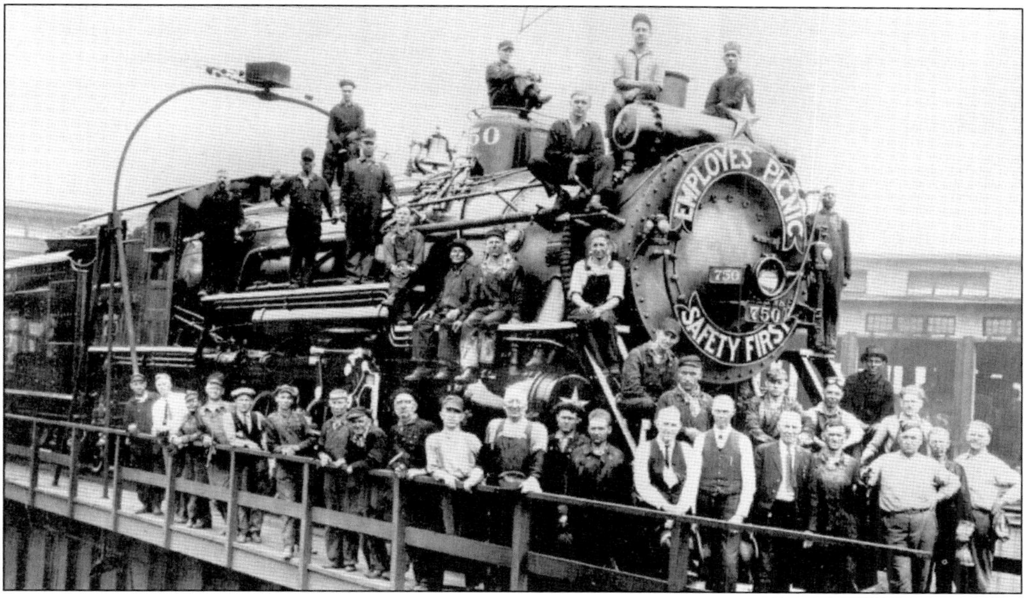

Engine No. 750 was dressed up for the annual employee picnic held at the Dellwood Park in Lockport on July 20, 1927. The locomotive was shown on the turntable at Kirk Yard, where it was ready to be coupled to a special passenger train hauling employees and their families to the picnic grounds.

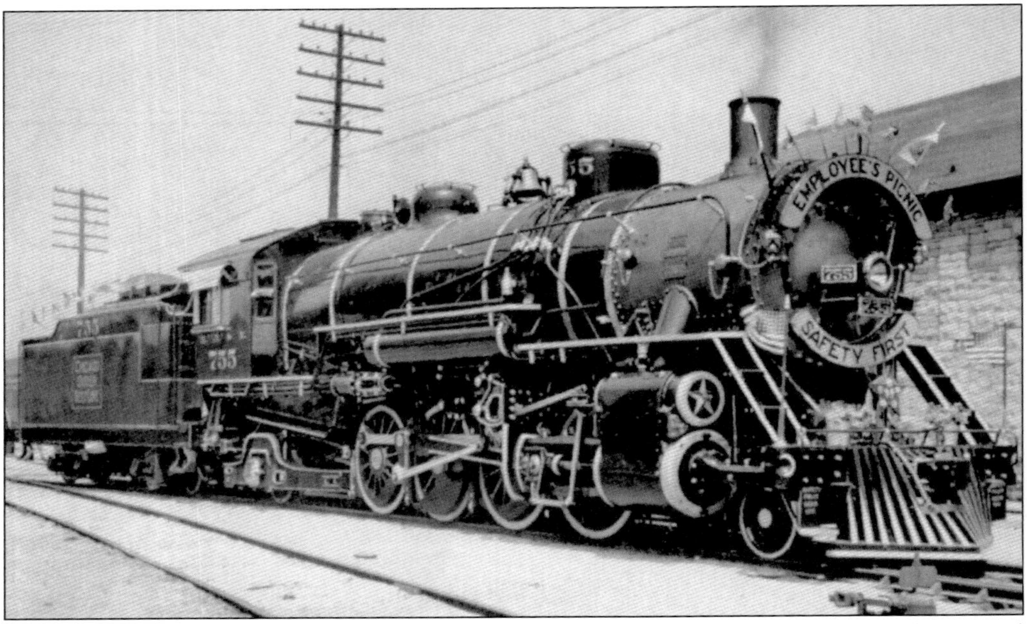

In 1929, 2-8-2 755 was one of the engines doing the honors on a picnic train. The special trains would sometimes take their passengers to Collins Street in Joliet, where Chicago and Joliet Electric interurban cars were boarded for a short run up to Dellwood Park in Lockport. Attendance at the picnics sometimes totaled over 20,000 employees and families with special trains coming from Gary, South Chicago, Waukegan, and even Rossville.

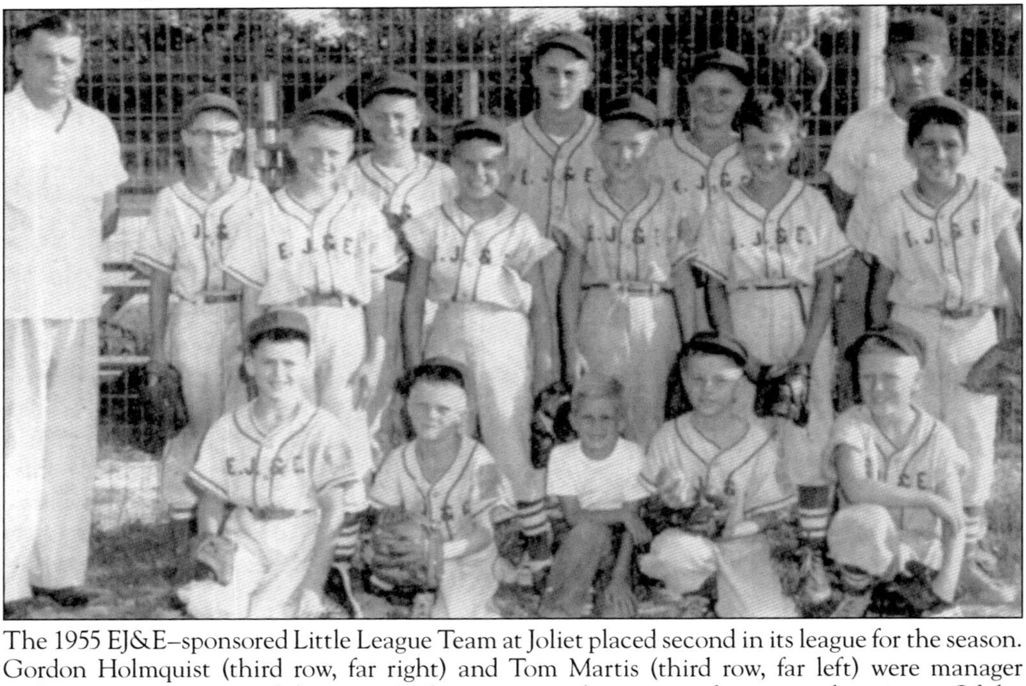

The 1955 EJ&E–sponsored Little League Team at Joliet placed second in its league for the season. Gordon Holmquist (third row, far right) and Tom Martis (third row, far left) were manager and assistant managers of the team. Holmquist was a locomotive fireman and engineer. Of the 14 players, 5 were sons of EJ&E employees.

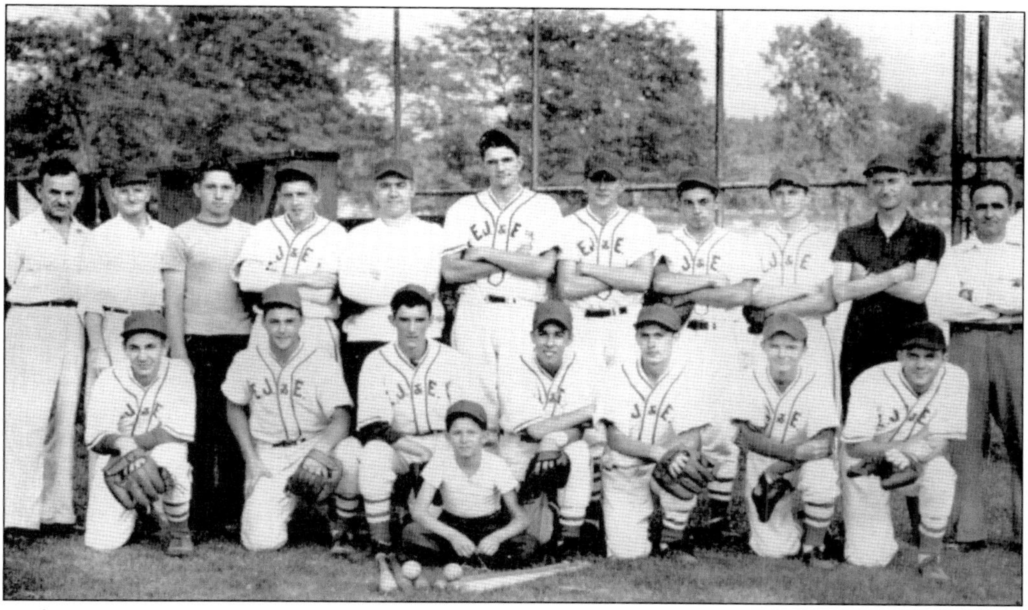

In the summer of 1948, the EJ&E American Legion Junior Baseball Team was hopeful of winning state and national championships.

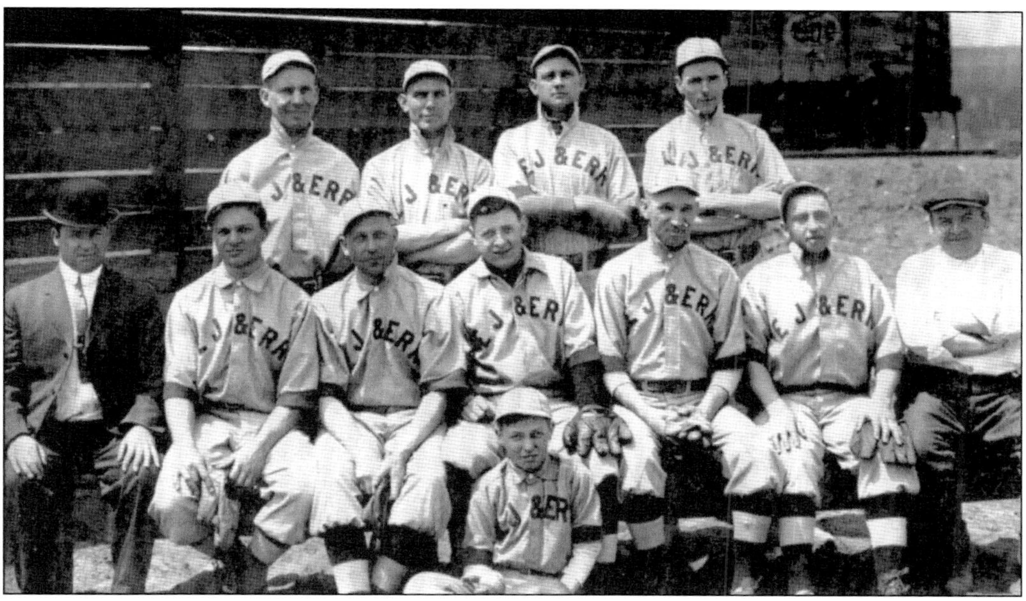

Young boys' baseball teams were not the only athletic activities sponsored by the EJ&E. In 1913, this team of employees competed in the Gary City League. The EJ&E supported many sports activities.

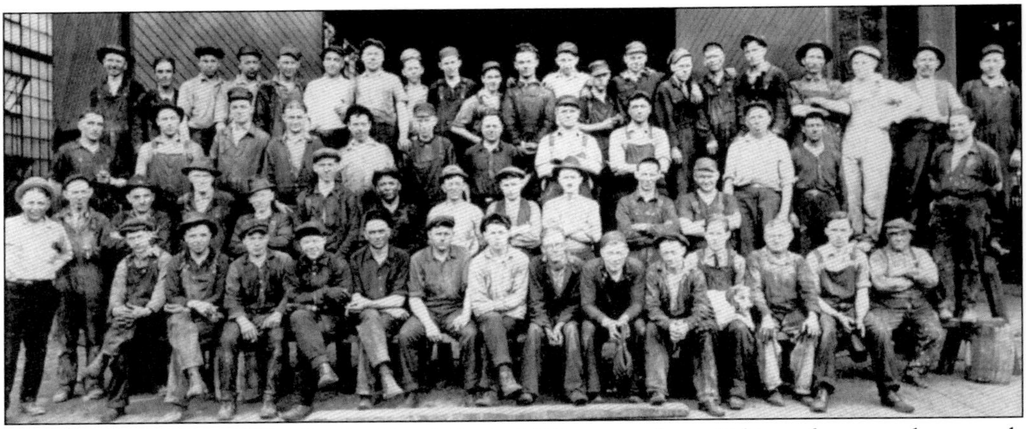

Back shop employees of the EJ&E at East Joliet in 1922 are seen here. Taking of a group photograph was always a special occasion. These men did the extensive overhaul work on locomotives. They were able to literally take one apart and put it back together again.

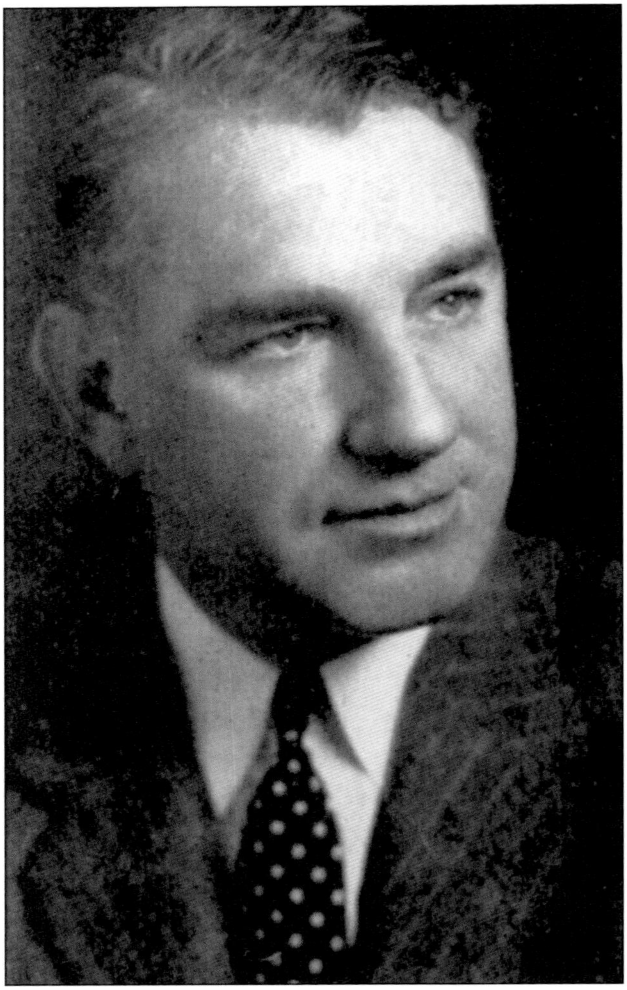

Thomas Delaney Beven, elected EJ&E president in 1946, guided the railroad through a period of tremendous growth. He was a man who would let other employees share the limelight and would recognize them for a job well done. The *J-Milepost* magazine was started in 1948, and over the years, Beven shared the inside front cover space with many employees for all departments. He was so well liked that a station point on the Illinois River line was named for him.

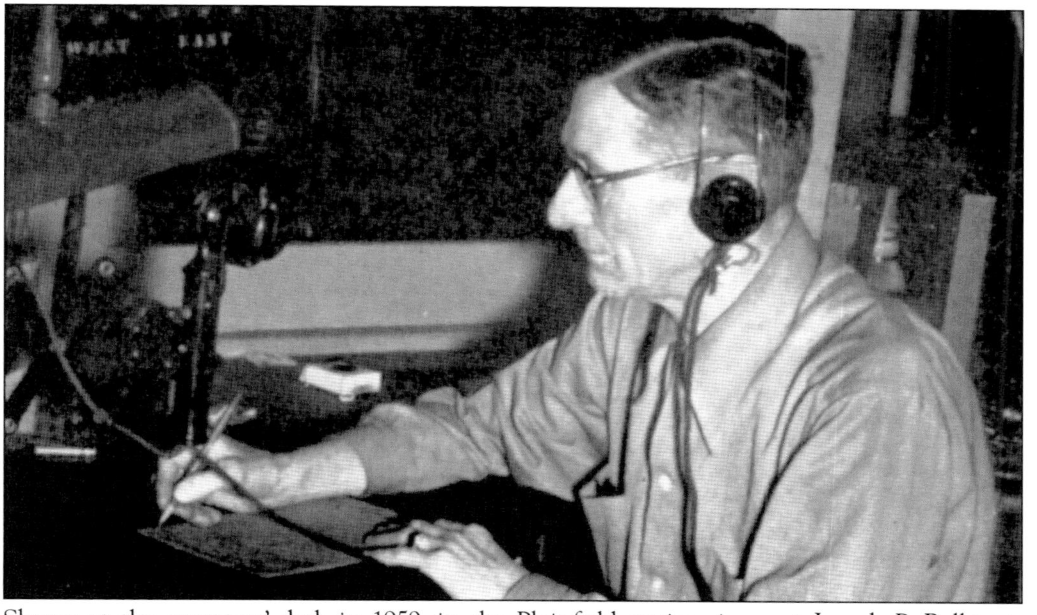

Shown at the operators' desk in 1959, in the Plainfield station, is agent Joseph P. Balbinot. He started working on the EJ&E in 1927. Balbinot prevented a derailment when he spotted a dragging brake beam under a freight car. Superintendent Thomas Murphy of the Joliet Division made sure that he was commended for his alertness and quick action in averting what could have been a serious accident.

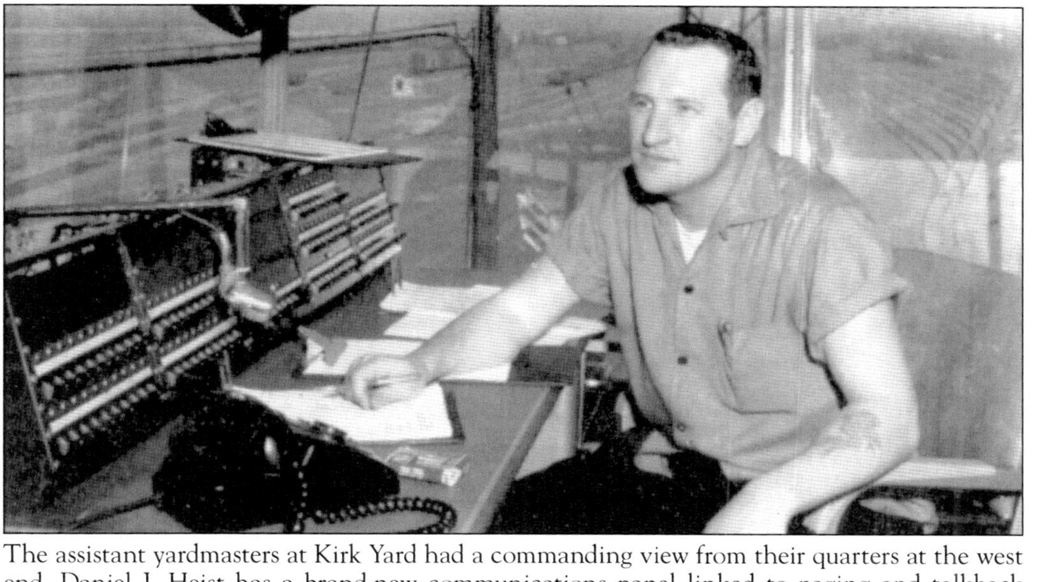

The assistant yardmasters at Kirk Yard had a commanding view from their quarters at the west end. Daniel J. Heist has a brand-new communications panel linked to paging and talkback speakers along the tracks. The facility was completed in 1958.

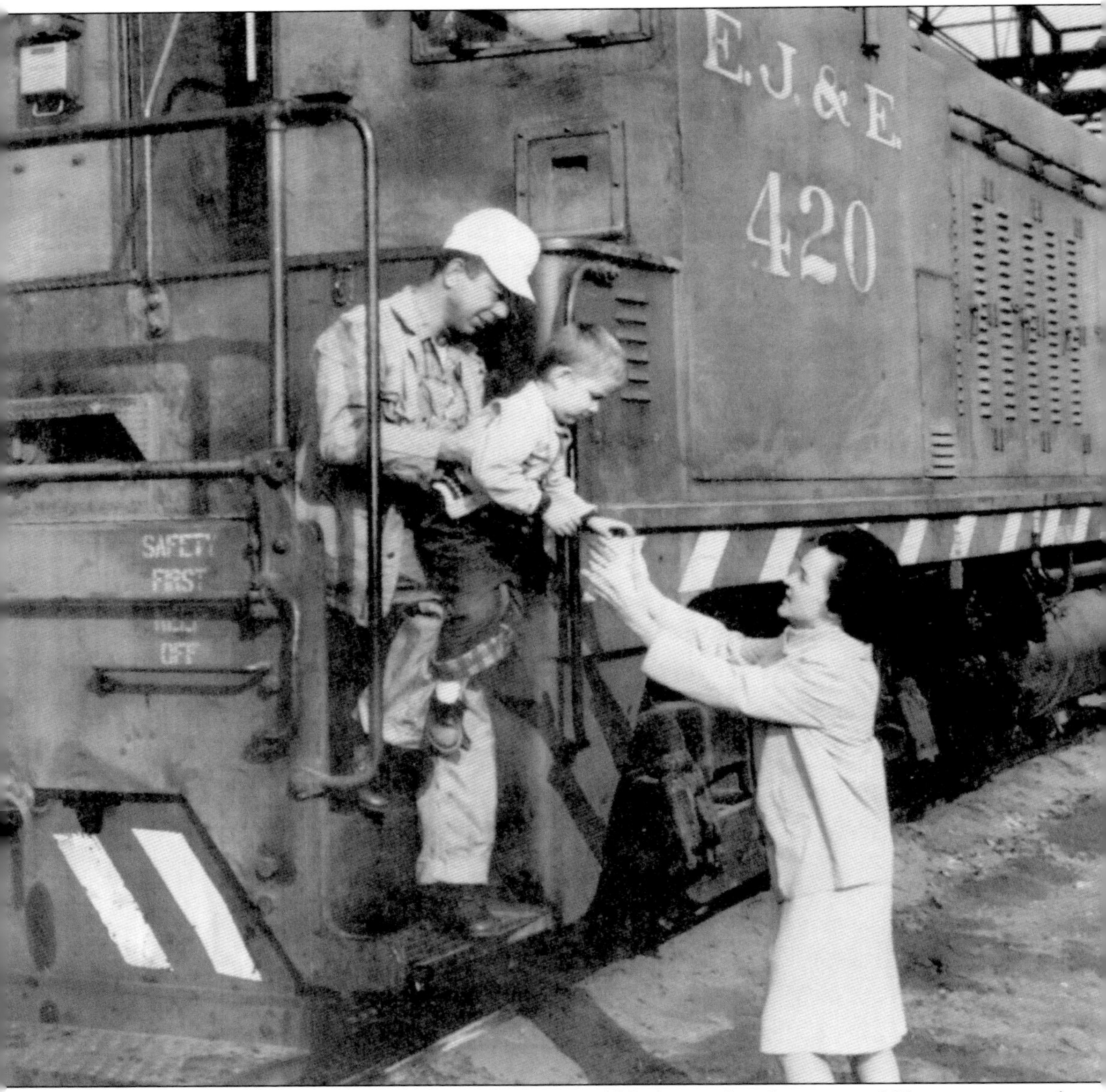

Thanks to the alertness of Gary engineman Harold Jackson, this three-year-old boy was spotted wandering near the EJ&E tracks in East Chicago in the summer of 1963. Jackson notified the local police, who were previously alerted by the boy's parents that the child was missing. This photograph shows the engineman returning the boy to his mother.

Helping on-line communities has always been an EJ&E tradition. In December 1965, 36,000 pounds of clothing were gathered from 24 parishes in the Joliet Catholic Diocese to be sent overseas for needy families. Overseeing the loading is, standing center, Rev. Msgr. Matthias J. Butala, pastor of St. Joseph's Church in Joliet. Holding the large box is Frank Scheid and standing in the freight car are Richard and Leonard Venturo.

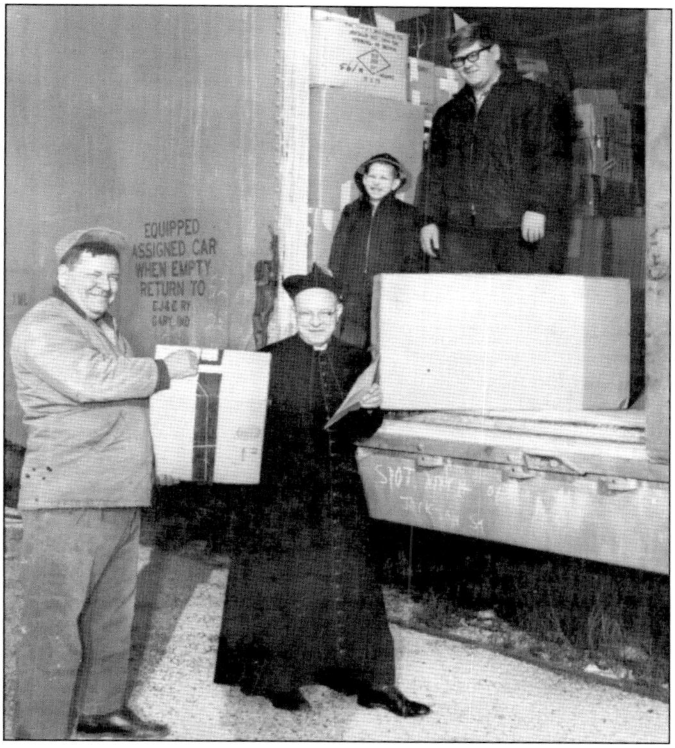

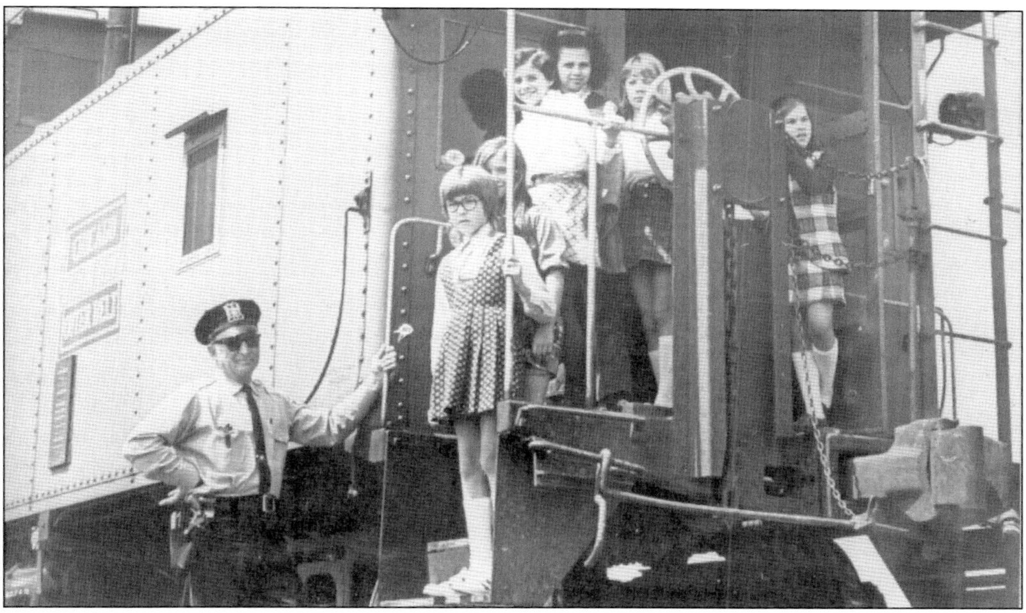

In April 1972, fifth-grade students from the Minooka Elementary School were given the opportunity to inspect caboose No. 529 under the supervision of special agent James Telfer. Students had come out to visit the train, which ran past the school grounds. Arrangements were made with the railroad in advance to stop the train so that the students could learn about railroading. Over 90 students had visited the train.

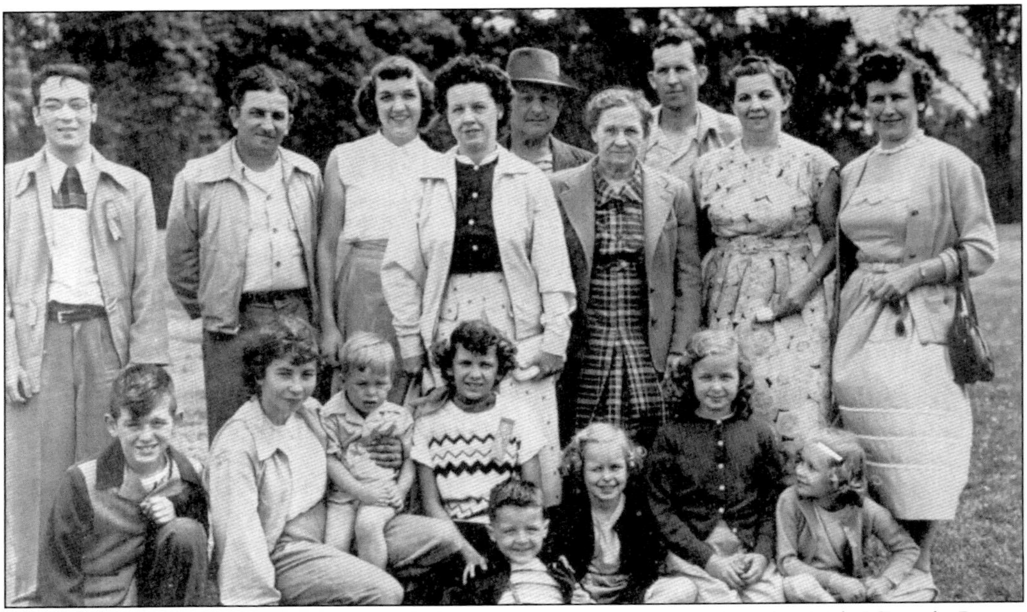

The family of car repairman Robert Schwartz of Gary was pictured at the 36th J Family Picnic in 1951. The affair was held on Sunday, August 5 at the Pilcher and Highland Parks in Joliet. Over 14,000 attended. A 14-car train brought families from South Chicago and Gary. Another came down from Waukegan.

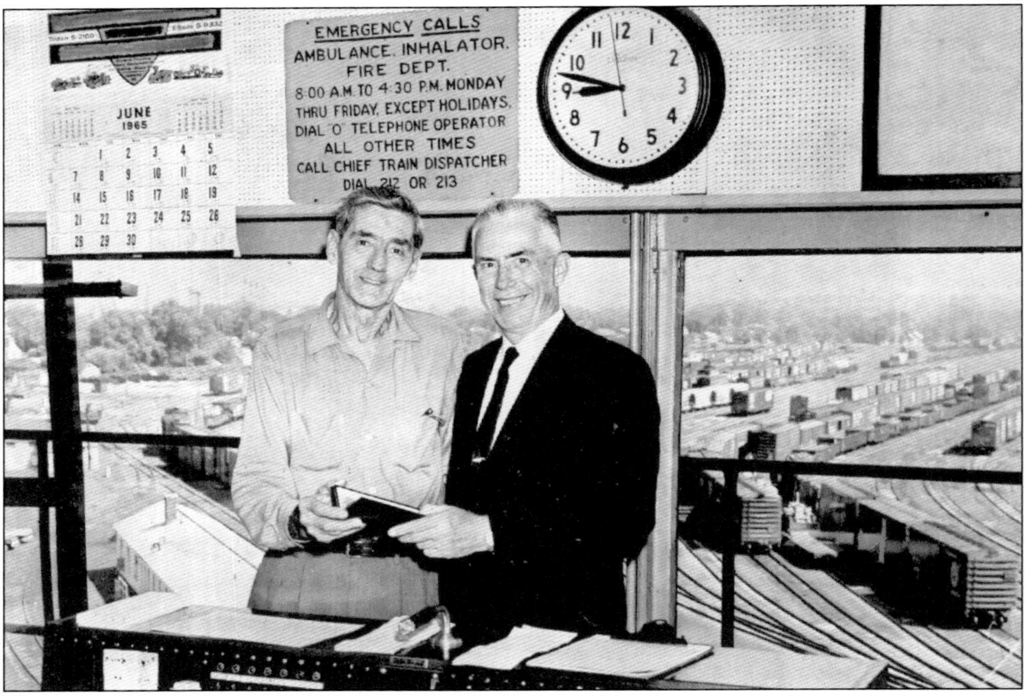

Pins and watches were presented to employees with 10, 25, 35, 45, and 50 years of service. In June 1965, general superintendent Vern Christensen (right) presents East Joliet assistant yardmaster George Sticker with a Ball railroad watch for 45 years of service.

Communication between engine and yard personnel was greatly improved by a two-way radio system that was first installed at South Chicago in 1959. It greatly enhanced the scheduling of pickups at customer locations and the handling of emergencies. In August 1962, engineman Thomas Davis was at the controls of engine No. 443 with engine foreman Joseph Plummer on the private line radio talking to the yardmaster.

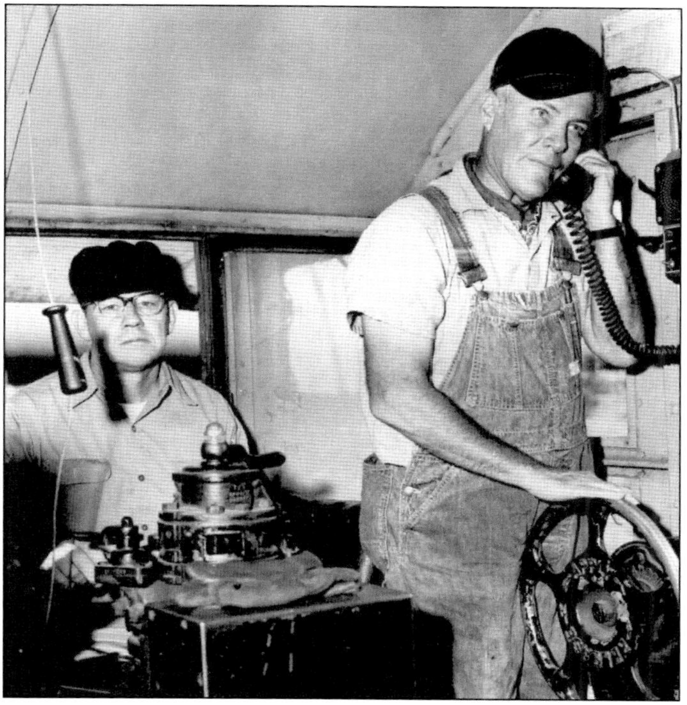

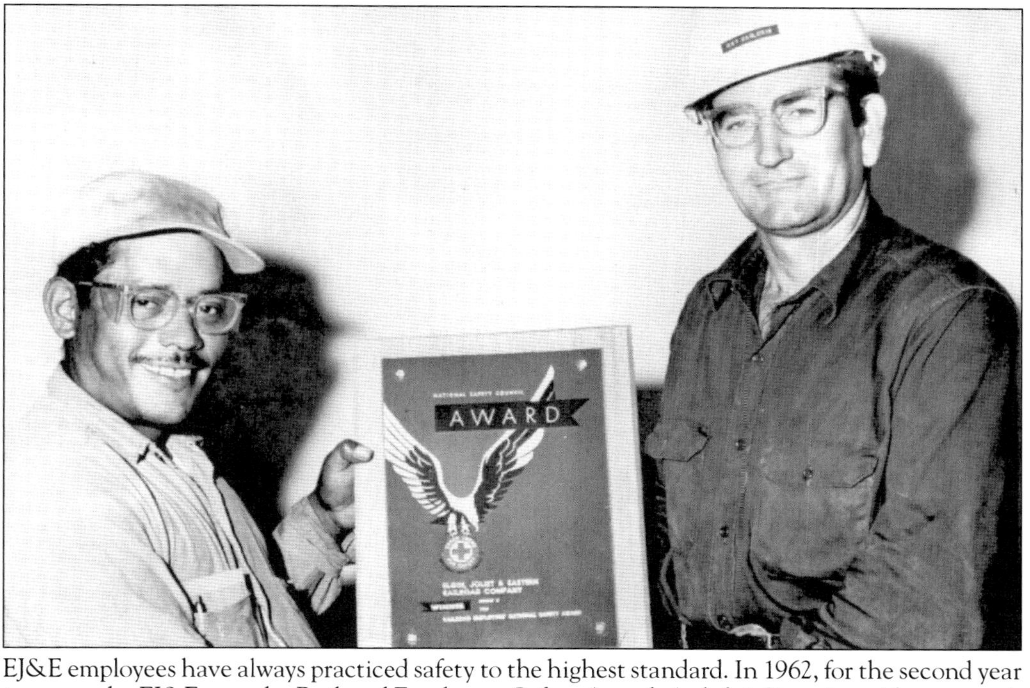

EJ&E employees have always practiced safety to the highest standard. In 1962, for the second year in a row, the EJ&E won the Railroad Employees Safety Award. At left is Francisco Alvarez, track foreman-East Joliet, and to the right is Roy Hazlerig, traveling lineman, Western Subdivision. Both are holding the plaque that recognizes the Joliet division Maintenance of Way Department for working through all of 1962 without a single reportable lost time injury.

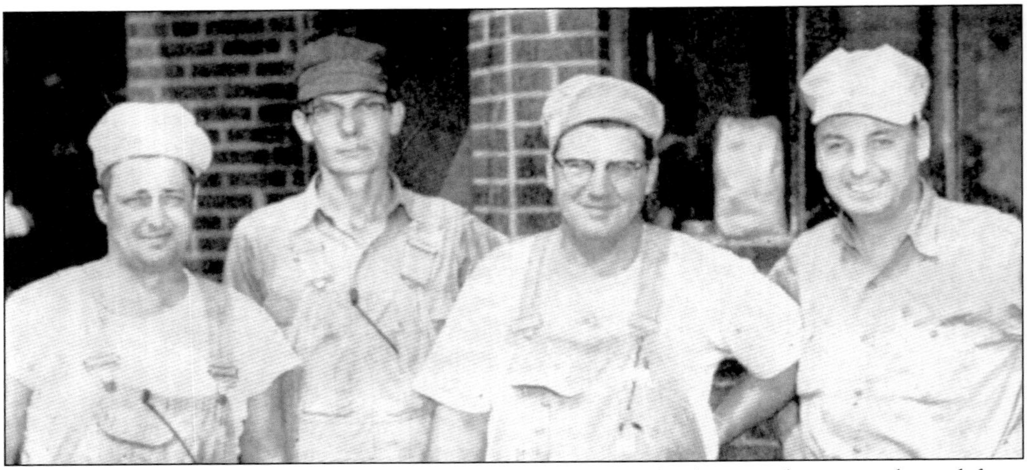

In September 1955, this EJ&E crew was part of train No. 51 about to leave westbound from Matteson. Seen here are, from left to right, Bill Young, Bill Cheney, Russ Spreitzer, and Frank Wagner.

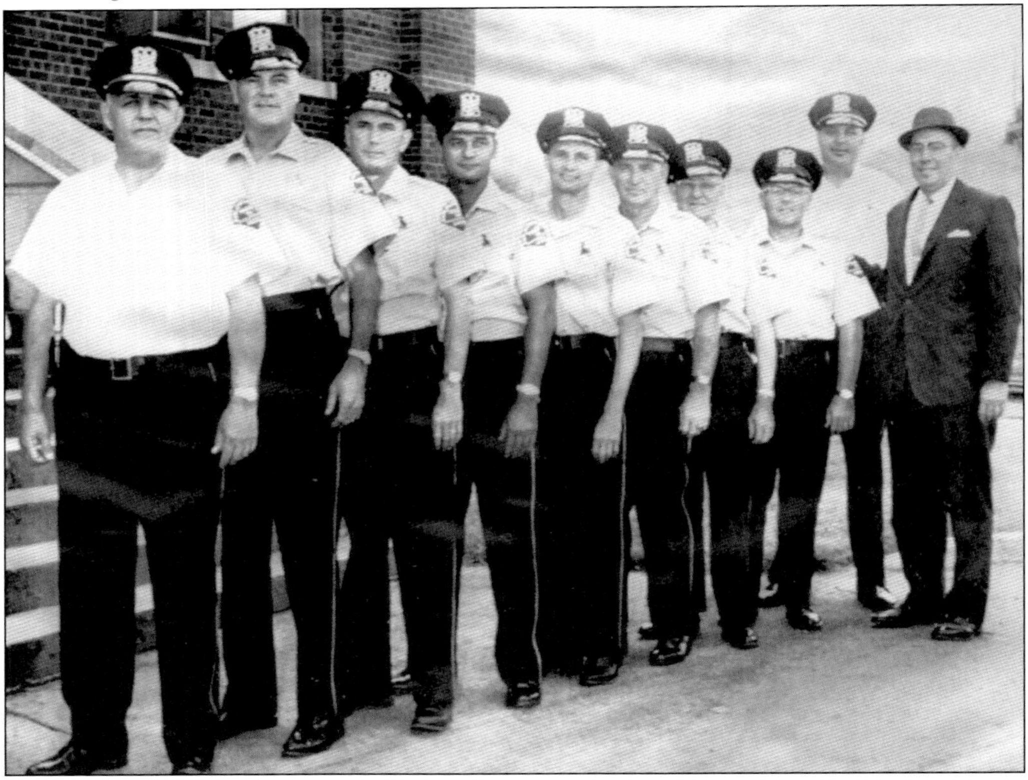

Policing the railroad can be a challenging and dangerous occupation. The EJ&E police are obligated to prevent and detect crime, protect life and property, investigate theft, and make proper arrests, to name a few of their responsibilities. In September 1965, these EJ&E police officers posed for the camera. They are, from left to right, Robert Barrowman, Robert Chidsey, Paul Havens, Sherman Marques, George O'Reilly, James Telfer, John Gleason, Kenneth Southcomb, Robert Simpson, and Frank Matthys.

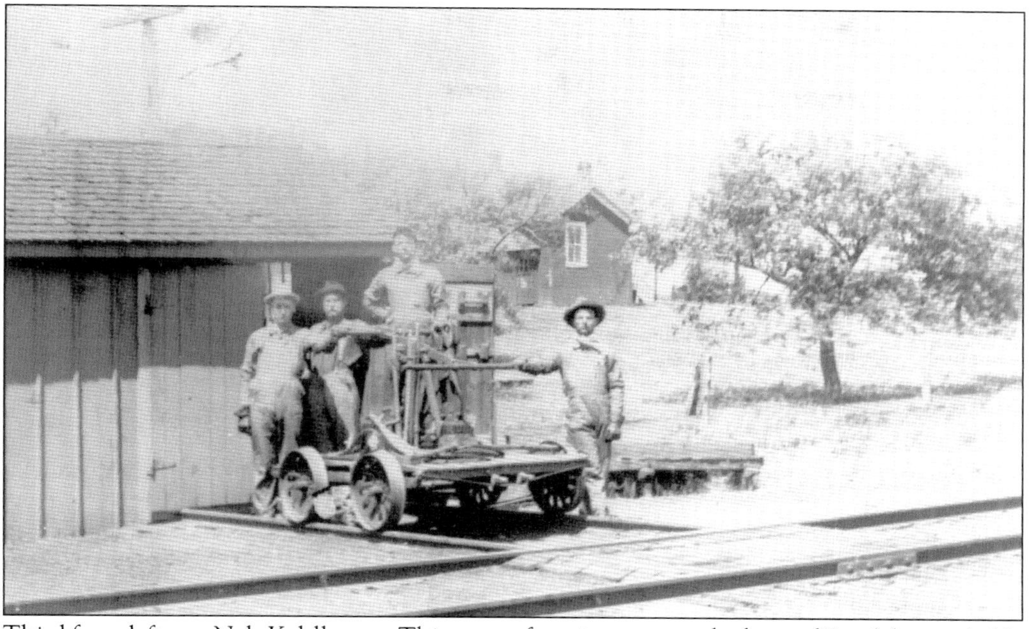

Third from left was Nels Kohlhagen. This gang of section men worked out of Frankfort probably around 1910. The EJ&E double tracked the railroad east of Joliet at that time. Section gangs, with track cars like the one in the photograph, were responsible for maintaining track, switches, road crossings, fence lines, and so forth.

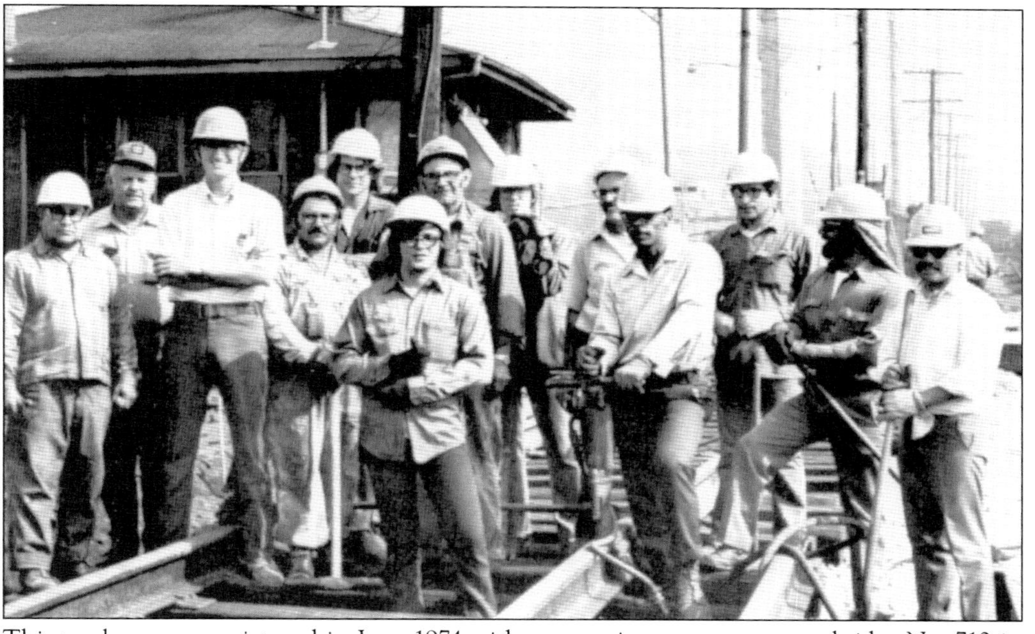

This track crew was pictured in June 1974 with a surveying party near new bridge No. 710 in South Chicago. Pictured are, from left to right, laborer Victor Vega, rodman Walt Cheney Jr., engineer Fred Tijan, trackman Nick Mihalariss, Alan Radochonski, Robert Purdy, foreman Frank Manno, trackman Gerald Driscoll, Paul Pesilskis, J. B. Kimbrough, Adan Flores, Roberto Melgoza, and Antonio Corona.

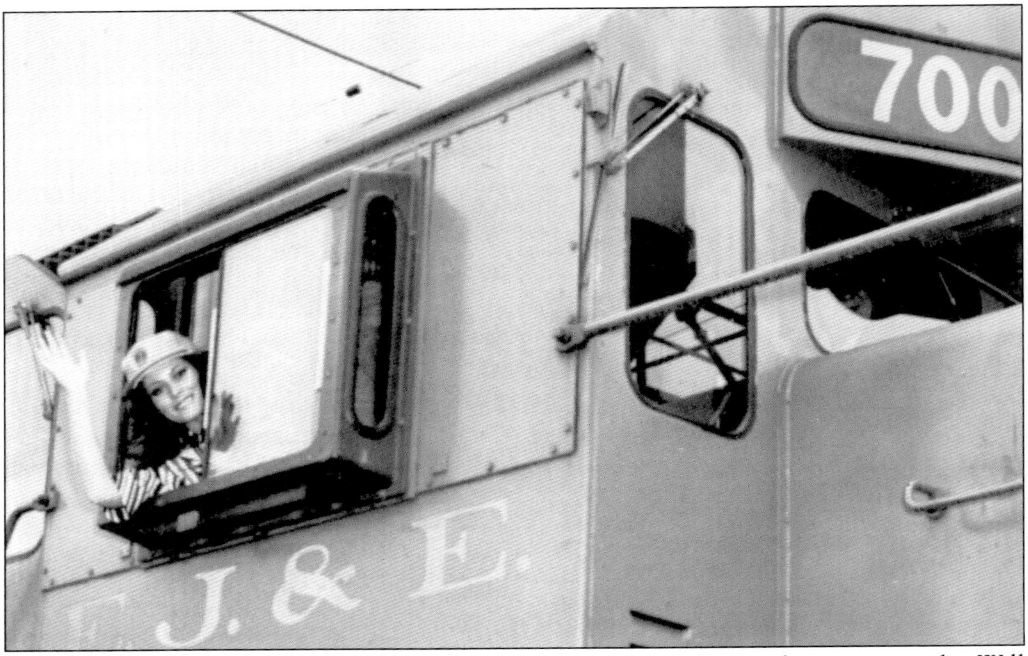

Summer Bartholomew, Miss U.S.A. 1975, came to the East Joliet yard to promote the Will County United Crusade in August of that year. Contributions were made by the "J-Givers" to help various charitable organizations in the area.

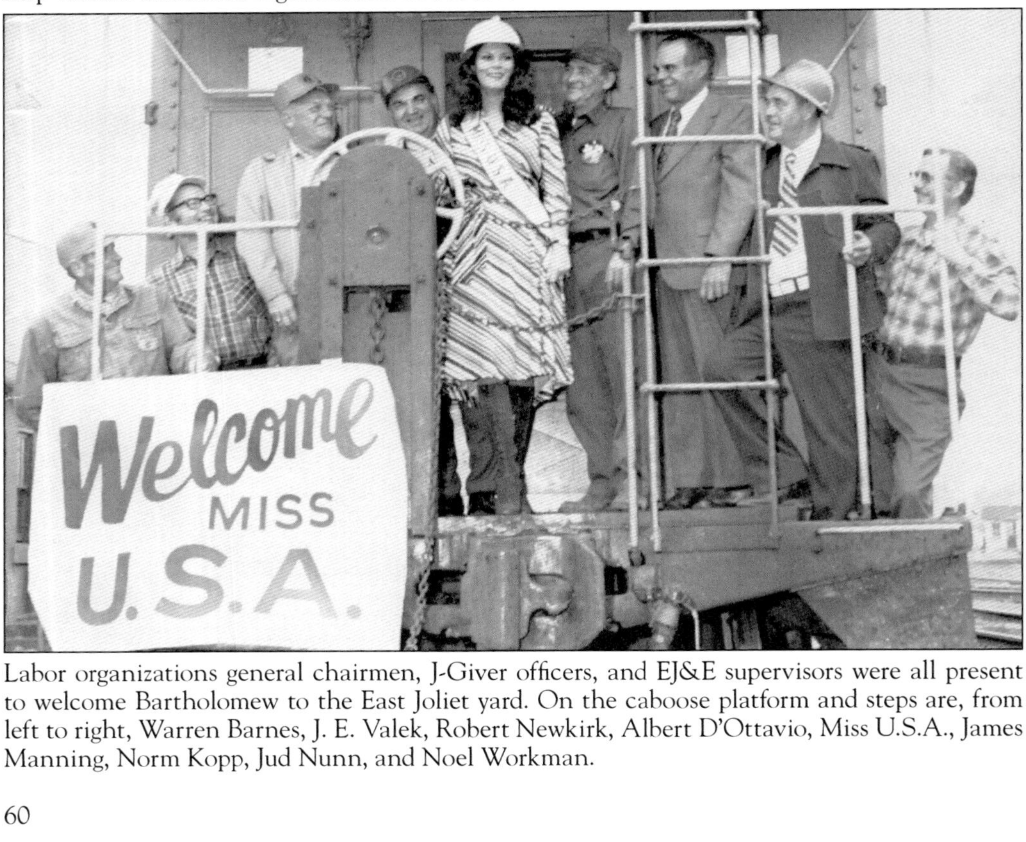

Labor organizations general chairmen, J-Giver officers, and EJ&E supervisors were all present to welcome Bartholomew to the East Joliet yard. On the caboose platform and steps are, from left to right, Warren Barnes, J. E. Valek, Robert Newkirk, Albert D'Ottavio, Miss U.S.A., James Manning, Norm Kopp, Jud Nunn, and Noel Workman.

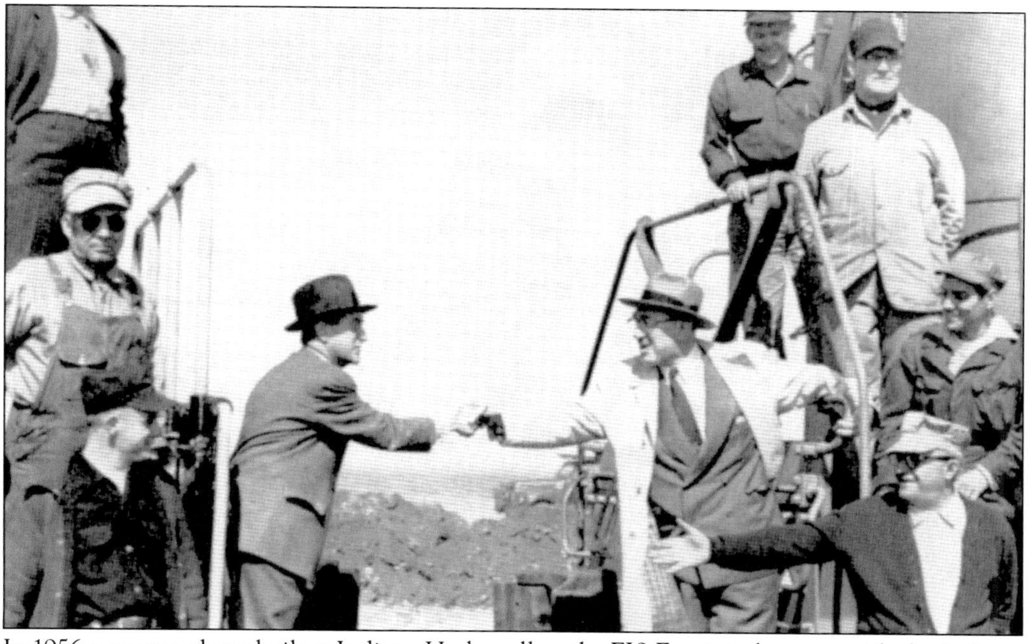

In 1956, a new yard was built at Indiana Harbor allow the EJ&E to jointly serve, with the Indiana Harbor Belt Railroad (IHB), the Inland Steel company plants. President Block of Inland Steel (left) and president Thomas Beven (right) of the EJ&E shook hands to mark the occasion.

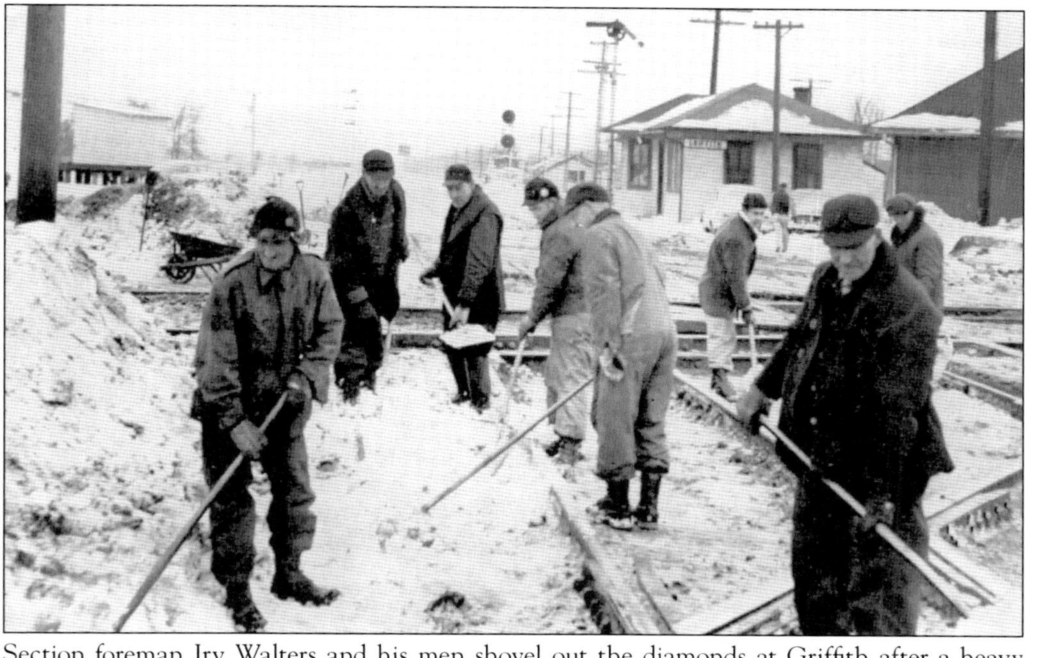

Section foreman Irv Walters and his men shovel out the diamonds at Griffith after a heavy snowstorm hit the area on December 21, 1951. Snow drifts over 10 feet high were common west of Plainfield. The EJ&E was called on to run a rescue train out beyond Normantown, and two cabooses were filled with stranded motorists from nearby Route 30. The special train brought them all into Joliet, where they were given shelter.

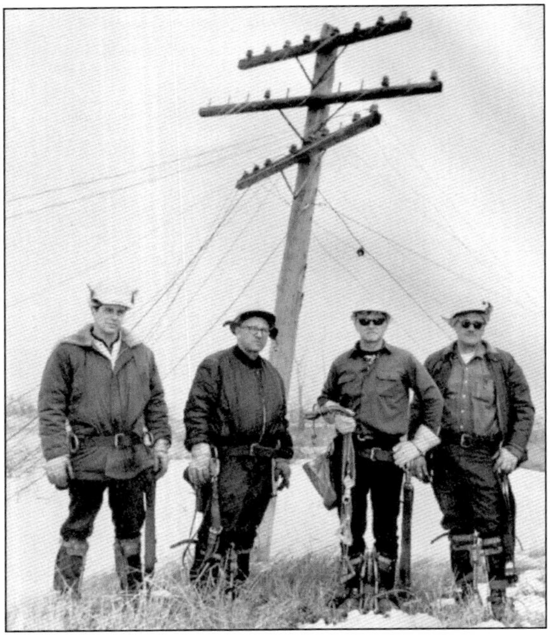

These linemen came from sister road Duluth, Missabe, and Iron Range Railroad (DM&IR) to help repair leaning poles and broken wires that were caused by heavy wet snow that had fallen on March 25, 1970. Borrowing workers and exchanging locomotives and other assets was a typical occurrence between the railroads that were owned by United States Steel Corporation. Seen here are, from left to right, mechanics in charge Richard Arris and Jim Patterson, linemen Harold Carlson, and Ted Leveille.

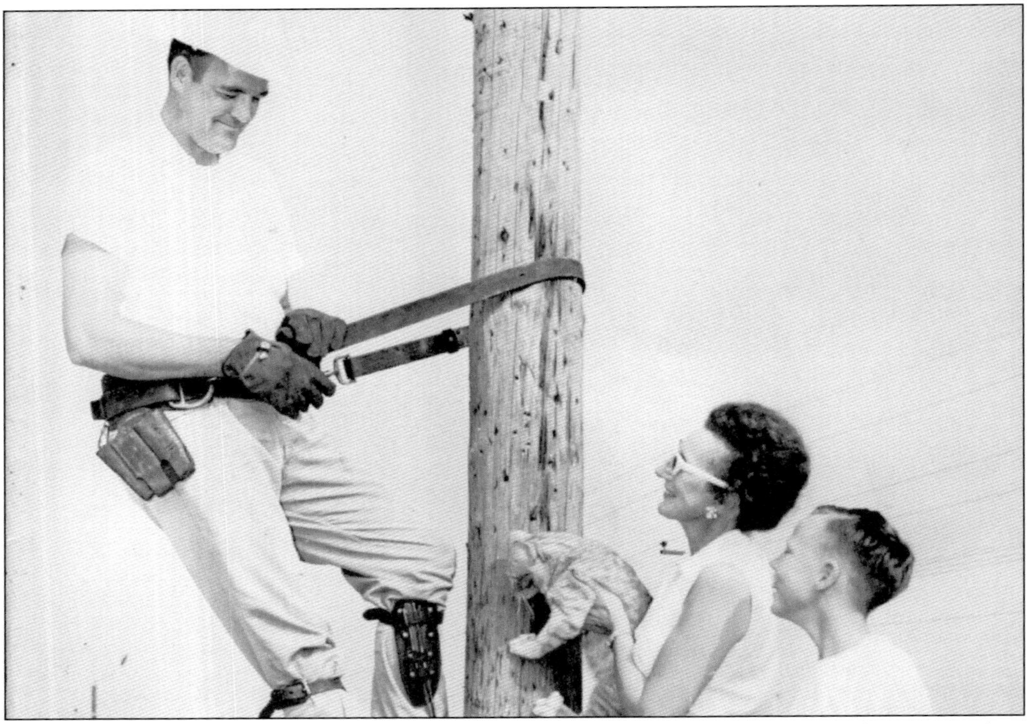

The EJ&E has always been a good neighbor to the communities along its right-of-way. Traveling lineman Leland "Lee" Graham is shown here returning a cat that had climbed atop a pole along the EJ&E tracks in Park Forest in July 1964. The cat was missing for several days and was too weak and frightened to come down from the pole. The owner of the cat had found help through the operator at Matteson, Don Heisler, who in turn notified Graham about the situation.

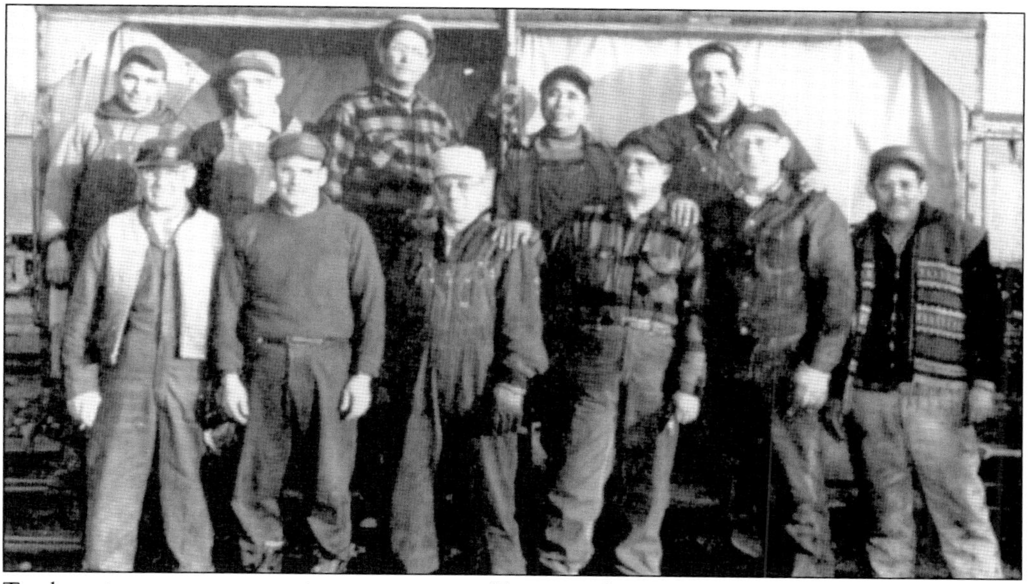

Track maintenance was an important part of keeping the trains running in a safe and timely mode. In April 1964, this group of men from the Track Department in South Chicago was photographed at the end of their workday. They are, from left to right, (first row) Stanley Jenske, Vidal Curiel, Anthony Peck, Guadalupe Loneli, Howard Jackson, and Ruben Sanchez; (second row) Harry Vardalos, Stefan Melnyczenko, Pedro Limon, Vincente Aguilar, and Carlos Velasquez.

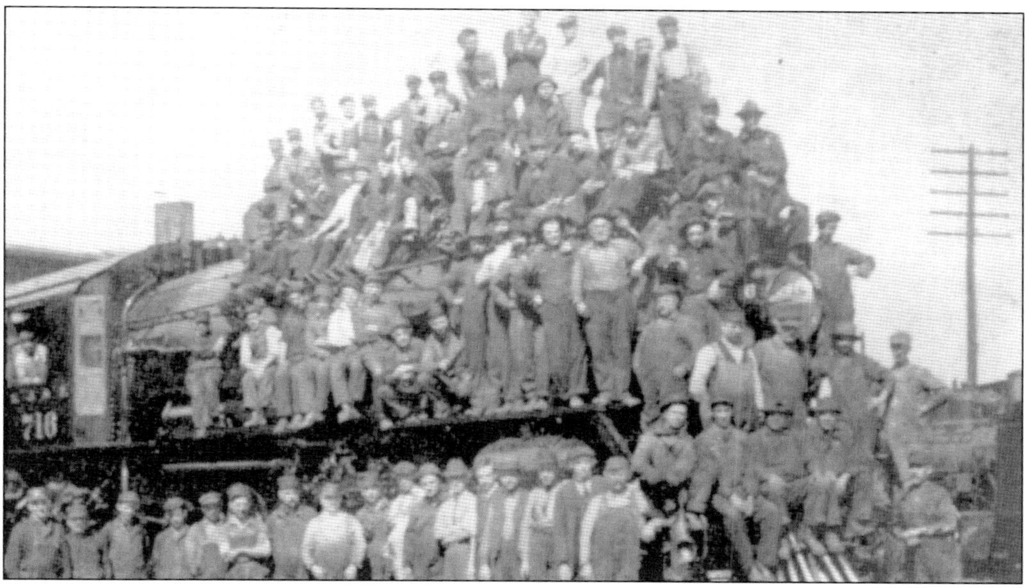

In 1913, everyone at the East Joliet engine house must have turned out at to be in the picture with the newly delivered No. 716. It was one of 20 2-8-2 Mikados built by the American Locomotive Company of Schenectady. The engines were equipped with Miller Train Control for operation on the C&EI railroad between Chicago Heights and Rossville. Automatic train control would stop a train if the engineer did not obey a wayside signal. The No. 716 was scrapped in 1946 after performing 33 years of service.

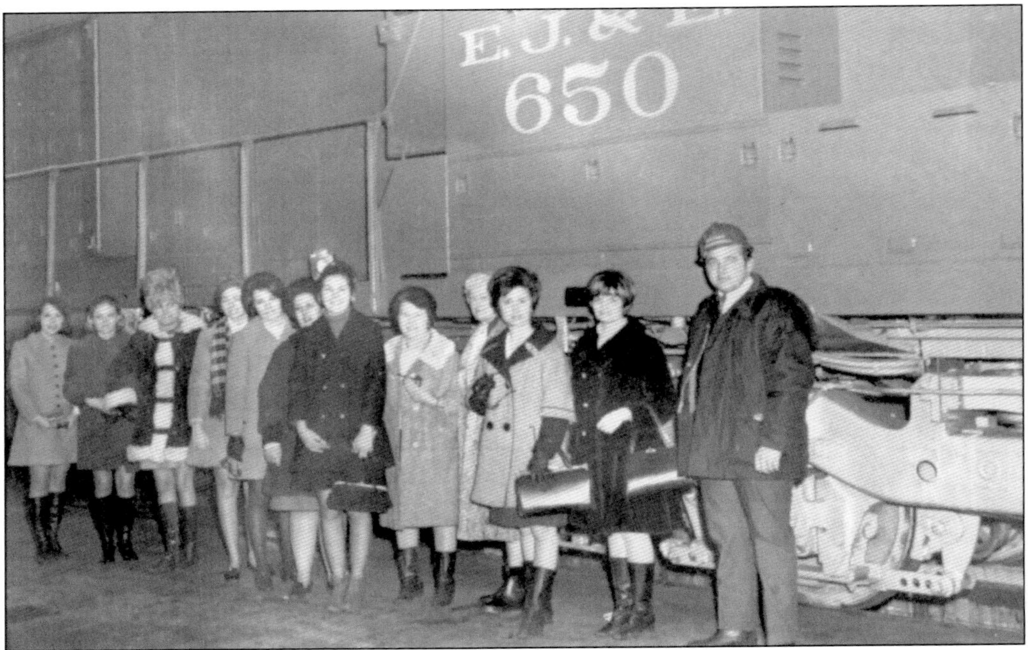

When the new six-axle SD38s were delivered in February 1970, female office workers at the company headquarters in Joliet were given an inspection tour of the new locomotives at the locomotive shops. Service engineer Roger Vitek from EMD is shown at the far right. These locomotives could reach a speed of 71 miles per hour, but the maximum allowable track speed on the EJ&E was 45 miles per hour.

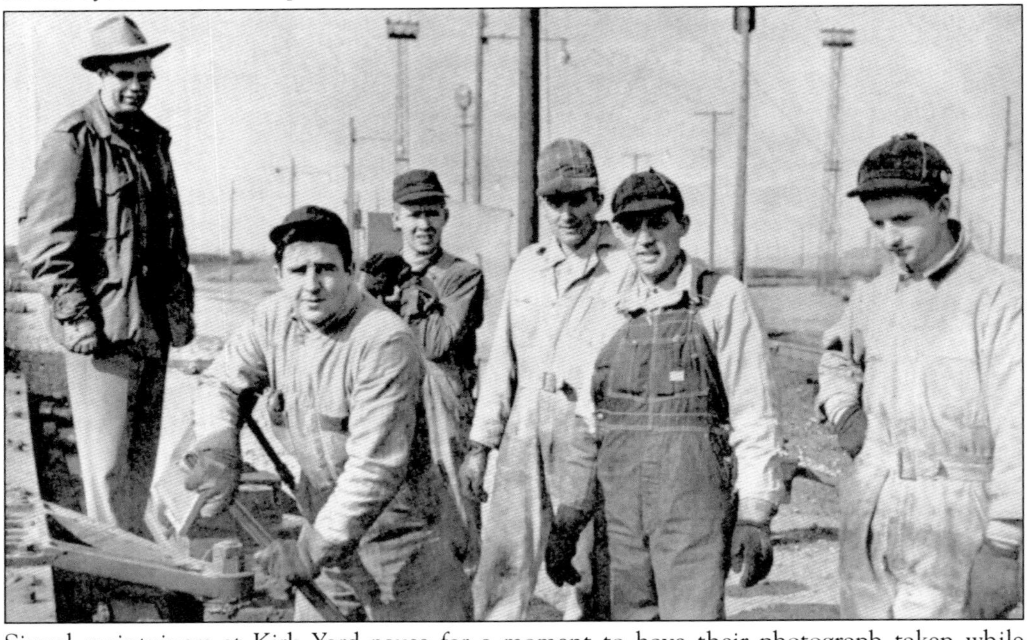

Signal maintainers at Kirk Yard pause for a moment to have their photograph taken while working on a hump retarder. Foreman Art Edson on the left keeps a watchful eye on (from left to right) Earl Norton, Jack Alger, Bob Grugel, Gilbert Kaiser, and Jim Santacroce.

Five

Along the Right-of-Way

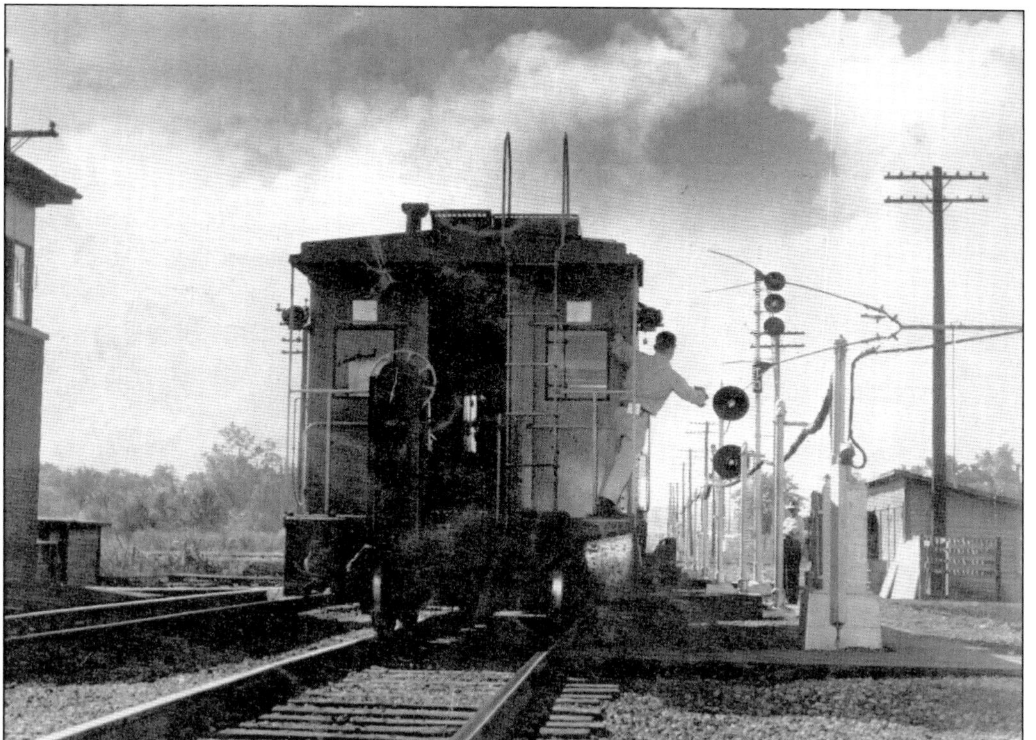

The conductor or flagman of an eastbound train leaving the East Joliet yard catches the train orders and clearance card for the train at the Rock Island tower. The three-aspect signal on the right displays a yellow light in the middle signifying the train crew must pick up orders. The two-aspect signal with the large banners governed the crossing of the Michigan Central Railroad tracks on the south side of Hickory Creek. The tower, the corner of which is visible on the left, controlled all the switches, derails, and signals at the crossings of the EJ&E with the Michigan Central and the Rock Island Railroads. The train was likely third class No. 42, the local freight, which ran daily from East Joliet to Kirk Yard and picked up and set out cars at stations along the way.

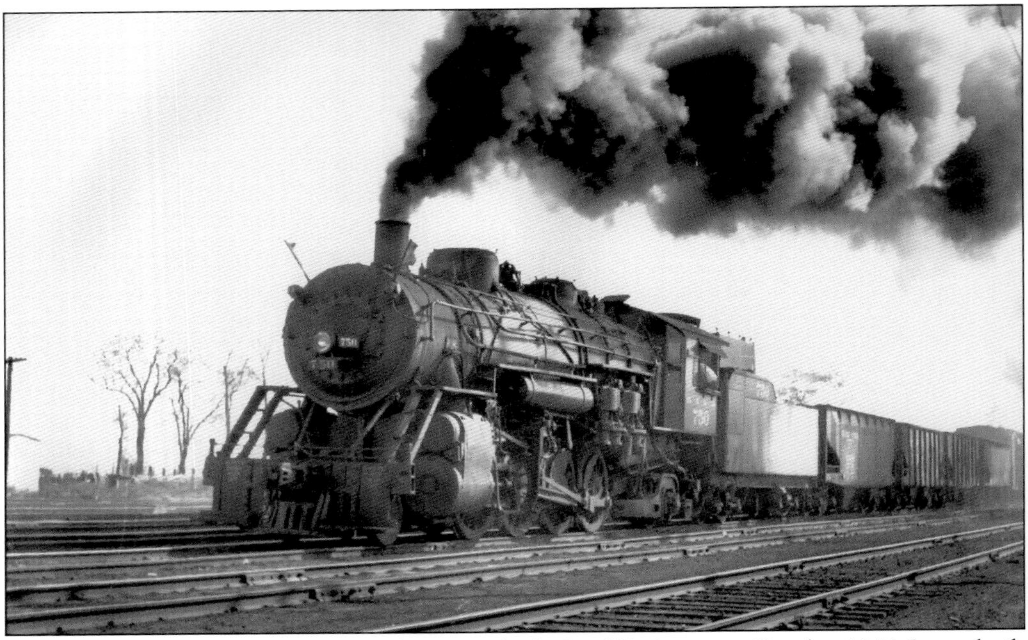

No. 750, a 2-8-2 Mikado type, is seen here as it looked in Waukegan in October 1946. It was built by the American Locomotive Company (Alco) in 1923 and was equipped with Miller Train Control for service on the C&EI down to Rossville. It was sold to sister road DM&IR in 1948. (Bill Raia collection.)

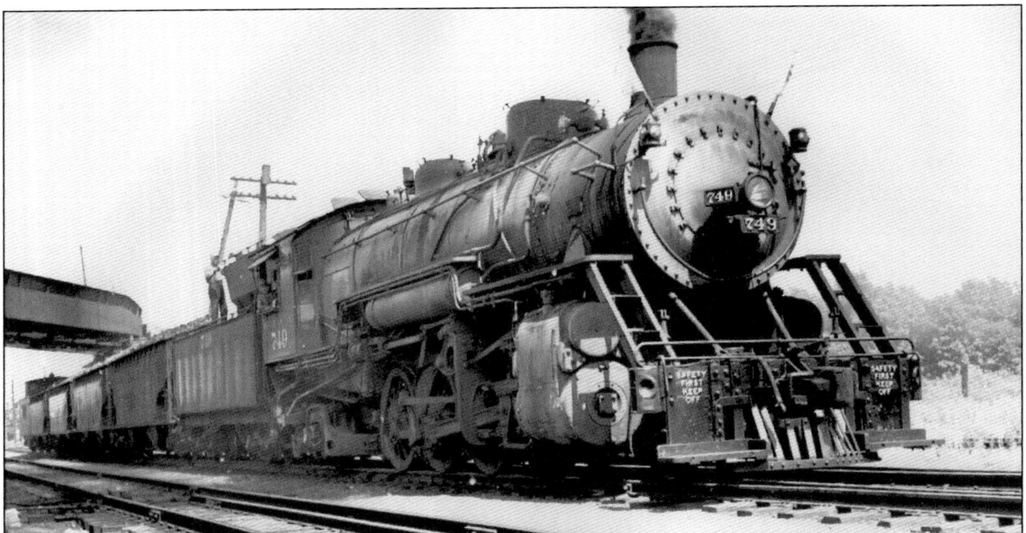

In October 1946, Mikado No. 749 heading southbound has just crossed under the Chicago, North Shore, and Milwaukee Railroad branch to Mundelein and was about to cross the Milwaukee Road main line at Rondout. The No. 749 was one of 26 Mikados sold to the DM&IR in the late 1940s. The 2-8-2s were the largest steam locomotives operated by the EJ&E. Searchlight signals were installed between Rondout and Barrington in 1937. (Bill Raia collection.)

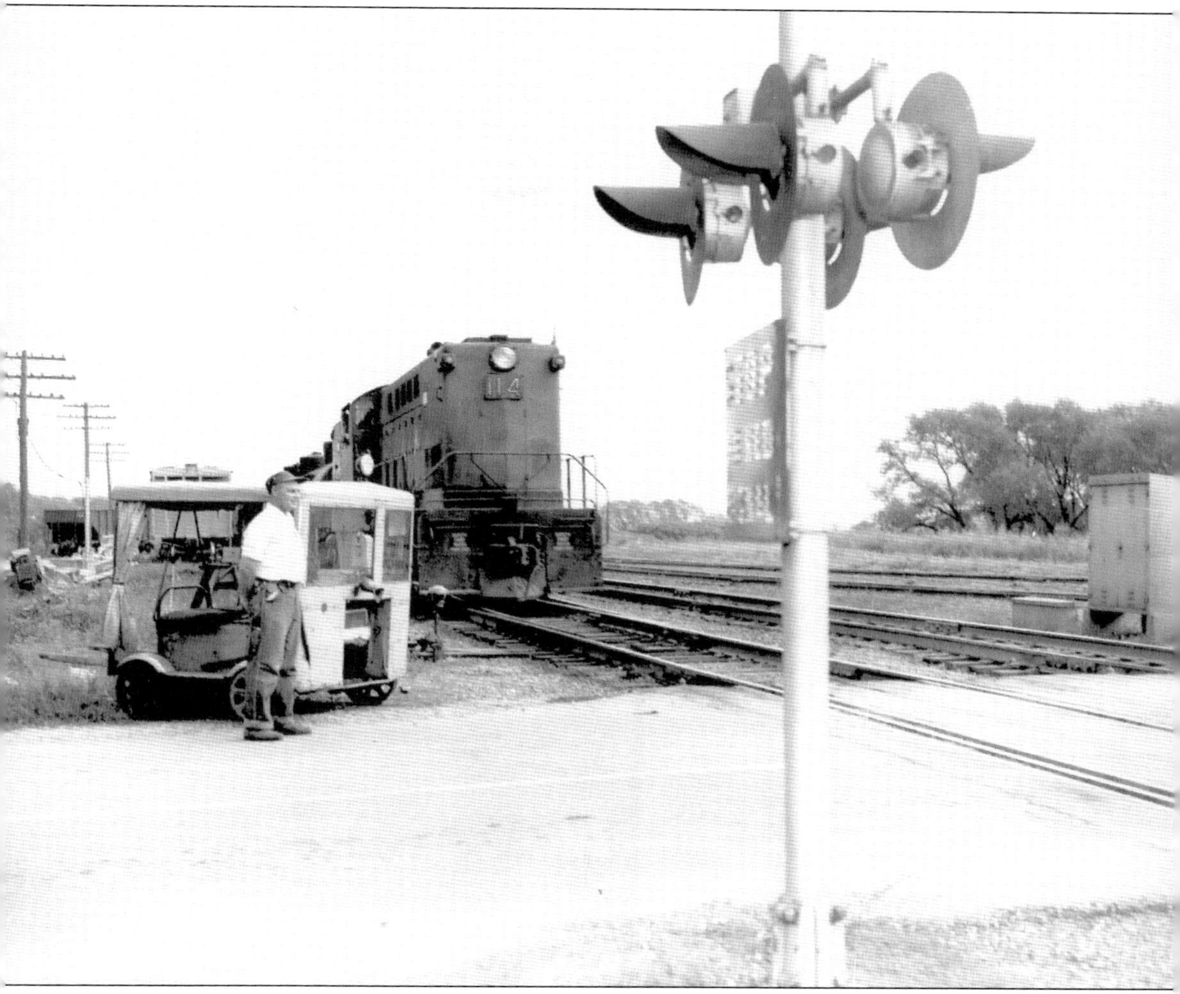

In September 1955, signal maintainer Gerald "Barney" Craig was at the Main Street crossing in Matteson. His inspection motor car was safely set aside to let a westbound freight train pass. Craig spotted an elderly person about to walk in front of an approaching train. He snatched the person from the train's path and saved her life.

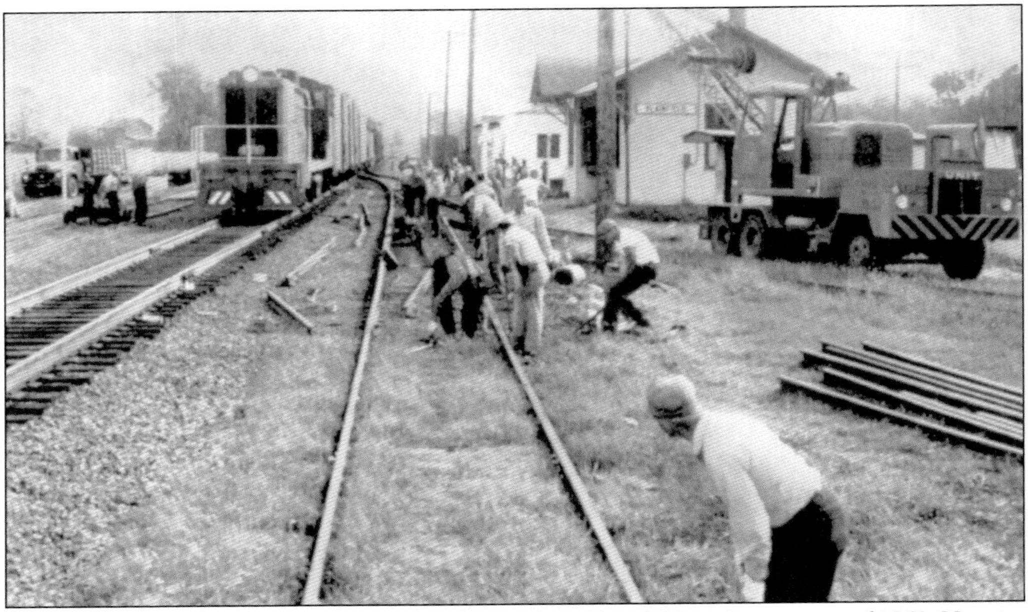

Maintenance of way track workers are hard at work in Plainfield in the summer of 1960. Heavier steel rail was being placed in the 33-car-long siding in anticipation of more frequent use after a Centralized Traffic Control signal system is installed. The train was en route from Joliet to Aurora and was being pulled by engine No. 479, a Baldwin model VO switching locomotive built during World War II. The truck on the right was a truck crane capable of lifting 15 tons. The EJ&E maintenance workers were, and still are, well equipped with the most modern equipment. The Plainfield station has been preserved by the local historical society. It has been relocated on the Illinois River Valley line by the Route 30 road crossing.

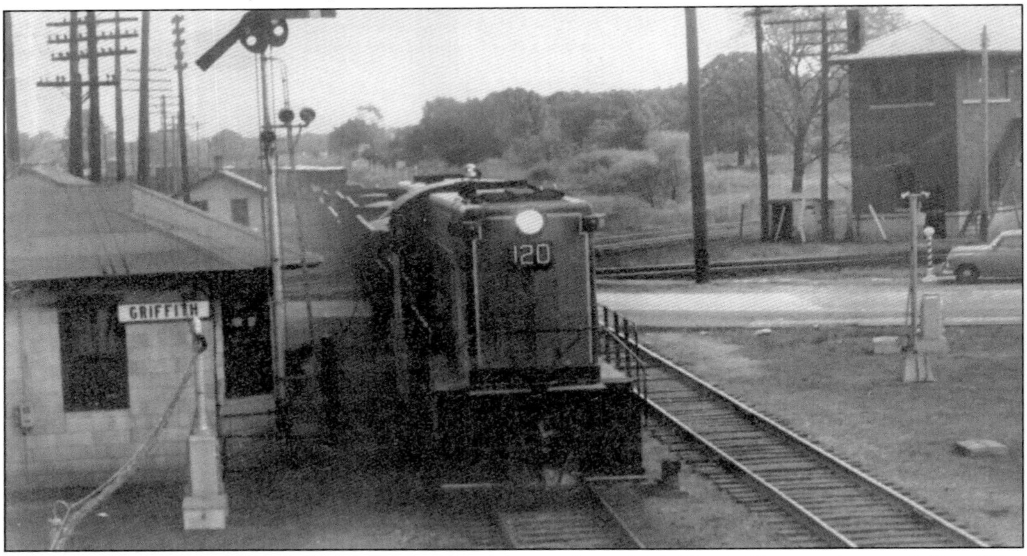

This was train No. 43 with locomotive 120 coming from Kirk Yard, Gary, going to Joliet. The left signal arm, which was in the yellow, 45-degree position, was for westbound trains. The operator Ralph Kauble is standing in front of the station handing up a clearance Form A and a train order or message.

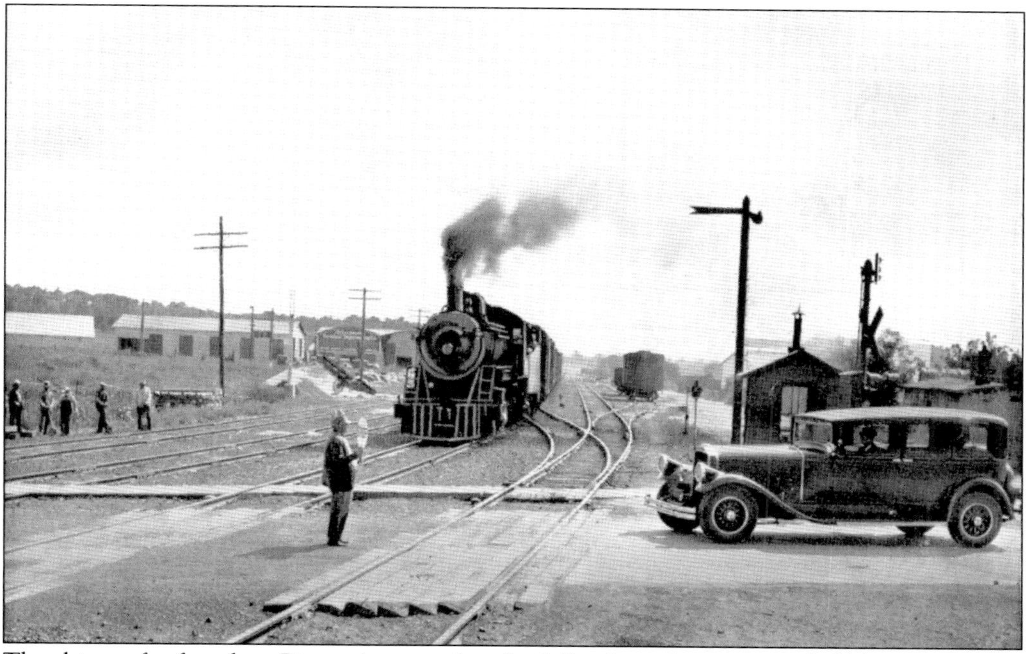

The driver of a four-door Pierce Arrow sedan dutifully obeys the stop sign held by the crossing watchman at Main Street in Barrington in June 1924. The railroad employed watchmen in many towns along the line when automobiles became a common mode of transportation. The train was westbound on the main track. The Barrington station was to the right, just out of the photograph.

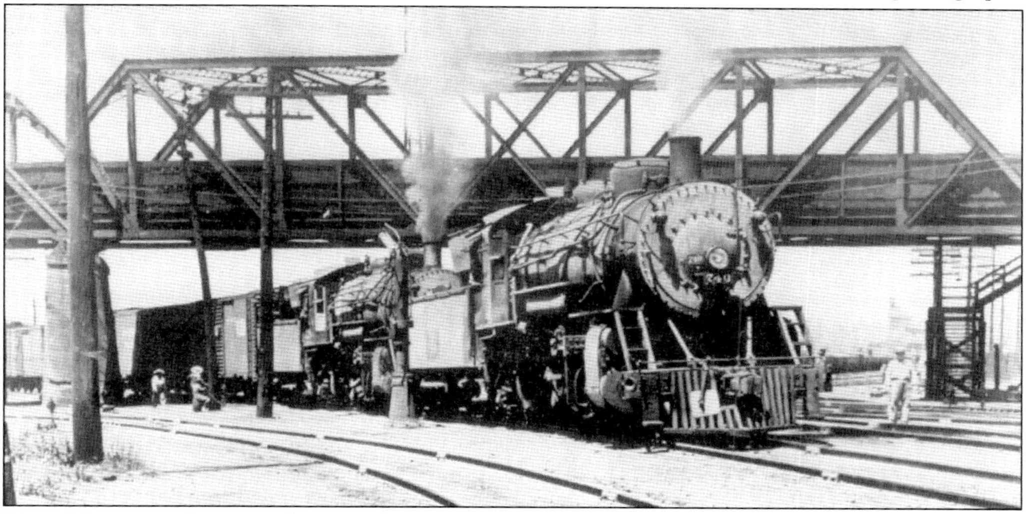

Train No. 4 seen here was leaving the East Joliet yard for Porter in the 1940s with helper engine No. 740 in the lead. Reportedly this was the last steam locomotive in the service of the EJ&E. Its final run was on May 27, 1949. The extra engines provided more pulling power for the stiff grade up and out of the Des Plaines River valley all the way to Frankfort. Eastbound trains could take on water for the steam locomotives at Frankfort. Joliet was the dividing point between the two subdivisions on the system. The Western Subdivision extended from Joliet to Waukegan, and included the Rockdale Branch, Coal City Branch, and the Aurora Branch. The Eastern Subdivision extended from Joliet to Gary and Porter.

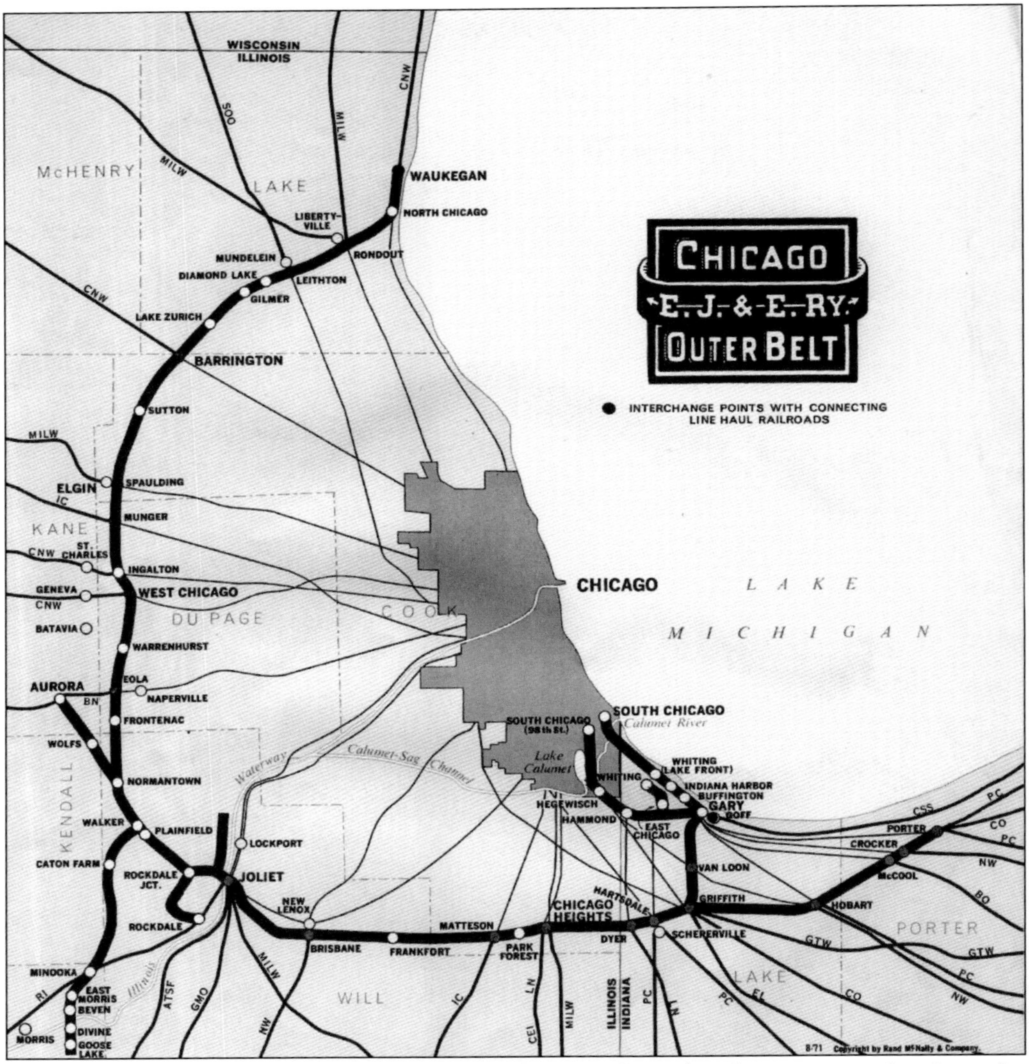

This map of the EJ&E was published in 1971, showing the railroads it connected with in the Chicago area. Serving as a bridge route for the interchanging of freight between railroads in the area has been an important function of the EJ&E. The semicircle of the railroad was essentially complete by 1893.

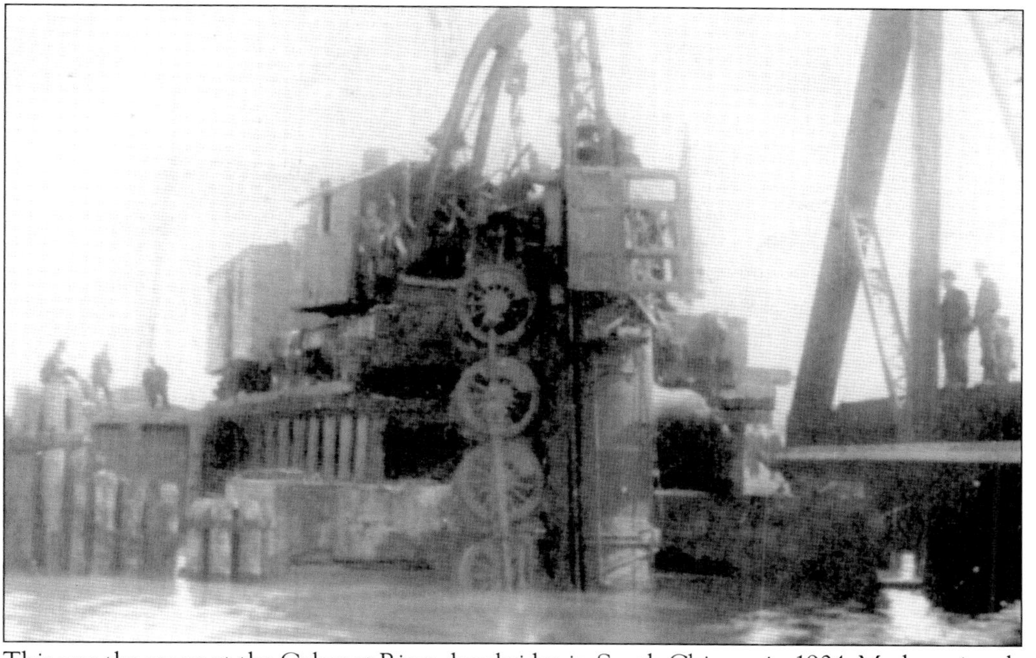

This was the scene at the Calumet River drawbridge in South Chicago in 1904. Modern signals and derails had not yet been installed there. Engineer John Busch on engine No. 543 was on board when the mishap occurred.

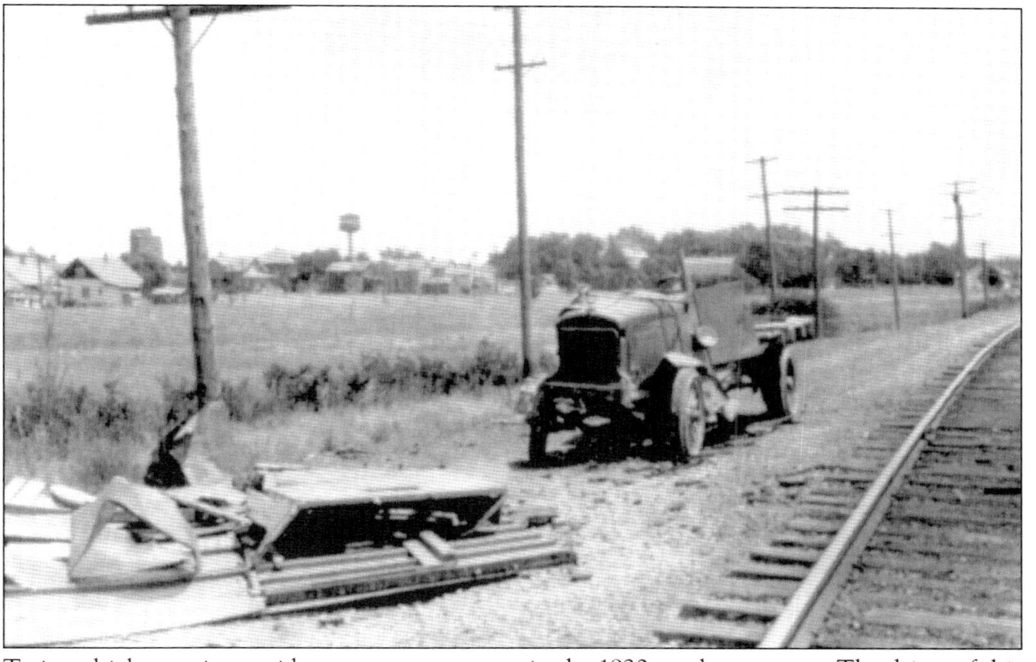

Train-vehicle crossing accidents were as common in the 1920s as they are now. The driver of this milk truck was killed instantly in June 1927, when his vehicle crossed in front of an eastbound EJ&E train at the Richton Road crossing in Matteson. The location was along a curve where a tree was believed to be obstructing the view of the approaching train.

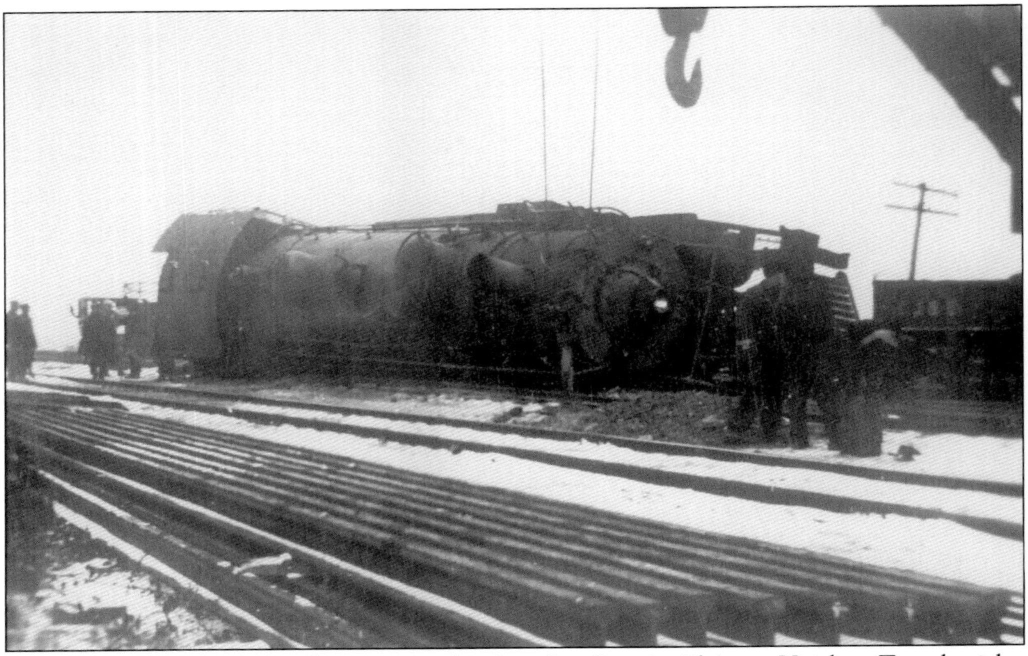

Steam locomotive No. 704 lies on its side after derailing in Chicago Heights. Two derricks, commonly referred to as "hooks," were necessary to right the engine and put it back on track. The location of the wreck was believed to be at the Chicago Heights Hill Yard by State Street crossing. (Howard Lenhardt.)

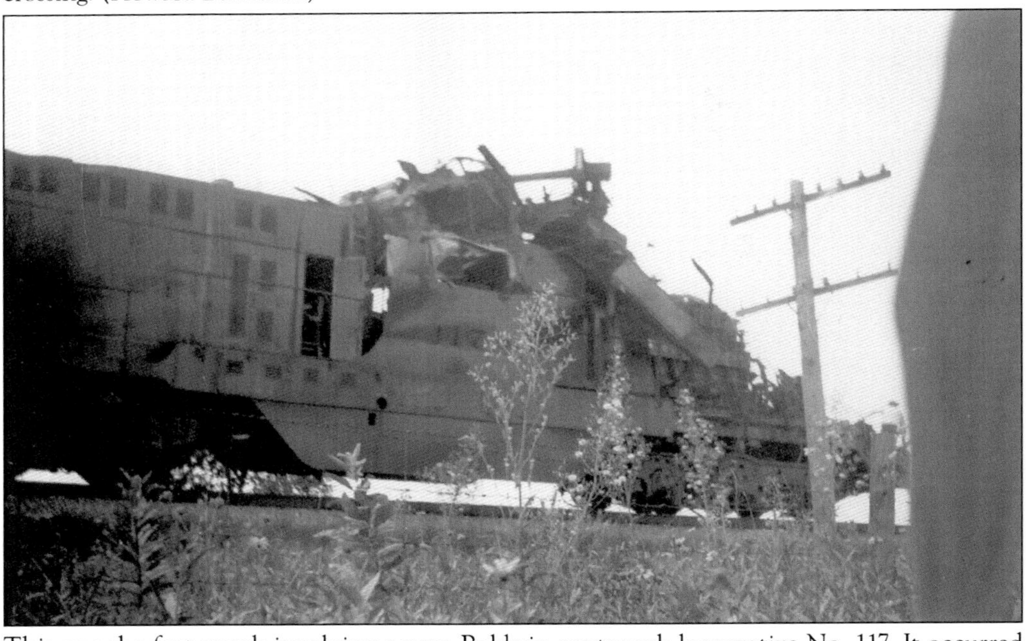

This was the first wreck involving a new, Baldwin center-cab locomotive No. 117. It occurred just east of Brisbane on the very foggy morning of August 29, 1948. A caboose was struck, which was pushed up on top of the locomotive. Nine side-dump coke hoppers and oil tank cars were derailed.

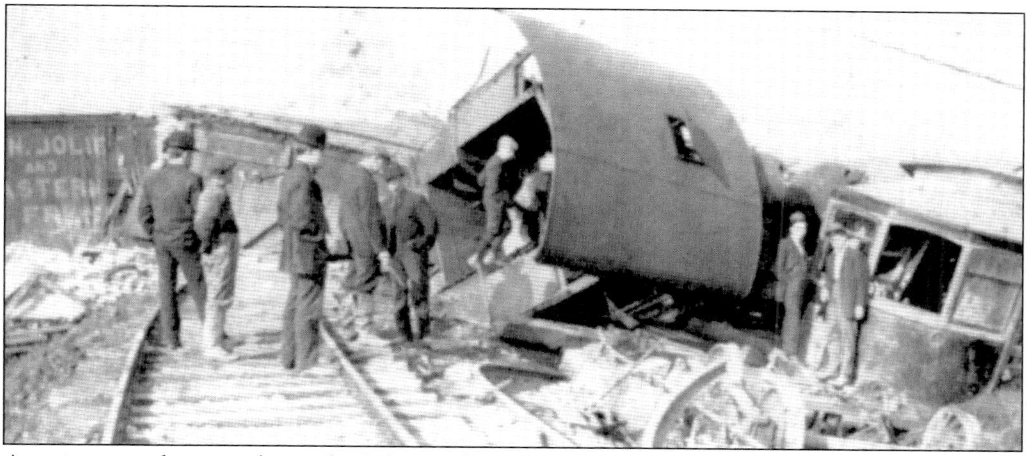

A serious accident involving the Joliet and Southern Interurban Railway and an EJ&E freight train on the Rockdale line occurred at 7:10 p.m. on June 4, 1908. The location of the accident was known as the "Big Slough." The interurban car was struck broadside at the crossing, causing EJ&E locomotive No. 29 to derail also. The signal was at stop and the derail open on the interurban line when the car ran past the signal.

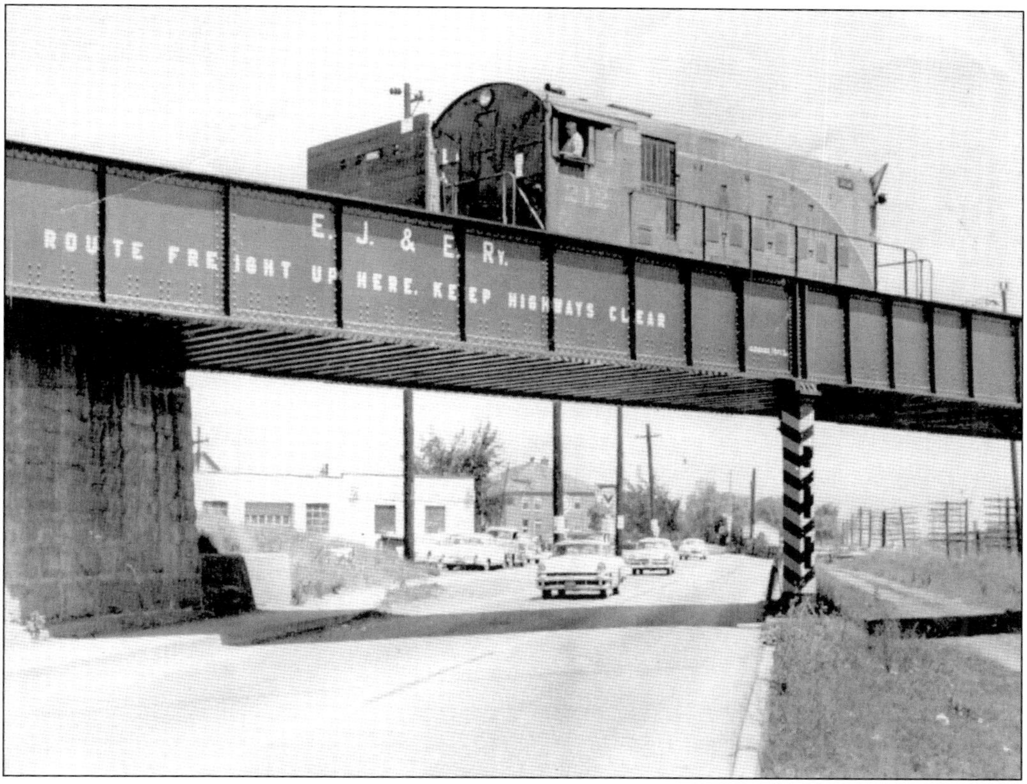

EJ&E locomotive No. 212 is pushing cars over Sheridan Road in North Chicago. The slogan on the bridge girder was credited to the assistant to president William E. Deaton. Other railroads were quick to also adopt the slogan. The engineer was Arthur J. Best, and the fireman was Frank Druba.

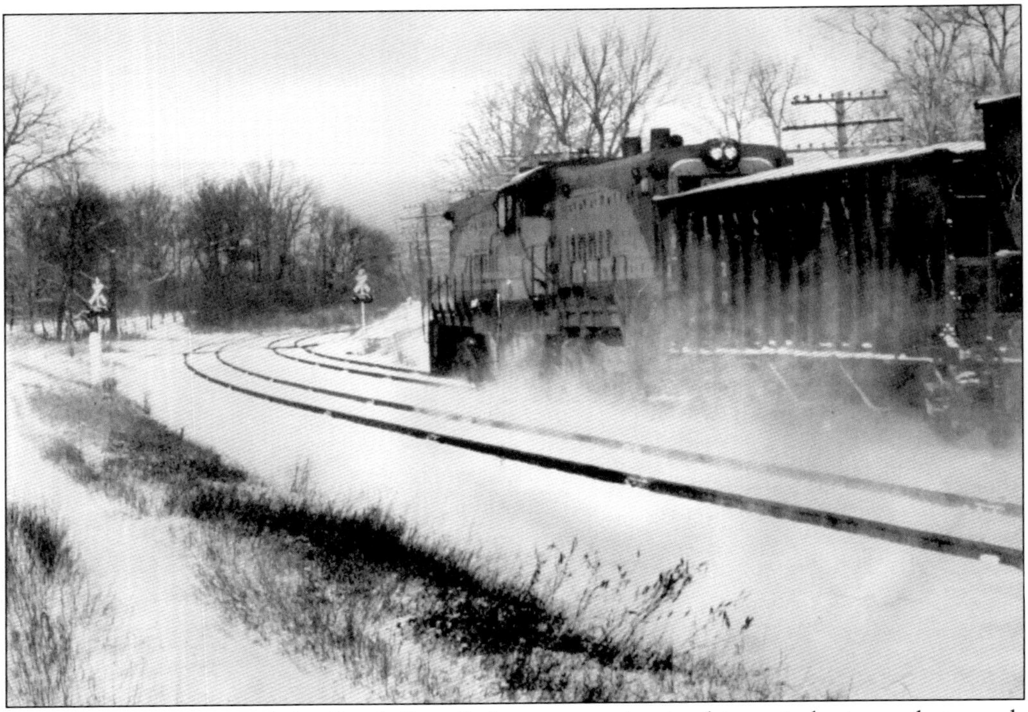

Extra 913 West is east of the South Rowell Avenue crossing in this typical winter photograph along the EJ&E in December 1969. It was en route from Gary to Joliet. Engine No. 913 was built in May 1948 and rebuilt by EMD in June 1958. Industrial Maintenance Service scrapped it in 1969.

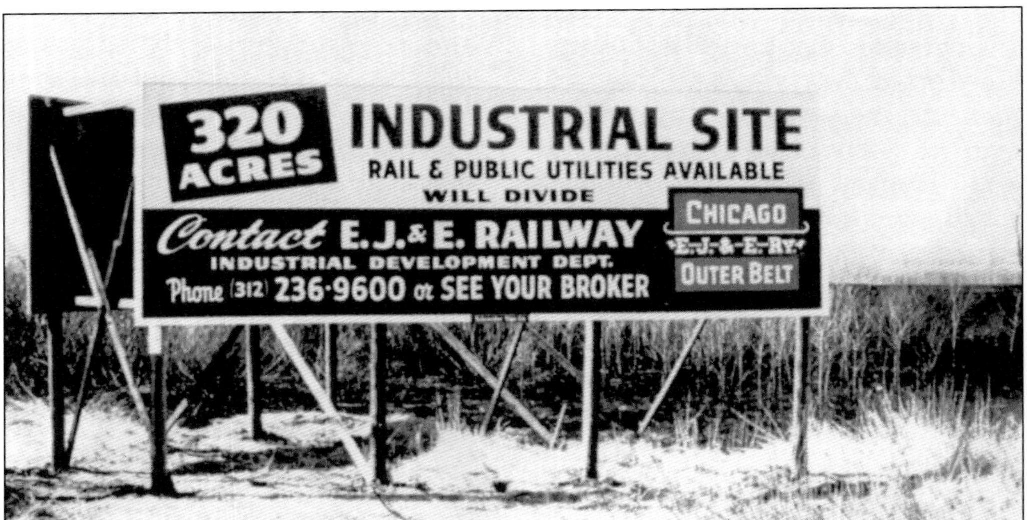

The EJ&E had taken a very active role in recruiting new industry to locate along its right-of-way. This billboard appeared in 1971 along the west side of Route 41 in Schererville, some distance south of the railroad's main line. This advertising had done much in developing unused railroad property, bringing real estate revenue along with freight car revenue to the railroad's financial statement.

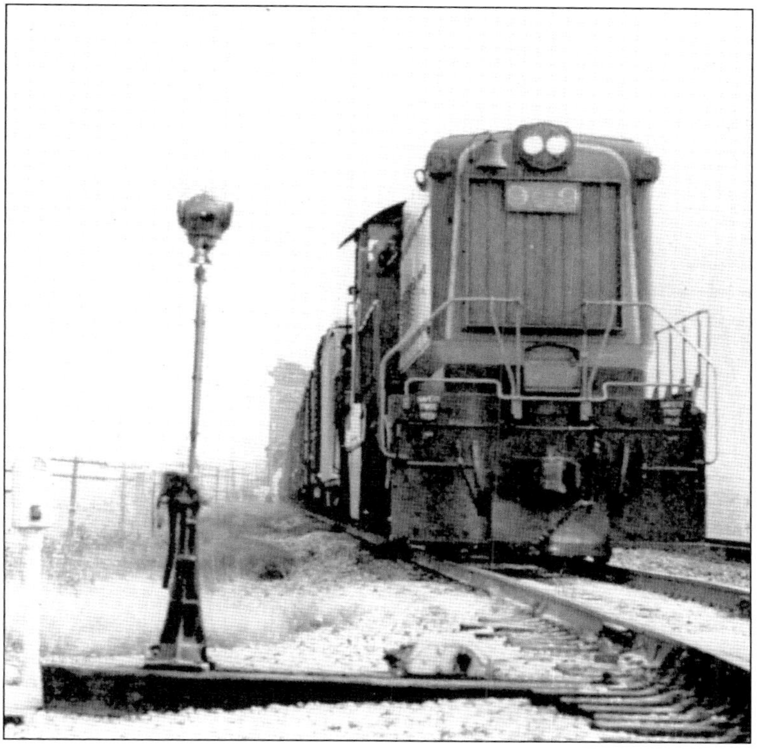

Engine No. 909 was leaving Joliet with train No. 17 heading west over bridge No. 198 in the fall of 1963. The train has a total of 28 loads and 8 empties for a total of 2,380 tons. Engine No. 909 was formerly No. 109, being reengined in 1958 with a EMD No. 567 engine. It was sold in December 1975 for scrap.

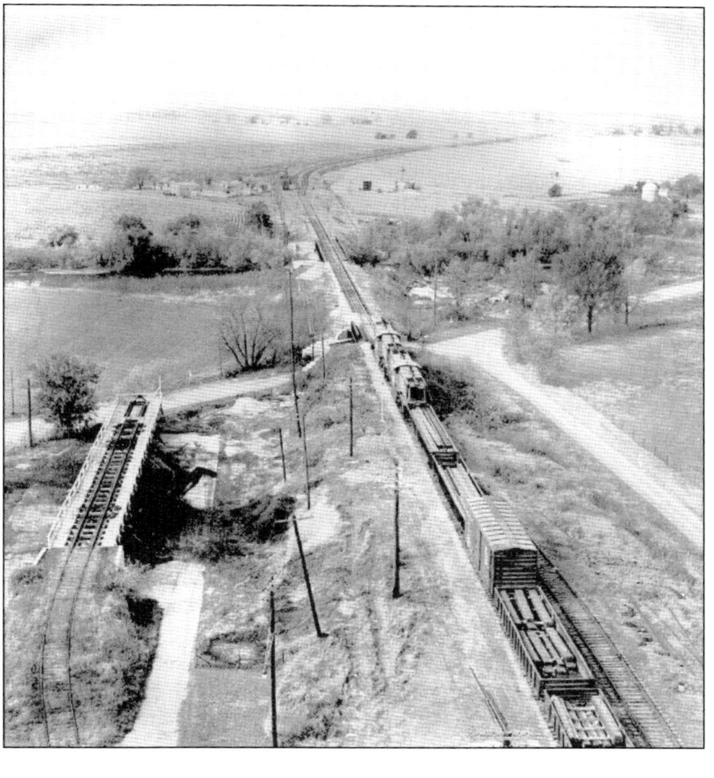

In October 1960, train No. 3 is shown heading toward Walker with locomotives No. 915 and No. 914 and was about to cross over Route 59 in Plainfield. This photograph was taken from atop the Plainfield Grain Company elevator. The Illinois River line can be seen branching off to the left. The elevator company's coal-unloading trestle was on the lower left.

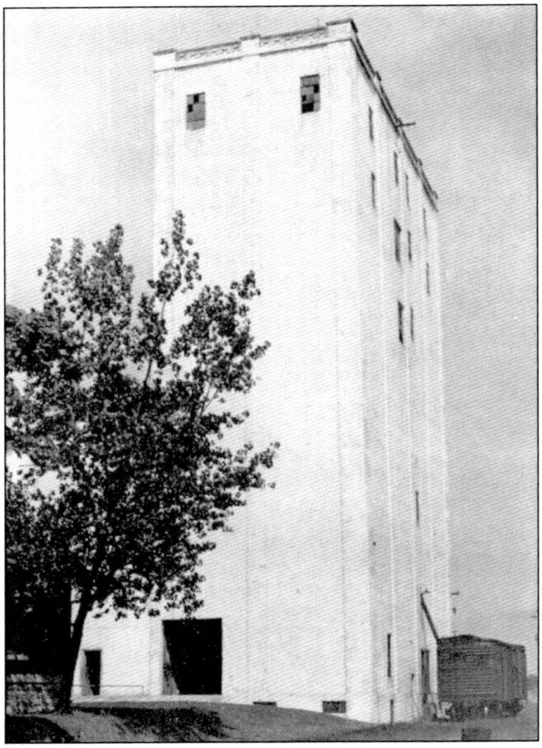

The concrete grain elevator in Plainfield stood 110 feet high and had a capacity of 90,000 bushels. There were many smaller elevators located in towns along the EJ&E. Over the years, subdivision development has covered many square miles of farm fields reducing the amount of grains grown along the railroad. Competition from the Illinois Waterway has also siphoned off traffic. Today Plainfield is a center of intense industrial development, and there are now many new customers for the EJ&E to serve.

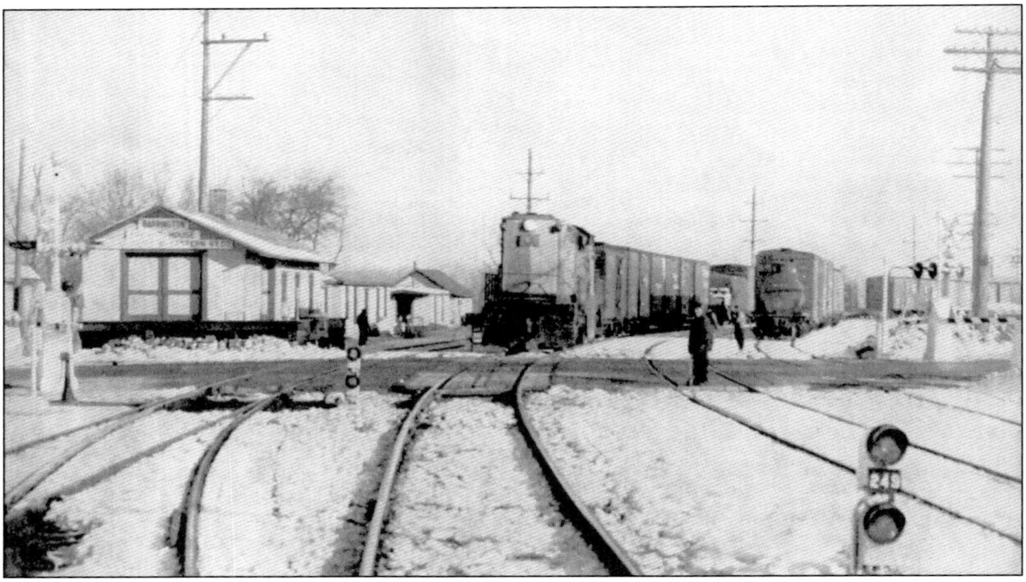

Conductor Tom Cole and his crew do some switching at Barrington during the winter of 1957–1958. They are eastbound with train No. 4 this day. The gates are down at the Main Street crossing in this view looking west. The EJ&E carded four, scheduled, second-class freight trains, plus a third-class local freight in each direction back then. It was a busy piece of railroad for a mostly single-track line. The engineer was Frank Konda, the fireman was George Smith, and the brakemen were Lee Hinchcliffe and Albert Johnson.

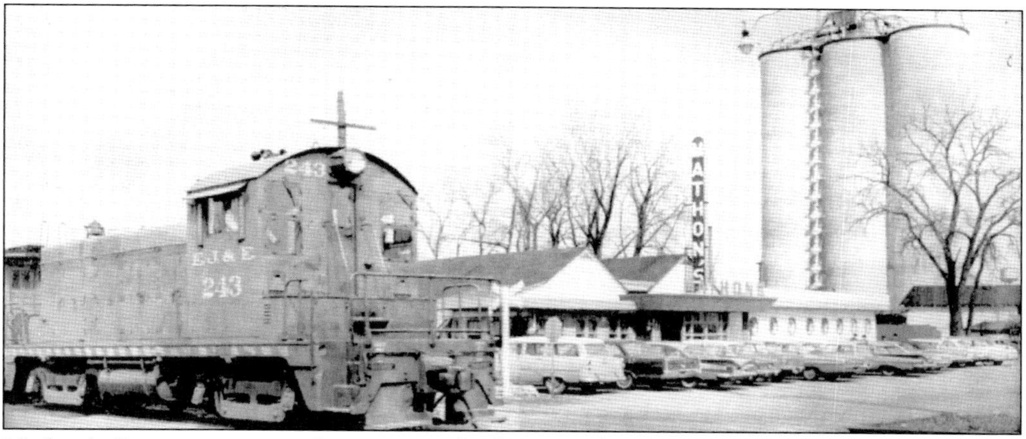

Mathon's Restaurant, specializing in seafood, was a familiar landmark along the EJ&E in Waukegan. Mathon Kyritsis opened it in 1939 on Clayton Street. The restaurateur employed his own fleet of fishing boats on Lake Michigan to catch perch, chubs, and smelt. He also had a reputation for being an accurate weather forecaster. EMD SW1 No. 243, built in 1941, was seen heading back to the Waukegan terminal after doing some switching at the Johns-Manville nearby in the spring of 1963.

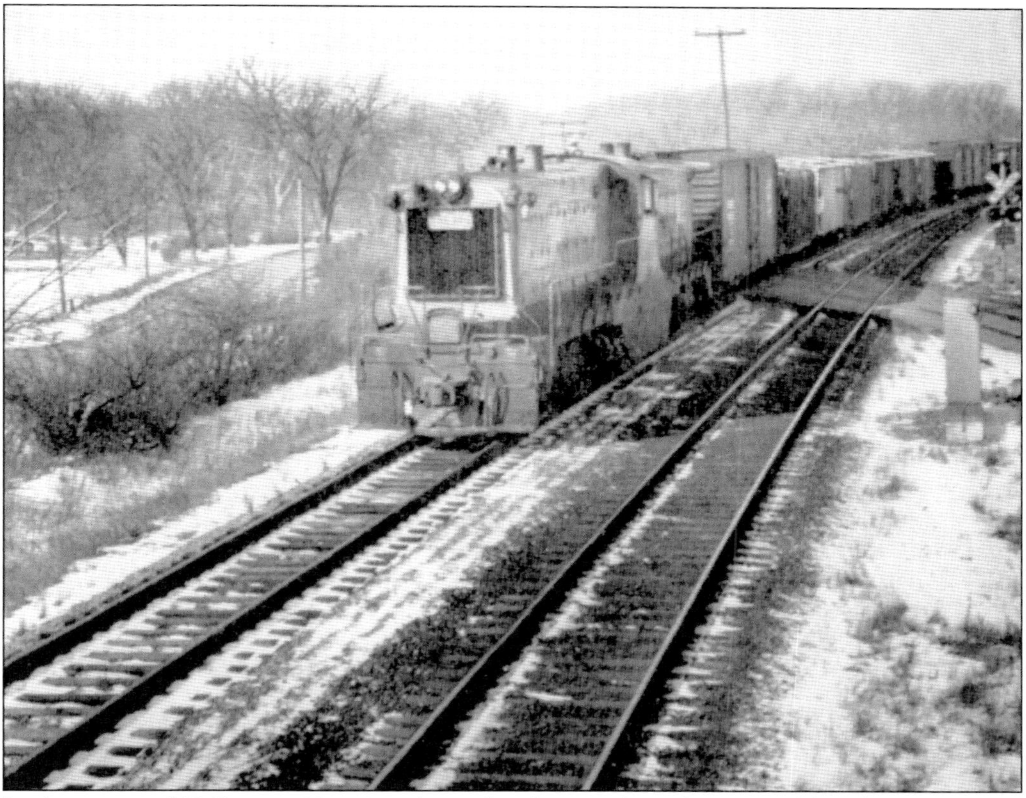

In the spring of 1963, train No. 42 is shown heading eastbound near Marble Falls with engine No. 906 leading. The center cab locomotives were the primary road power for EJ&E freights from 1948 to the early 1970s. No. 906 was retired and sold for scrap in 1974.

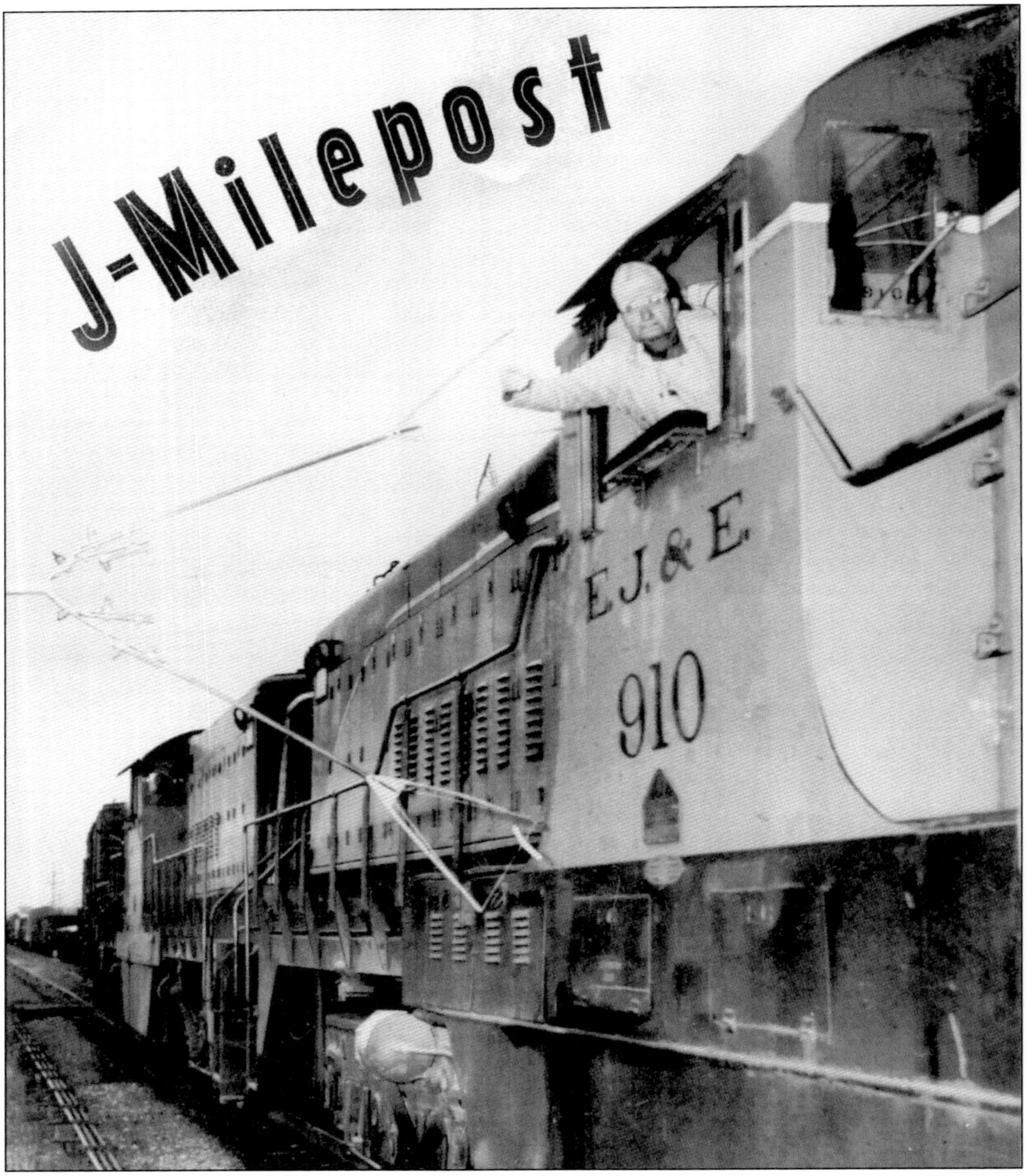

Engineman Courtney Smith was seen grabbing train orders in February 1963 at Leighton with train No. 3. Rebuilt engines No. 910 and No. 906 are pulling the train between East Joliet and Waukegan. Train orders were a time-honored tradition of running trains safely between stations before centralized traffic control or the track warrant system became the norm.

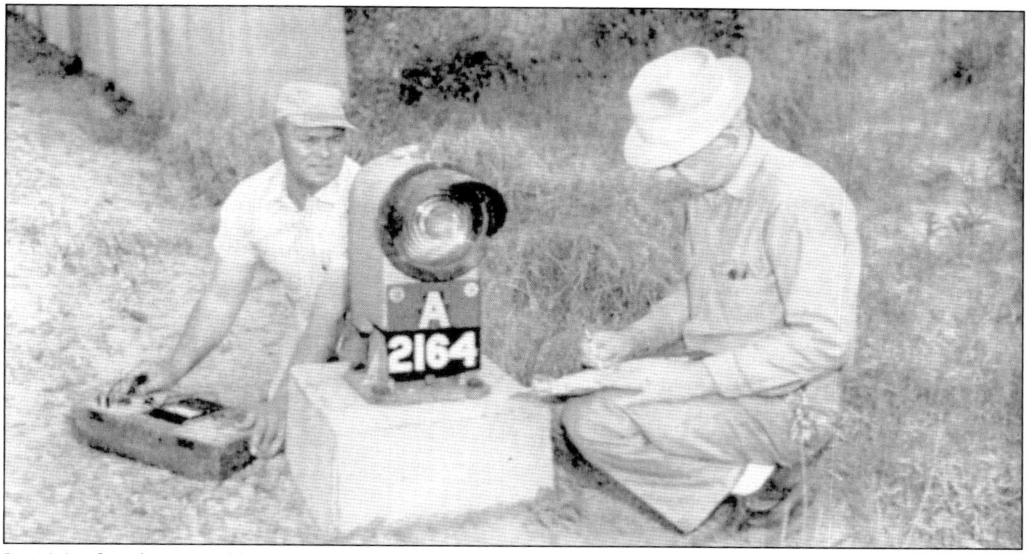

In 1961, fire destroyed bridge No. 613 over the Grand Calumet River at Cavanaugh. A temporary signal system was installed that authorized both westbound and eastbound trains to proceed through the construction area by signal indication only. This greatly expedited the traffic over this high-density part of the system. Lead signalman Gerald "Barney" Craig, left, and signal foreman Paul Elliott are testing the functions of signal A-2164, which was installed to control eastbound train movements while the new bridge was under construction.

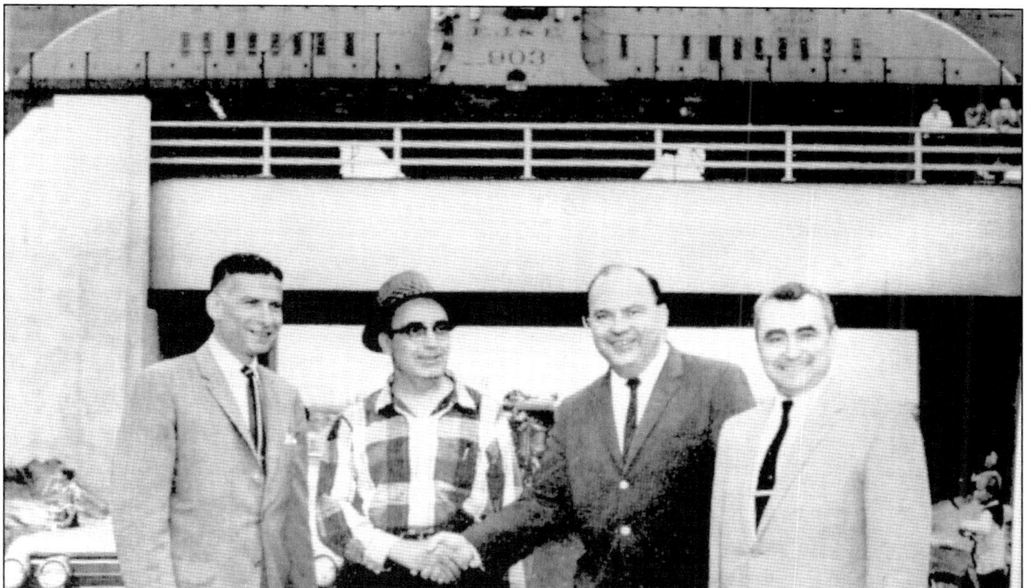
On July 4, 1962, a commemorative parade was given to celebrate the opening of the new Orchard Drive between Route 30 south to the EJ&E bridge in Park Forest. The bridge was completed over the drive a year earlier, but work still remained in building the road. On hand to celebrate the event are, from left to right, former village president Robert Dinerstein, EJ&E superintendent Louis Veronda, village president B. G. Cunningham, and former village president Henry Dietch. Centered on top of the bridge is locomotive No. 903.

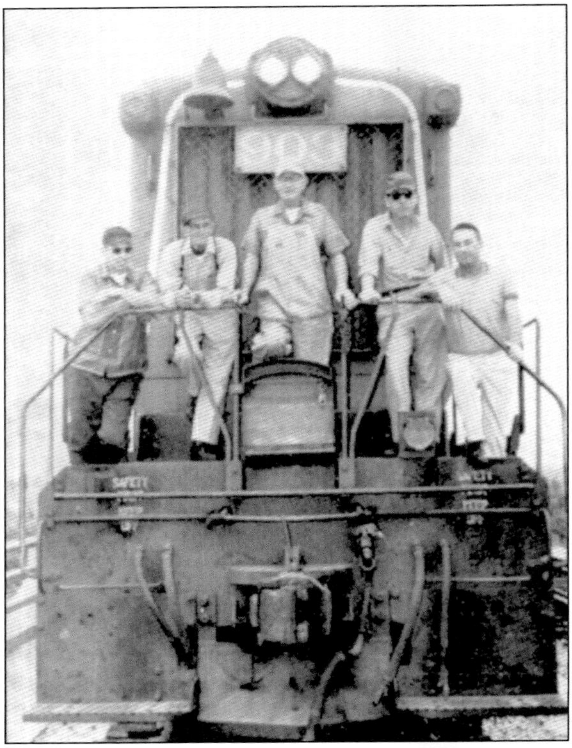

Participating in the opening of the new Orchard Drive are, from left to right, trainman Leo McCarney, conductor John Jones, enginemen John Demmond and Richard Reeves, and trainman Donald Whalen. The train's destination was Porter, and it was powered by the 2,000-horsepower No. 903.

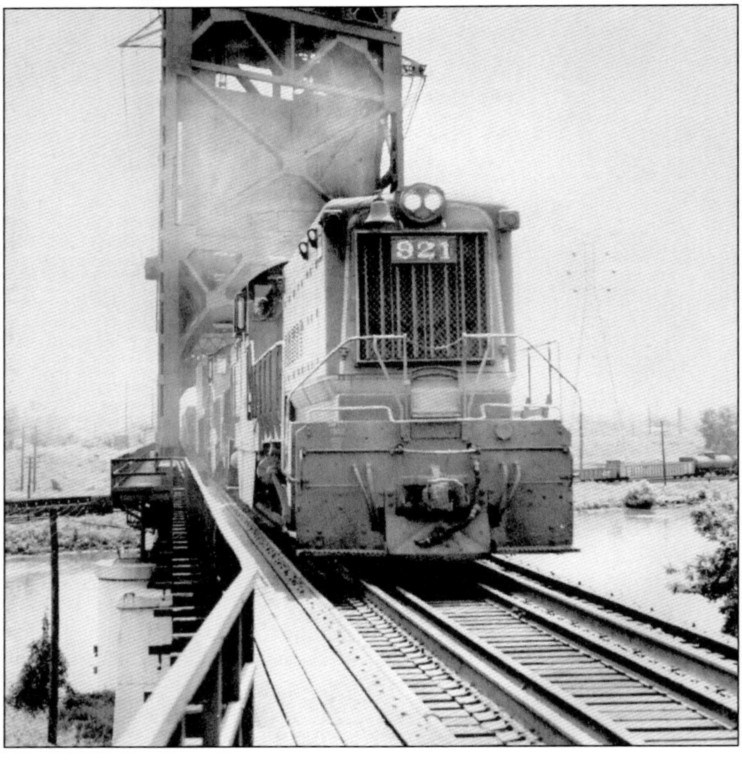

Engines No. 921 and No. 924 are shown pulling train No. 3 over the Illinois Waterway at East Joliet bound for Waukegan. The train had 106 loaded and 7 empty cars in the consist. A total of 4,000 horsepower was being used to pull the train. The engineman visible in the cab is Wendall Bishup. Engine No. 921 was rebuilt by EMD in 1957 and sold for scrap in 1976 after 19 years of dependable service.

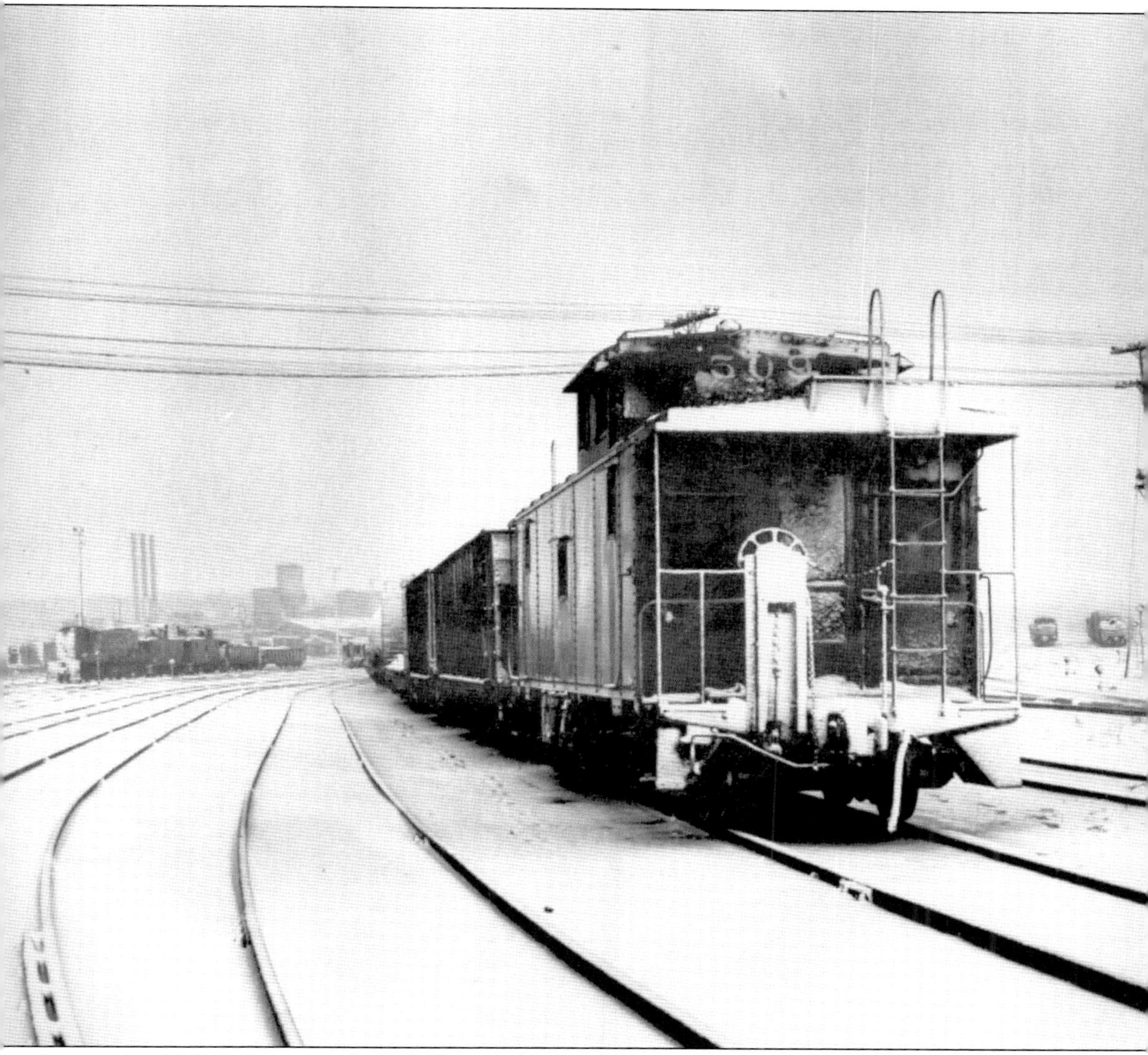

Train No. 12 has just arrived in the East Joliet yard from Waukegan in this wintry scene in December 1968. The markers have just been taken off the caboose and the crew was heading to the yard office to finish up their paper work and seek warmth from the blustery weather.

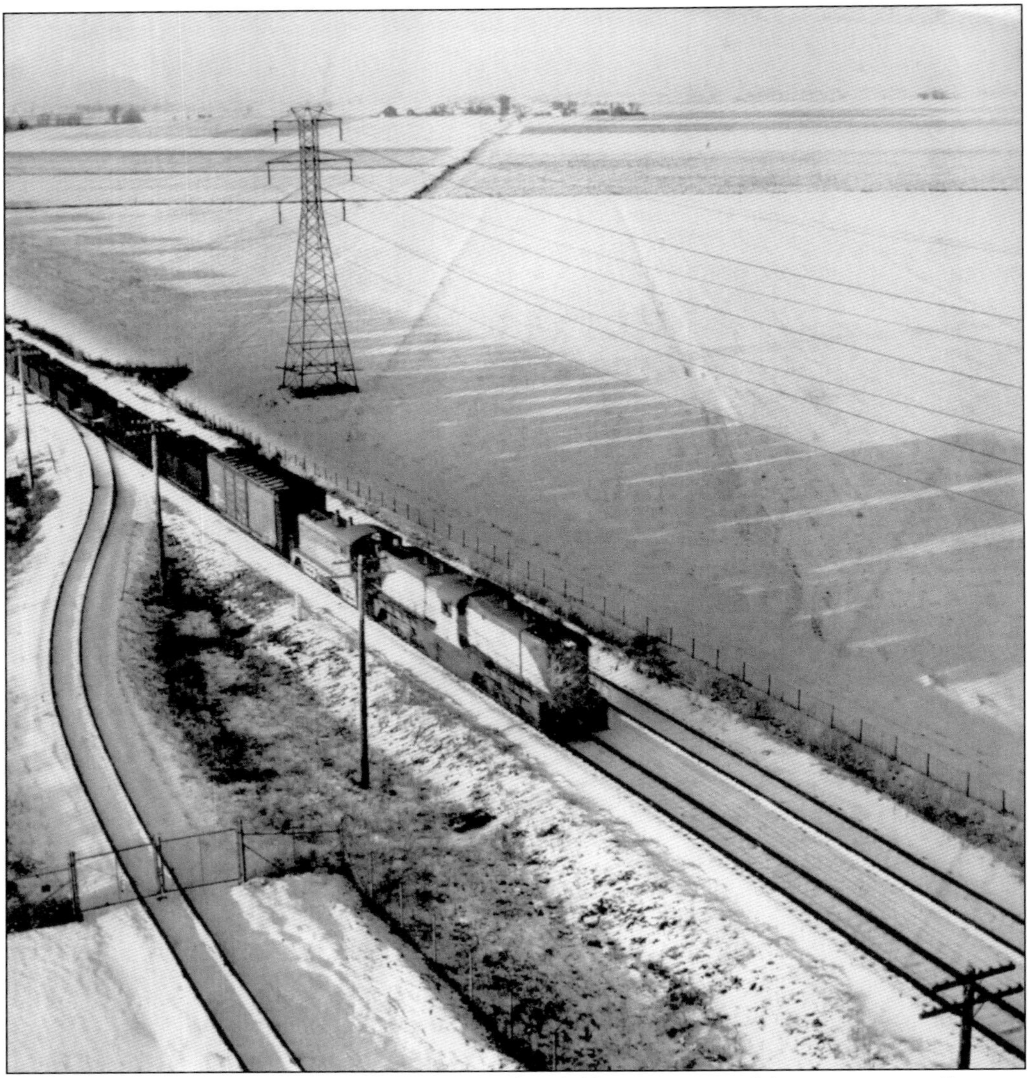

Train No. 6, shown here, was rolling through Plainfield on its way to Joliet on a wintry January 1966 day. The photographer was standing on top of the Lehigh Portland Cement storage bins looking in a northeast direction. Train No. 6 originated in Waukegan and was pulled by a reengined center cab and an EMD NW2 switcher. The EJ&E still occasionally uses switch engines on its freight trains to this day.

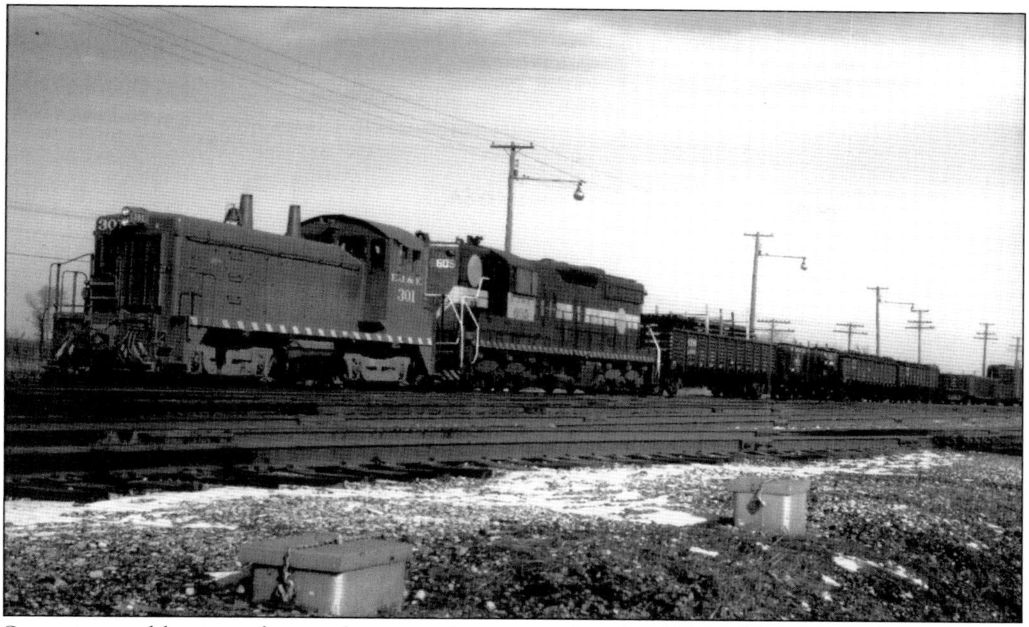

Swapping and leasing of power between the sister railroads of United States Steel Corporation has always been a common occurrence. In February 1968, SW1200 No. 301 together with leased SD9 No. 605, was one of nine SD9s leased during 1968–1972 to replace the aging Baldwin center-cab fleet.The SD9 was formerly DM&IR No. 108, which was acquired in 1968 by the EJ&E and later saw service on the Montana Rail Link. (Paul Meyer photograph.)

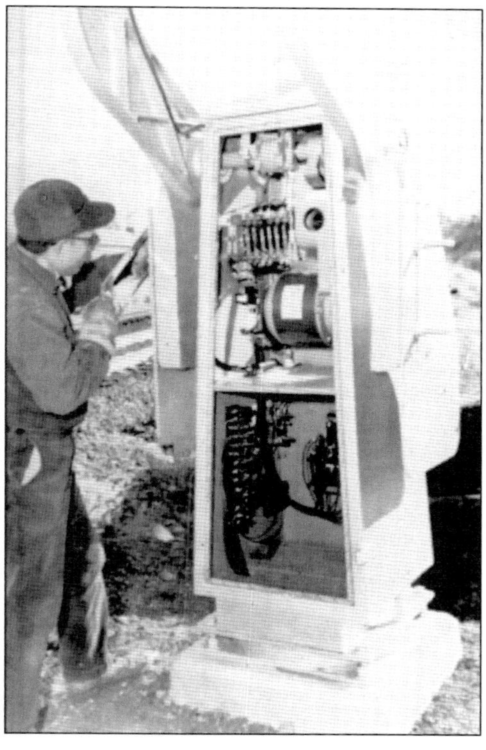

In the fall of 1965, new crossing gates were installed at Mills Road in southeast Joliet. The new crossing protection was installed due to the new east campus of the Joliet Township High School being less than a mile from the crossing. Signalman James Pennuto is shown sawing off the protruding ends of the bolts that will be holding the counterweights for the gate arms.

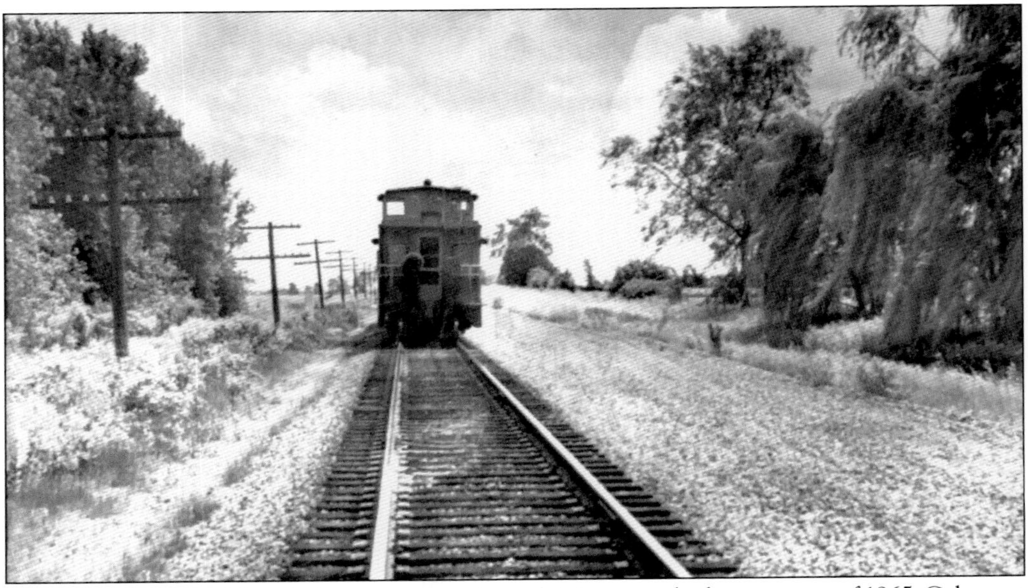

The caboose of train No. 6 is shown passing through Wayne in the late summer of 1965. Cabooses were all but gone by 1985 on road freights but were still used on local switch runs that required a lot of switching or backup movements over road crossings.

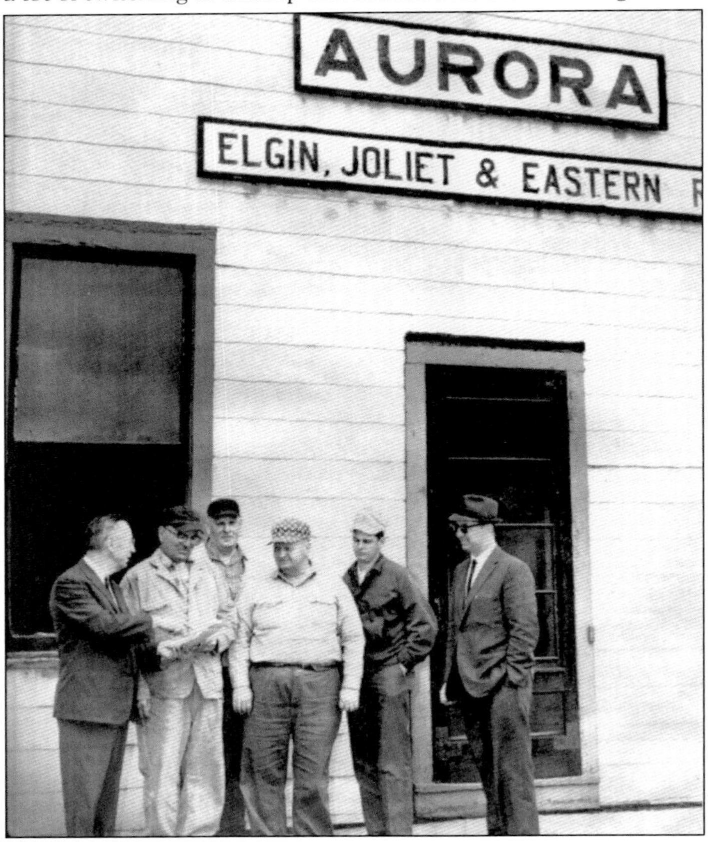

In May 1886, the City of Aurora granted the Joliet, Aurora, and Northern Railroad the right to operate into their city. This was the first section of what would later become the EJ&E. The intentions were to build the line northwesterly across Illinois to Dubuque, but these plans were never carried forward. Passenger trains ran on this line between Aurora and Joliet until about 1907. In the summer of 1965, crew members of the Aurora run are pictured standing by the freight depot. They are, from left to right, agent Harry Cron, enginemen Al Zettergren and John Krohn, trainmen Barry Allison and Andy Kapinus, and trainmaster Bob Chamberlin.

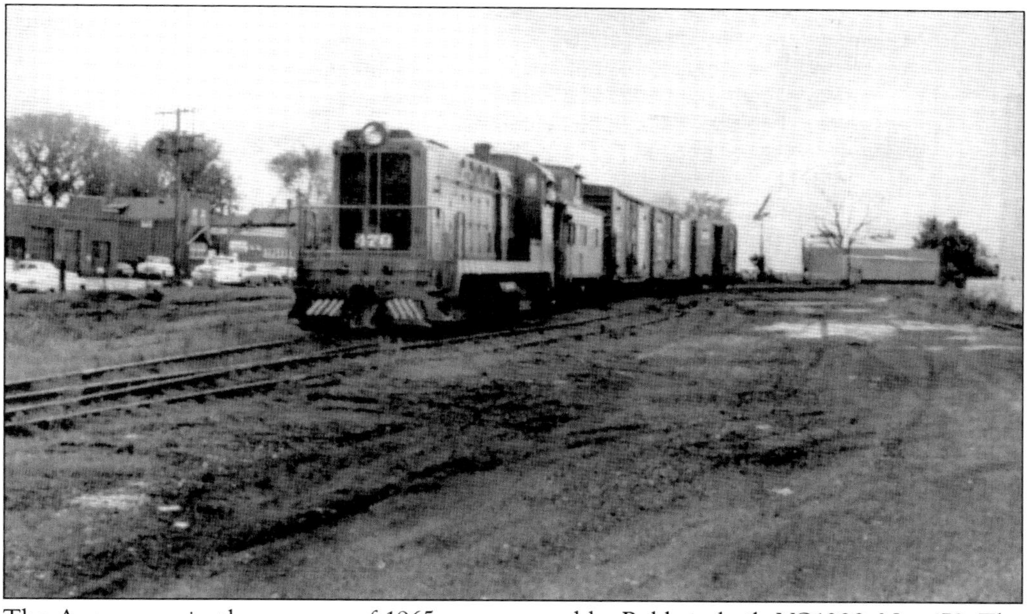

The Aurora run in the summer of 1965 was powered by Baldwin-built VO1000, No. 479. The train is shown in the yard at Aurora near the depot. For the return trip to Joliet, the diesel will be "run around" the caboose and cars in the yard. The west end of the Aurora branch was abandoned by the spring of 1977. Service to a station called Wolfs did continue until 1985. At one time the Chicago, Milwaukee, and Gary Railway (later Milwaukee Road) had trackage rights on the EJ&E between Joliet and Aurora.

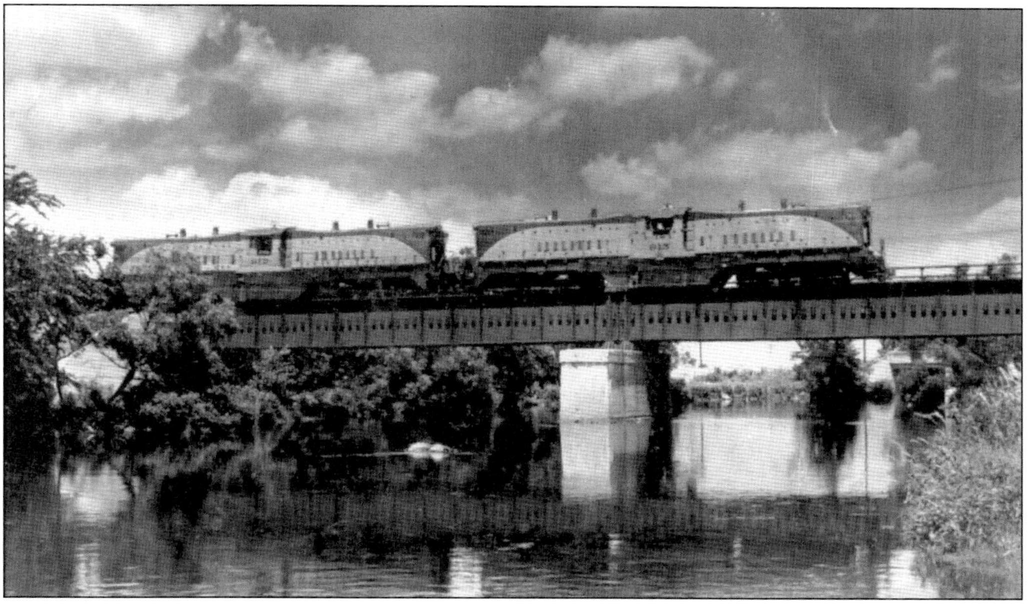

Despite its reputation of being an industrial railroad, the EJ&E did have some tranquil locations along its right-of-way. This scene shows the No. 915 and No. 912 pulling train No. 4 across the Du Page River at Plainfield during the summer of 1964. The train was bound for Joliet and consisted of 36 loads and 61 empties.

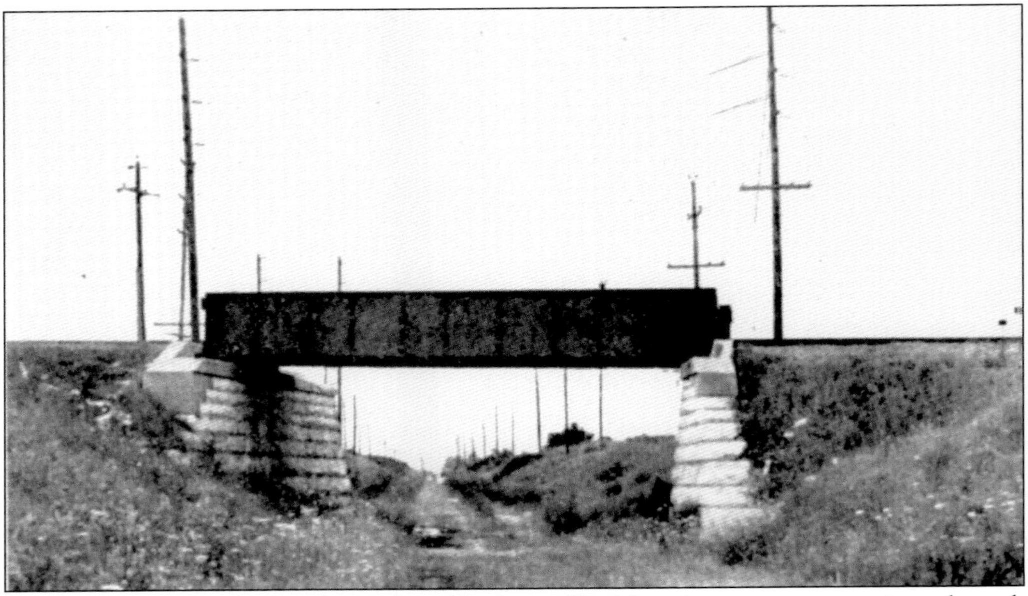

During the summer of 1964, the track and bridge and building departments were given the task of removing the bridge that spanned the abandoned Chicago, Aurora and Elgin Interurban line near Aurora. The bridge was built in 1901 and was the narrowest on the EJ&E system. The task of removing the bridge, filling the opening with slag, and relaying the ties and rail was done in a seven-hour period.

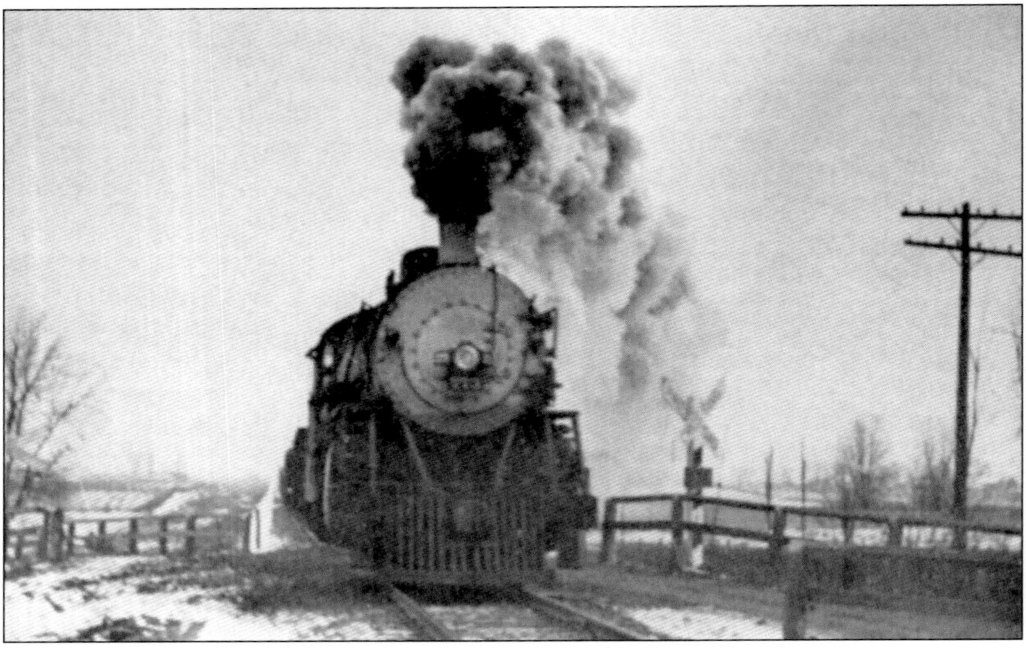

In the early 1940s, EJ&E employee John Cleary at the Sutton Road crossing near South Barrington took this Christmas scene. Train No. 6 was heading for Joliet with engine No. 773 in the lead. The Baldwin-built locomotive was one of the last 2-8-2 Mikados delivered to the EJ&E. It was built in 1930 and sold to the DM&IR in 1948.

Bridge No. 710 (left), was a swing bridge built in 1896 to span the Calumet River at South Chicago. In March 1974, it was replaced with a steel lift bridge (right). The new span was 242 feet long, 22 feet wide, and was fabricated by United States Steel Corporation's American Bridge Division, adjacent to the Kirk Yard. Ships traversing the river to and from Lake Michigan frequently struck the old bridge.

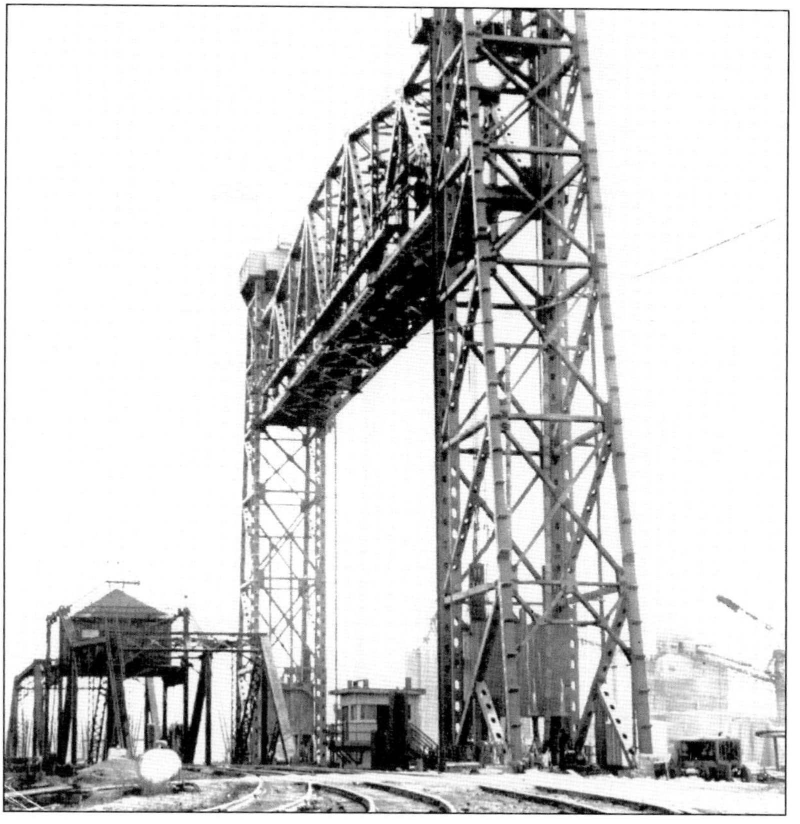

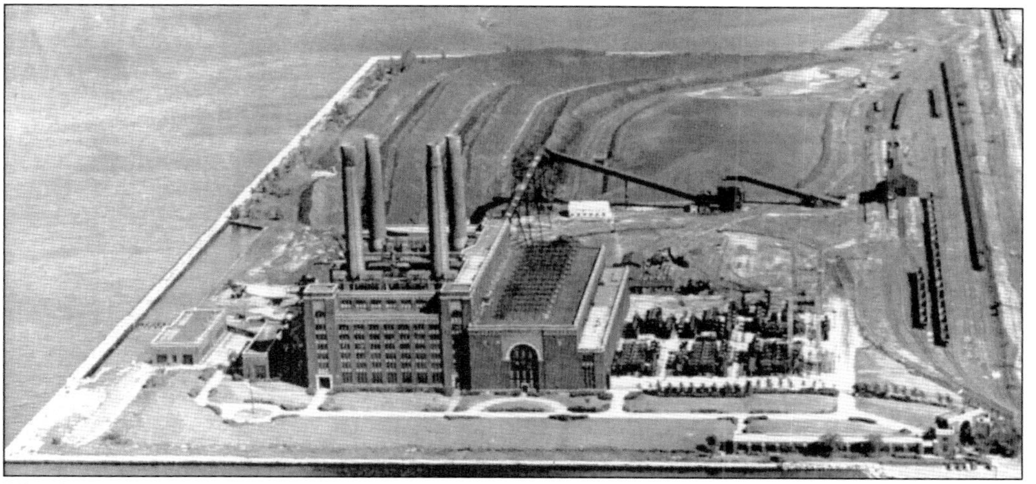

The State Line generating station in Hammond, Indiana, was built in 1929. Currently the total generating capacity is 490 megawatts, or enough to power 60,000 homes.

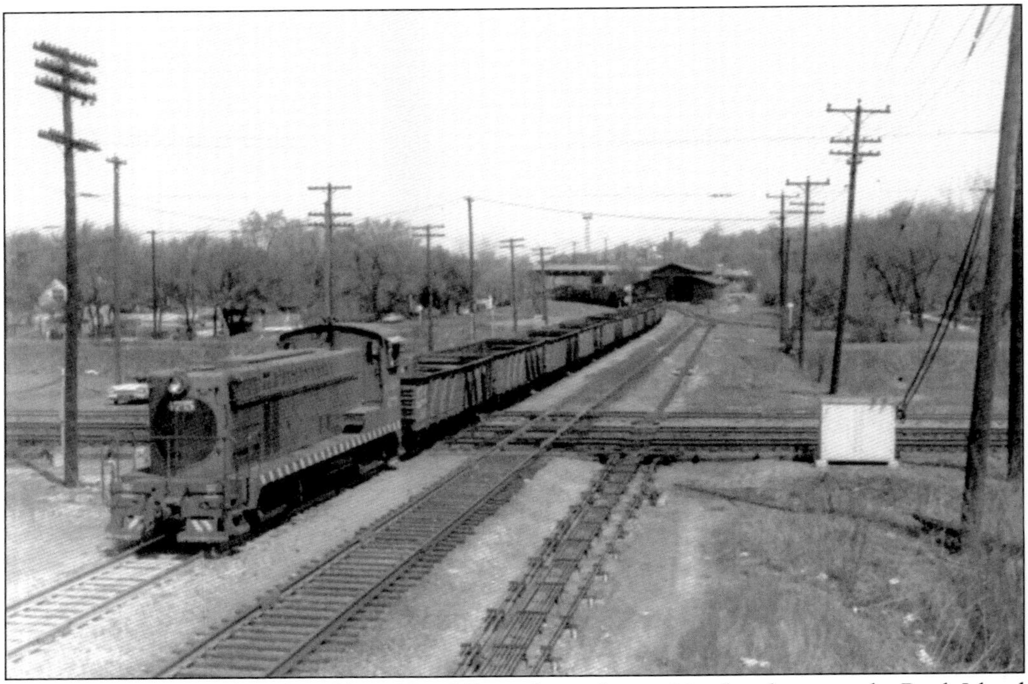

The East Joliet yard job with Baldwin No. 475 was shown here taking headroom at the Rock Island tower in the summer of 1958. Long strings of freight cars were occasionally pulled out of one track and put back in another, requiring that the crew pull way out to the tower. (R. A. Eisenbrandt.)

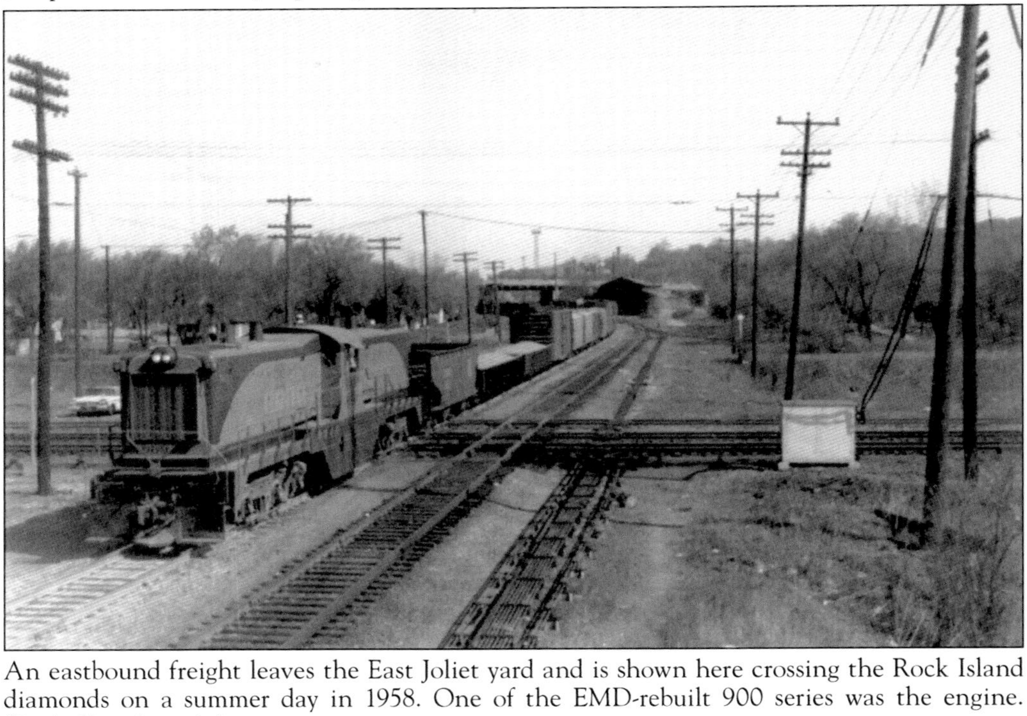

An eastbound freight leaves the East Joliet yard and is shown here crossing the Rock Island diamonds on a summer day in 1958. One of the EMD-rebuilt 900 series was the engine. (R. A. Eisenbrandt.)

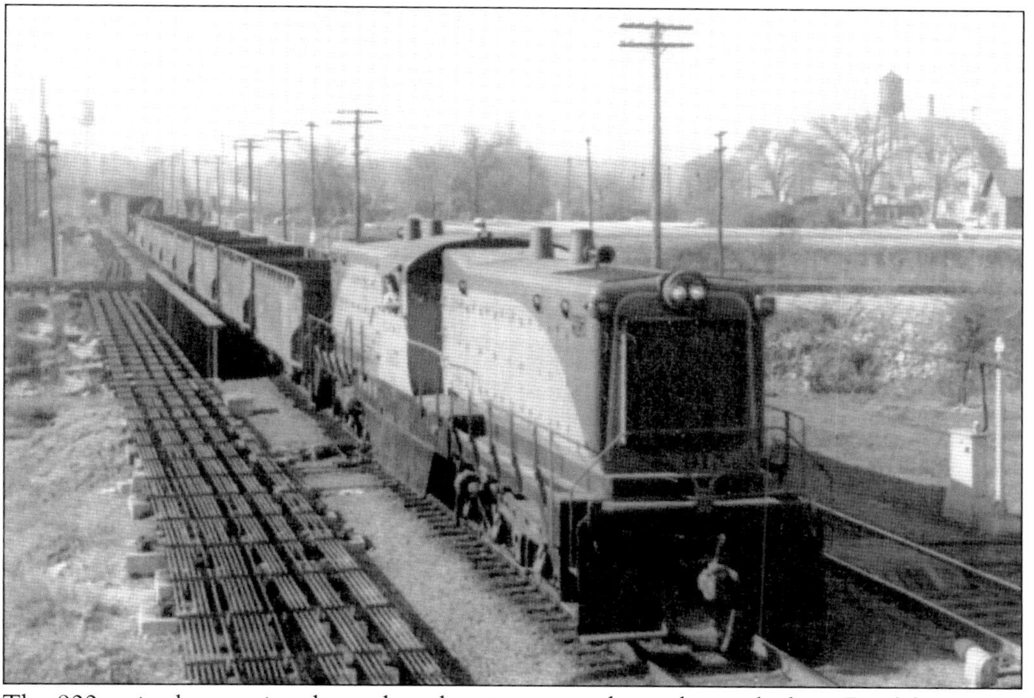

The 900 series locomotive shown here has just come down the grade from Frankfort and is entering the East Joliet yard. The pipeline connecting the tower levers to the derails and switches was visible on the left side of the tracks. Before two-way radios became common, the towerman displayed yard track numbers in a box located in a window. Train crews then knew on which track they were to yard their train. (R. A. Eisenbrandt.)

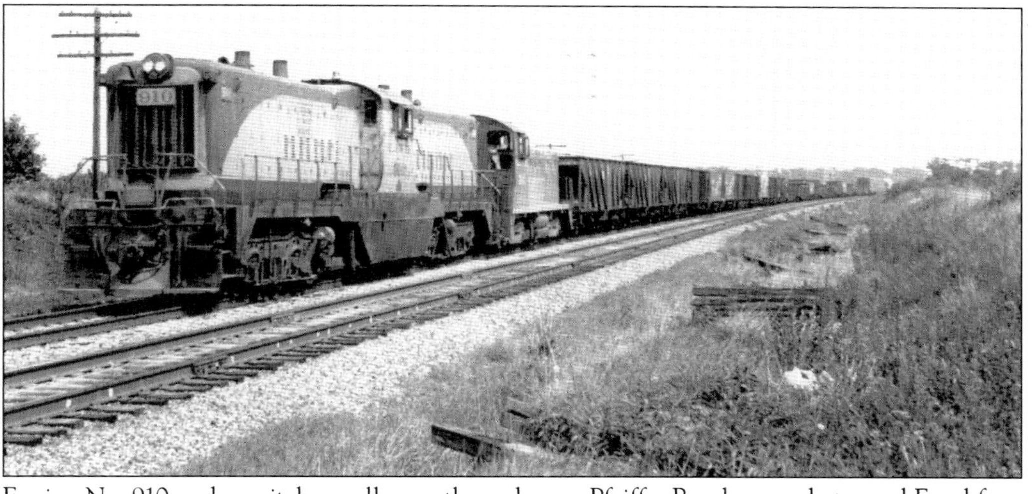

Engine No. 910 and a switcher pull a westbound, near Pfeiffer Road, upgrade toward Frankfort. The highest elevation on the east end of the EJ&E was at Frankfort where the elevation was 765 feet above sea level at the Center Road crossing. Crosstie replacement had been done a few months before, as the old ties are still lying along trackside. The ties will be hauled away later. Some will be sold to landscapers; others may be turned into wood chips. (R. A. Eisenbrandt.)

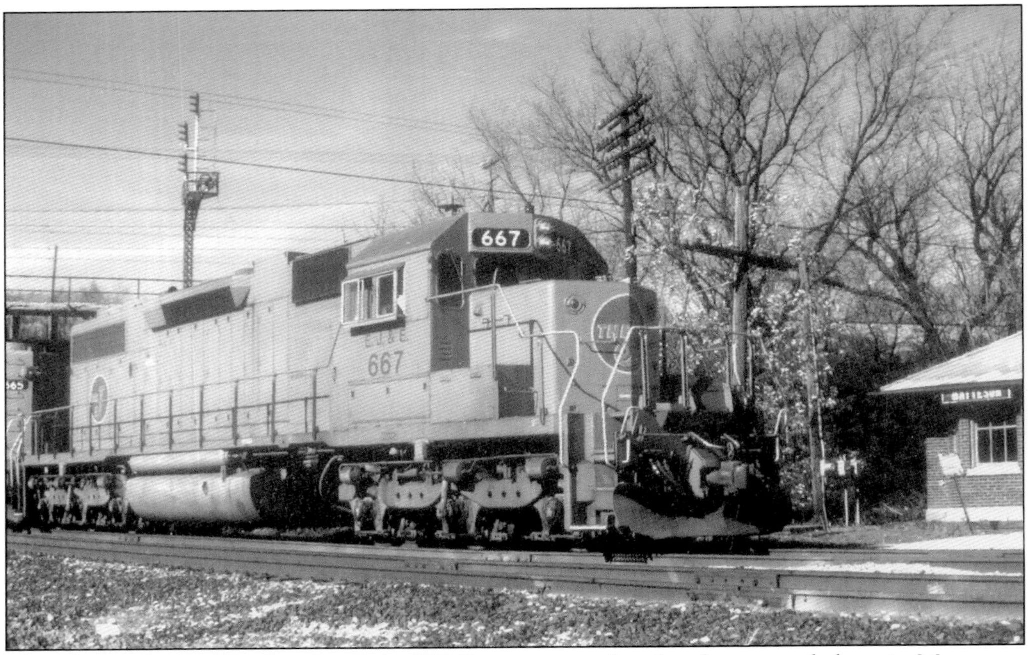

The Illinois Central Railroad and the EJ&E once crossed each other at grade here in Matteson. In 1922, the Illinois Central Railroad elevated its right-of-way, eliminating the crossing and interlocking tower that once controlled the location. Each railroad maintained a small yard for the interchange of freight cars between the railroads. No. 667 and No. 665 are headed east passing the brick EJ&E freight depot that was constructed shortly after the Illinois Central Railroad elevation. (Paul Meyer photograph.)

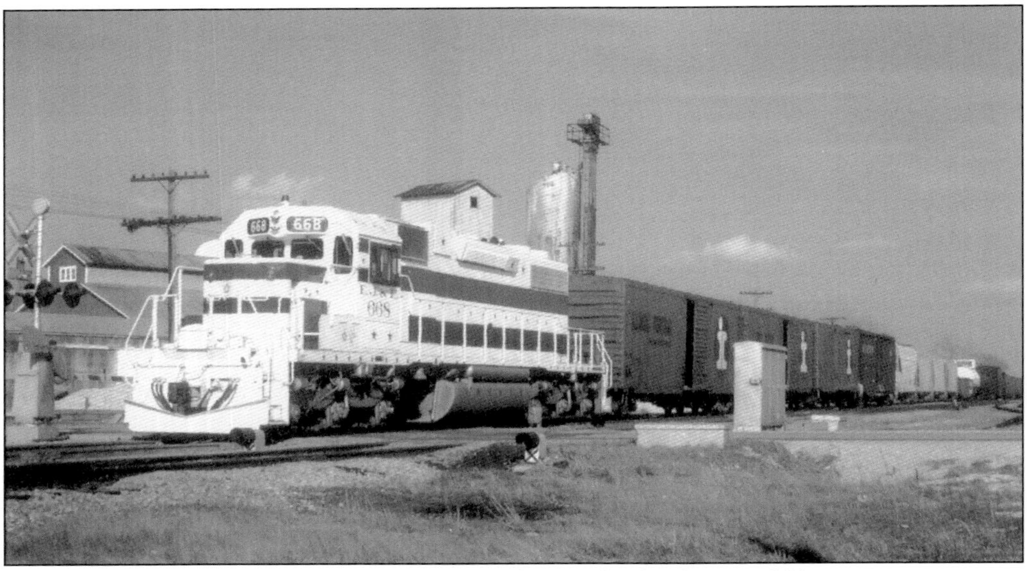

Engine No. 668 was painted into a patriotic scheme of red, white, and blue to commemorate the bicentennial year of 1976. The westbound train was at Matteson's Main Street crossing as the crew picks up cars from the interchange with the Illinois Central. In the background is the Matteson Lumber Yard. (Paul Meyer photograph.)

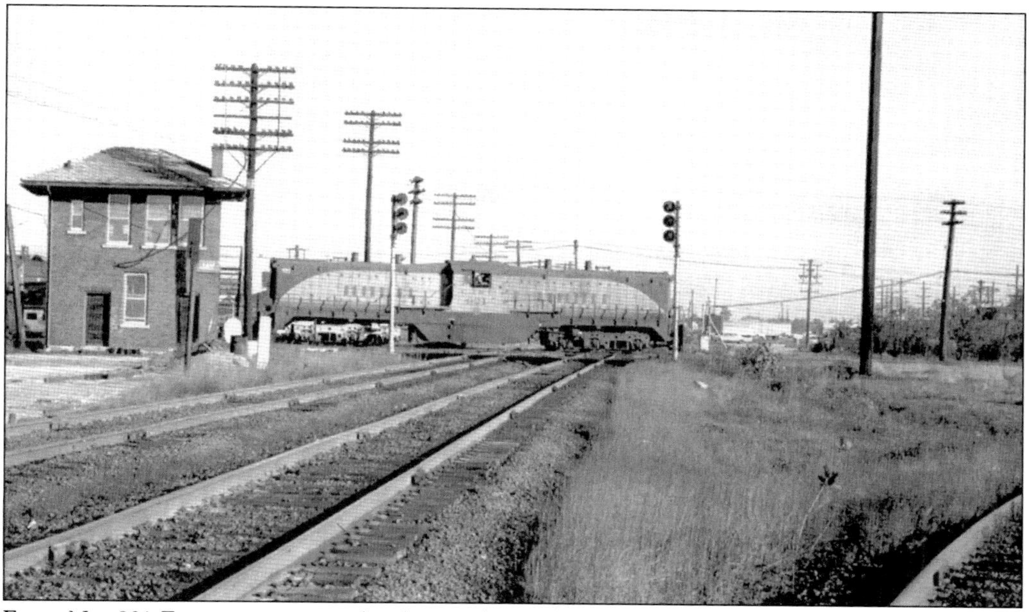

Extra No. 921 East starts across the diamonds at Chicago Heights. Once known as the C&EI, the north-south line later belonged to the Missouri Pacific Railroad, and is now part of the Union Pacific. Trackage rights allowed the Louisville and Nashville Railroad (L&N), and then the Seaboard System to share the route. Now the CSXT also operates through there. The tower still stands though no longer manned by operators. The EJ&E train dispatcher in Joliet remotely controls the signals and switches. (R. A. Eisenbrandt.)

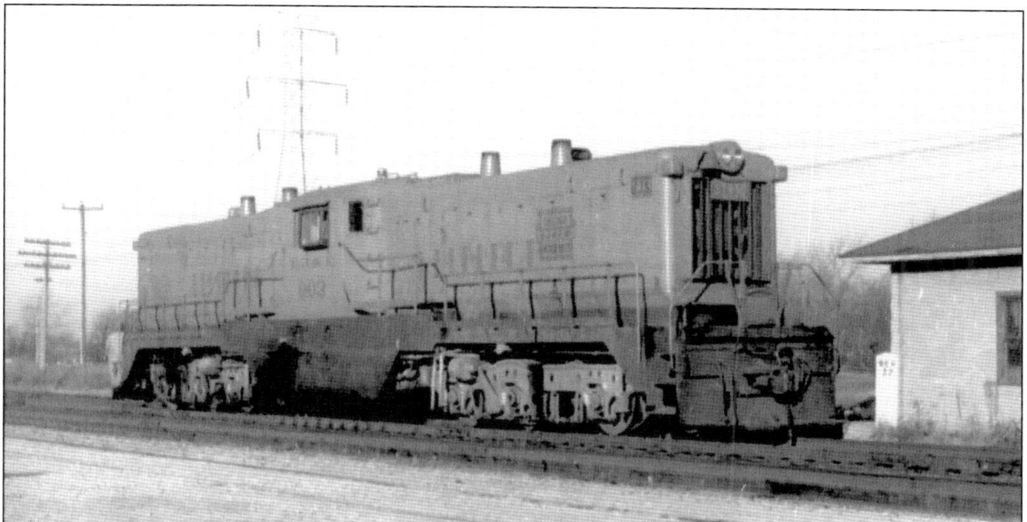

The EJ&E has several local industries in Frankfort over the years. The most notable has been the Mobil Plastics division plant east of Center Road. Here extra No. 903 makes a crossover move in the process of running around some cars to be spotted on an industry track. The building on the right was the old pump house. Trains with steam locomotives once took on water here after the hard climb up from Joliet. The Village of Frankfort purchased the well and property in 1950 for $3,500. (R. A. Eisenbrandt.)

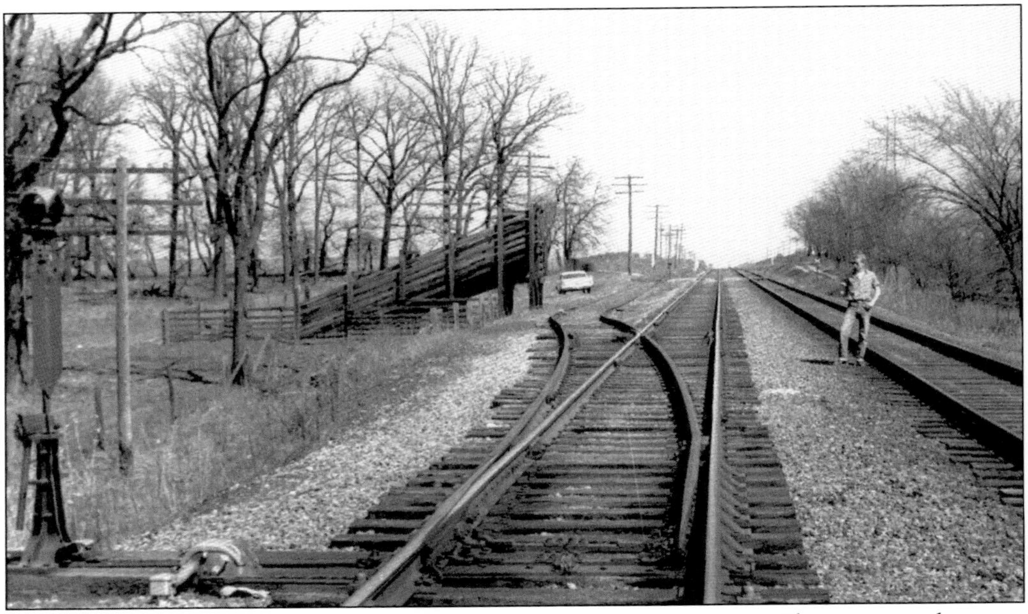

This view was looking east toward the Harlem Avenue road crossing. The private siding was known as McGlashen's Spur and was 627 feet in length. It could hold about 15 41-foot-long freight cars. The McGlashen family owned over 300 acres on both sides of the EJ&E. The farms were used to fatten cattle and other livestock for market, hence the stock pens and ramp. Carloads of stale Cracker Jack popcorn, used to feed the livestock, were often brought in from Chicago. (R. A. Eisenbrandt.)

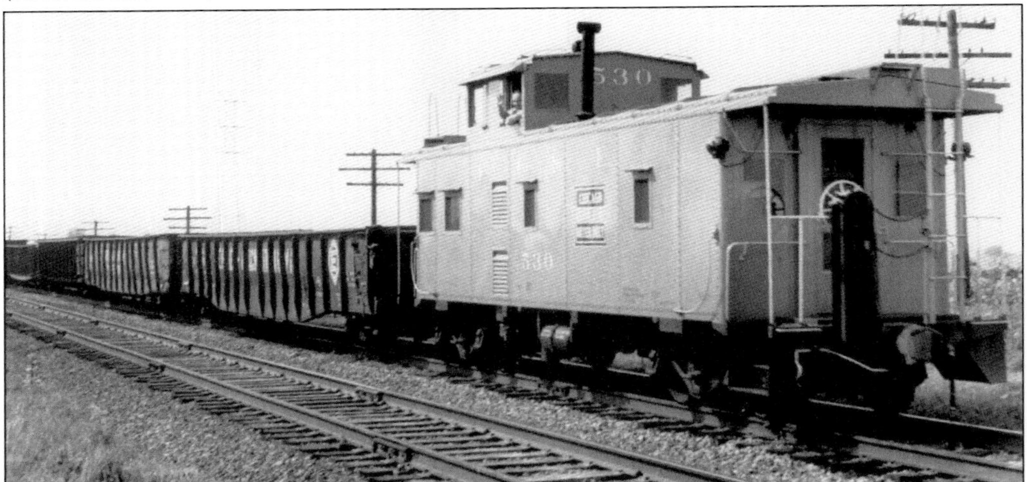

A comfortable caboose like No. 530 was the pride of a conductor and his crew. The EJ&E ordered 50 of the all-steel cupola-type cars and started taking delivery in 1956. Each one cost $17,000. Propane gas–driven electric generators provided 110-volt current. There were electric fans, a gas refrigerator, a hot plate, a space heater, kitchen and bathroom type sinks, hot and cold running water, and a toilet compartment. There were also four bunks and cushioned seats. The floor was covered with asphalt tile, and the walls and ceiling were insulated. Each crew member had a steel locker, and there were additional storage compartments. Cabooses were once assigned to a specific conductor, and it was usually kept spotless. (R. A. Eisenbrandt.)

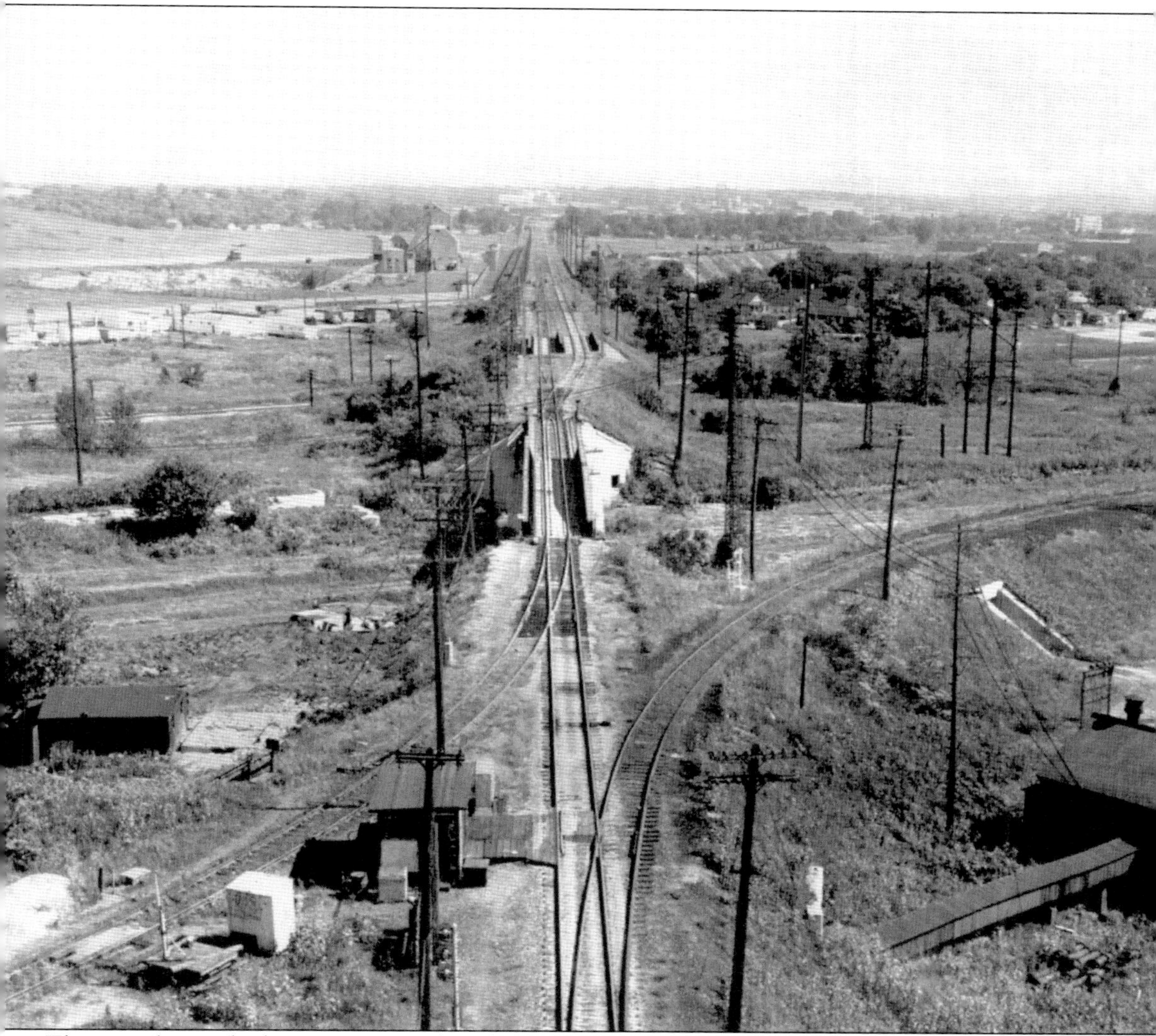

This aerial view looking east was taken from the bridge No. 198 over the Des Plaines River at Joliet in July 1961. The Silver Cross Hospital lies directly straight in the distance, with the tracks curving to the right and into the East Joliet yard. The lead to the Santa Fe interchange track was on the lower right with the one to the lower left leading into a former coke plant. The lift-type drawbridge was constructed in 1934 over both the Des Plaines River and the new Illinois Waterway.

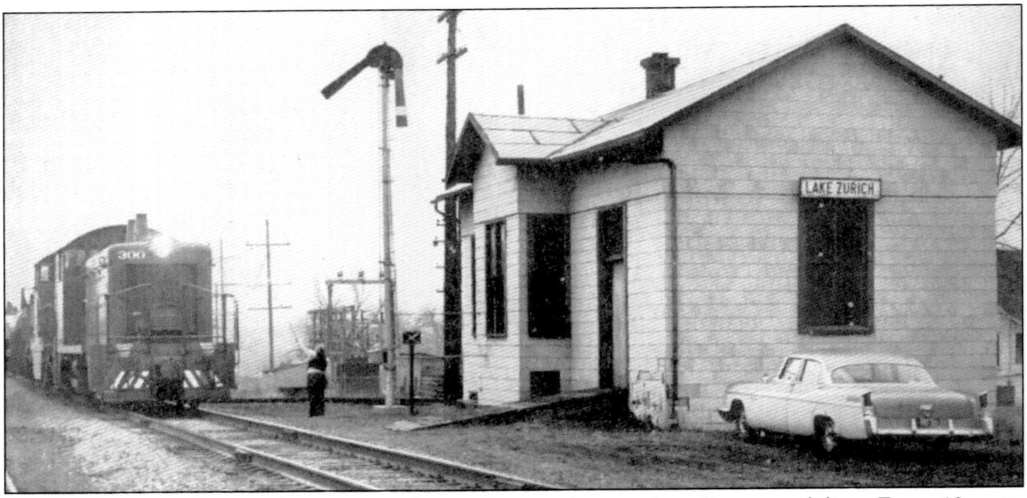

Agent Lester "Bucky" Walters was ready, in the time-honored tradition, to deliver Form 19 train orders to train No. 3 at the Lake Zurich depot in January 1963. The train was about to cross Route 22, Main Street, bound for Waukegan. The crew was given the heads up by the position of the signal in front of the station that train orders would be waiting for them.

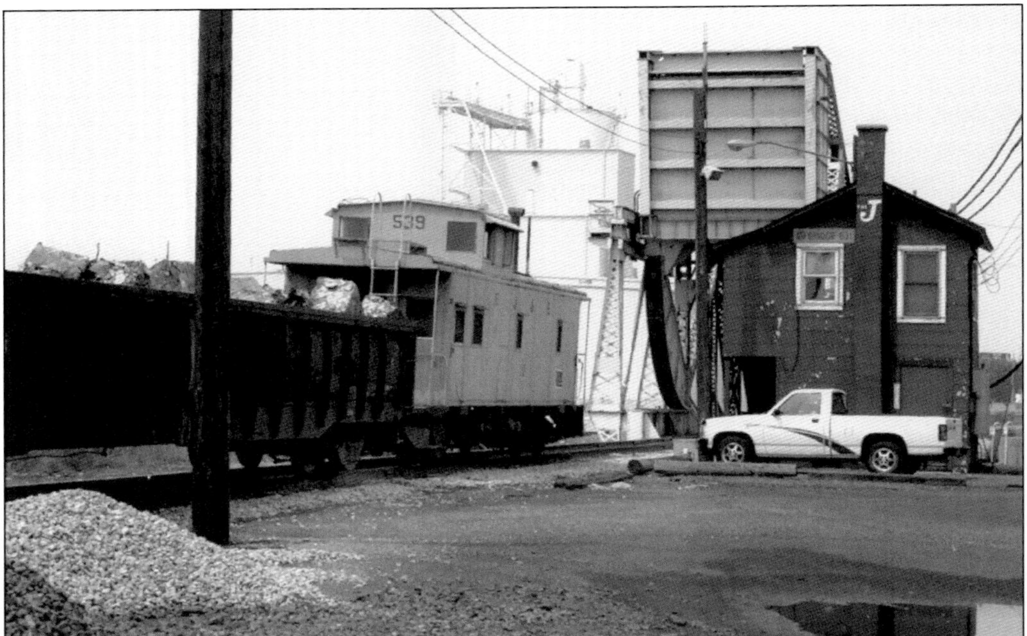

The Whiting line, which serves a refinery and other industries, was a viable part of the EJ&E. In this August 2000 view, the local switch job crossing lift bridge No. 631 over the Indiana Harbor Canal can be seen. This bridge was also shared with the IHB. The Whiting Yard was just to the north of this location. (Mark Stanek photograph.)

Six

Equipment of Steel for a Railroad of Steel

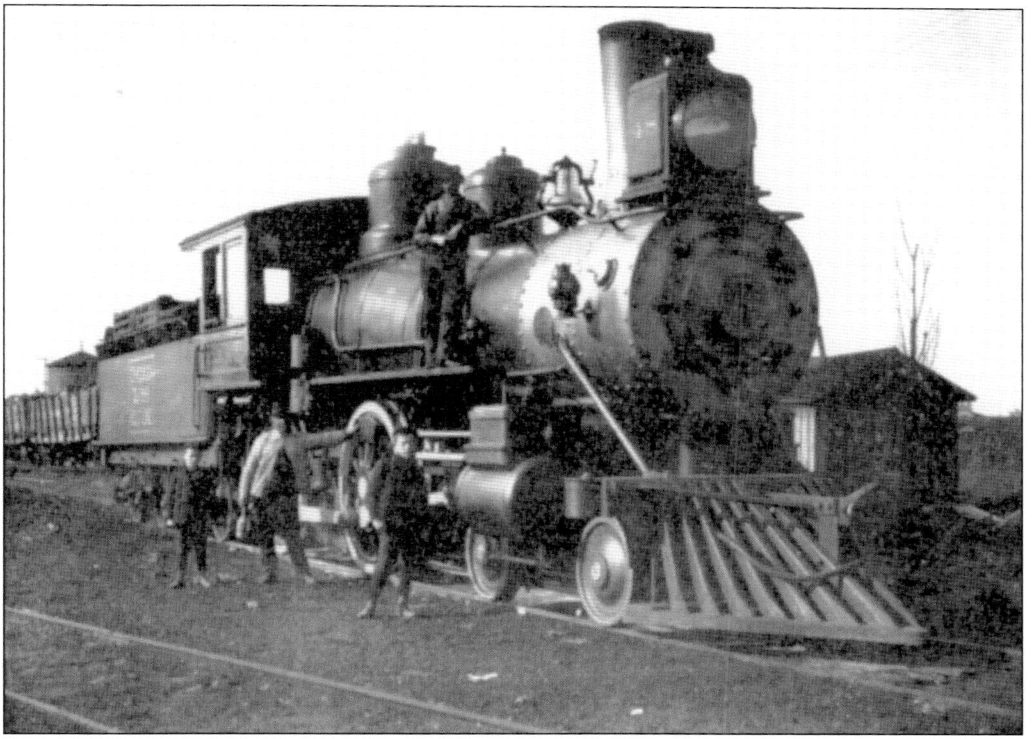

This photograph of engine No. 48 was believed to be have been taken in Waukegan around 1907. Alco manufactured it in 1904 for the CLS&E as No. 52. It was retired in late 1934 and scrapped the following year.

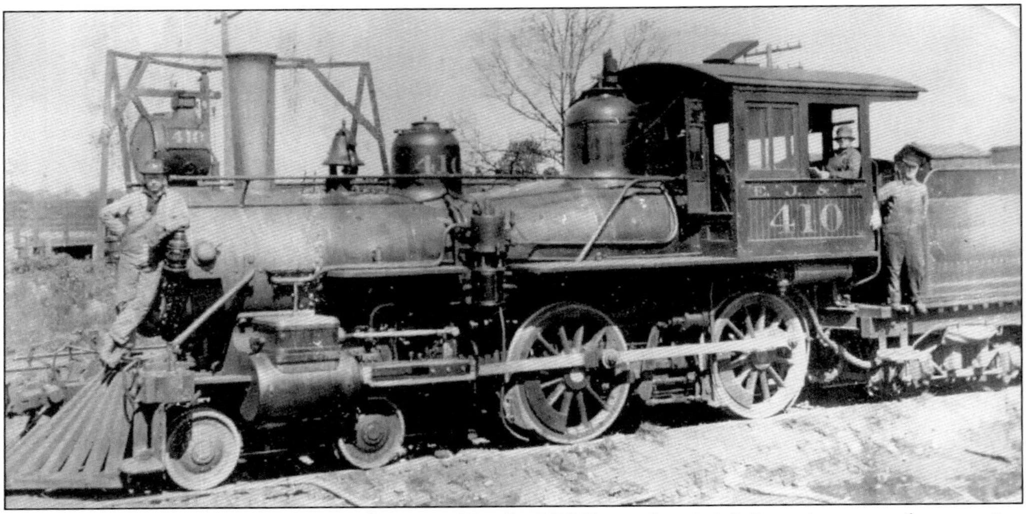

One of the earliest steam engines to be owned by the EJ&E was this 4-4-0 American-type locomotive built in 1887 by the Rhode Island Company. It was sold in 1918 to the J. T. Gardner Company.

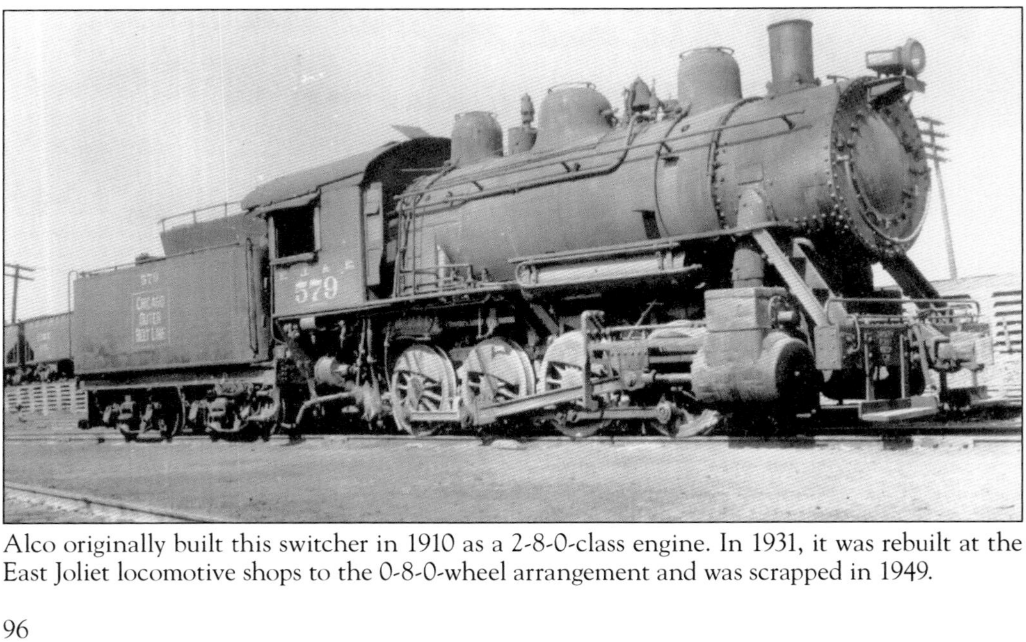

Alco originally built this switcher in 1910 as a 2-8-0-class engine. In 1931, it was rebuilt at the East Joliet locomotive shops to the 0-8-0-wheel arrangement and was scrapped in 1949.

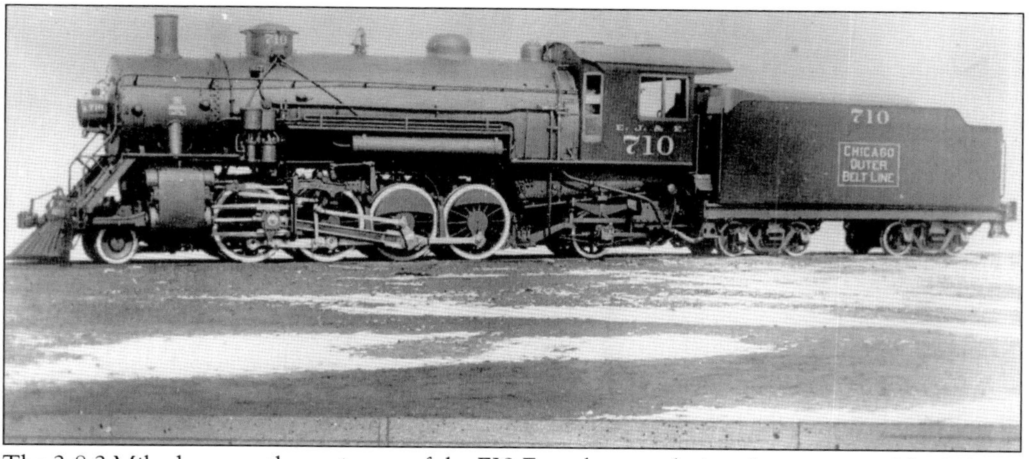

The 2-8-2 Mikados were the mainstay of the EJ&E road power during the steam era. No. 710 was built by Alco in 1913 and was equipped with the Miller Train Control for running on the C&EI track to Rossville. By October 1949, the last steam locomotives were retired from the EJ&E.

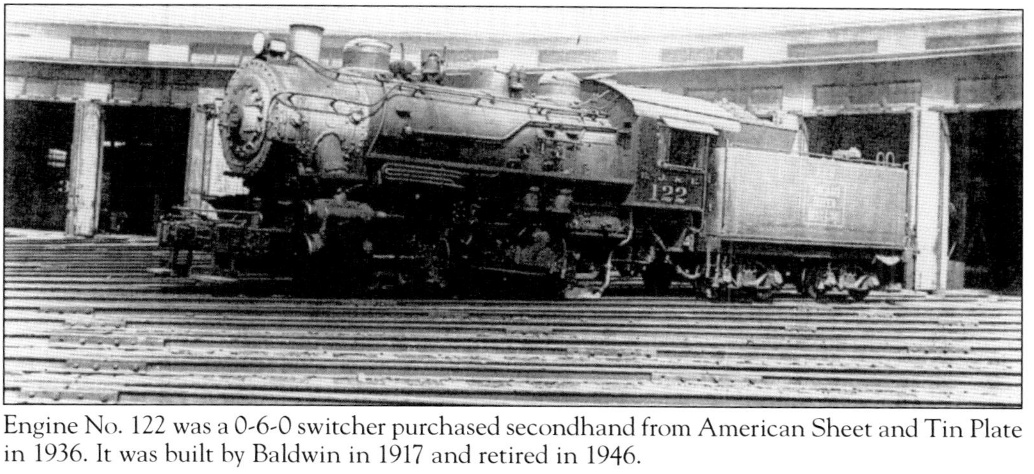

Engine No. 122 was a 0-6-0 switcher purchased secondhand from American Sheet and Tin Plate in 1936. It was built by Baldwin in 1917 and retired in 1946.

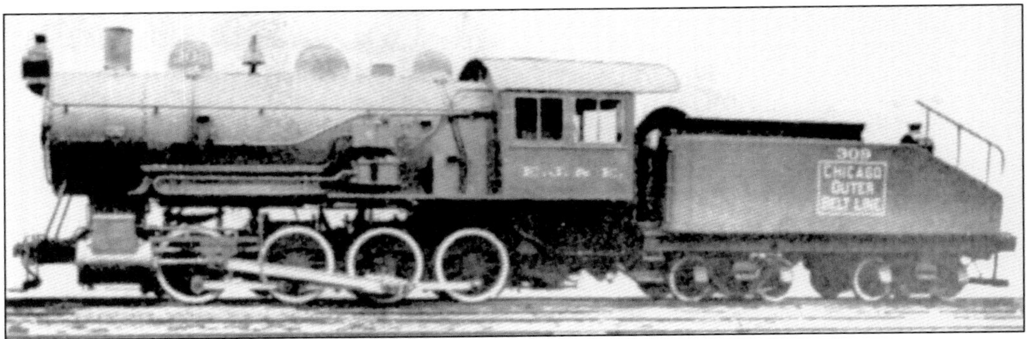

This builder's photograph is of 0-8-0 switcher 309, class AS, one of 11 built by Alco. The class had 51-inch drivers and 22-by-28-inch cylinders. The locomotives carried 200 pounds per square inch of steam pressure and weighed 91 tons.

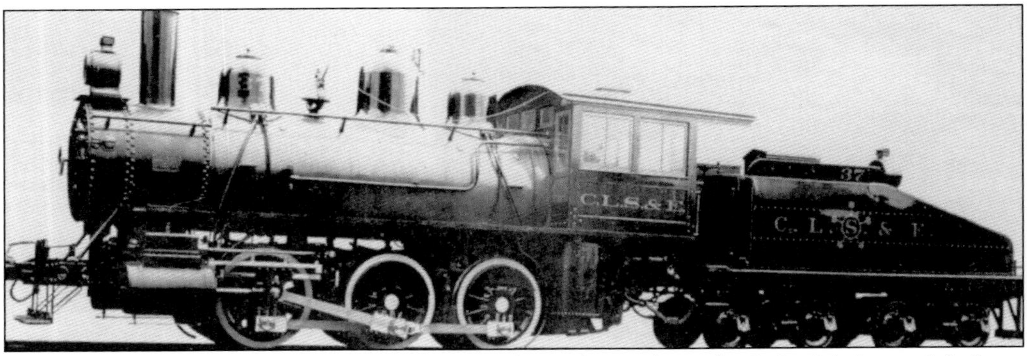

The CLS&E predecessor line to the EJ&E with trackage along the Lake Michigan lakefront connecting South Chicago with Gary. The CLS&E's predecessor was the C&BI, which obtained the trackage rights on the C&EI down to Rossville. The EJ&E had leased the CLS&E in 1909 and was merged into the system in 1938. No. 37 was a 0-6-0 car built by the Pittsburgh Locomotive Works in 1899. It later on became EJ&E No. 26 and was scrapped in 1927.

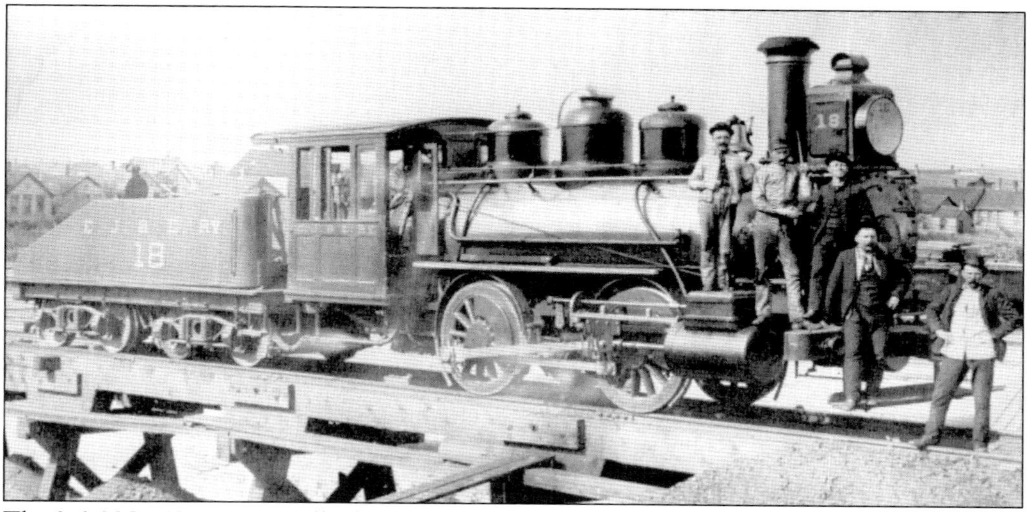

The 0-6-0 No. 18 was originally the CLS&E No. 31. It was built in 1892 and is seen here working in South Chicago. It was eventually sold to the J. T. Gardner Company in 1917.

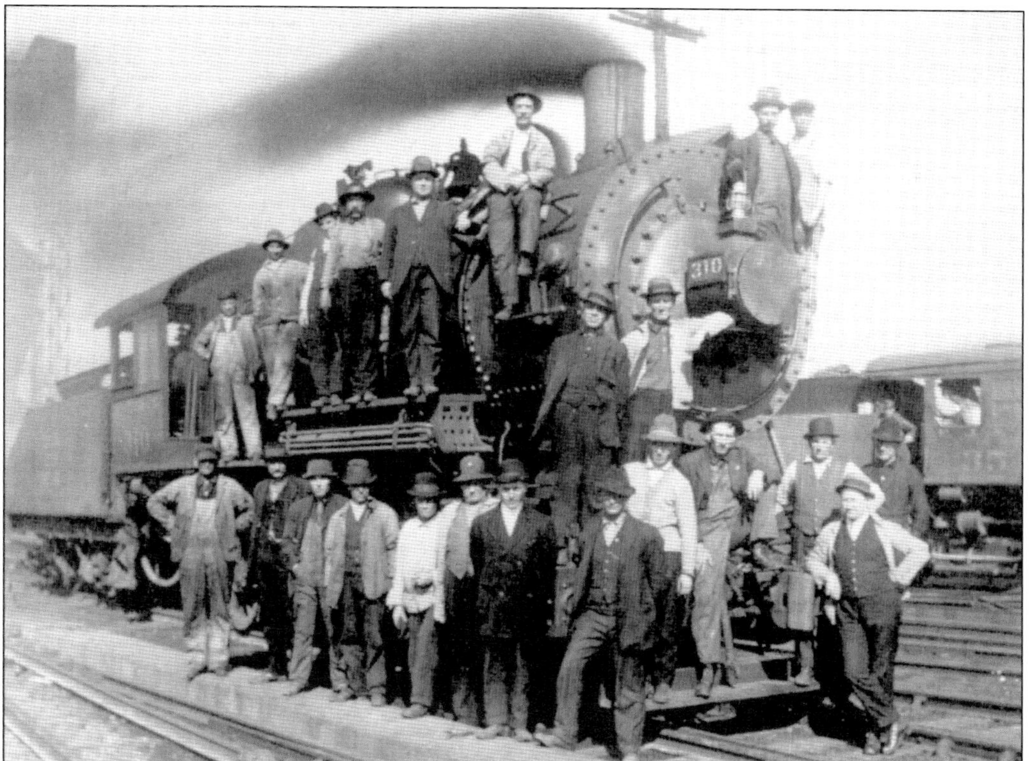

Most everyone climbed aboard switcher No. 310 at the East Joliet yard around 1915. The engine was built by Alco Pittsburgh in 1910 and was part of a group numbered from 302 to 311. It was retired in 1944 and scrapped the following year. The EJ&E owned 36 switchers of this type at one time. Most were scrapped at the time of dieselization in 1949.

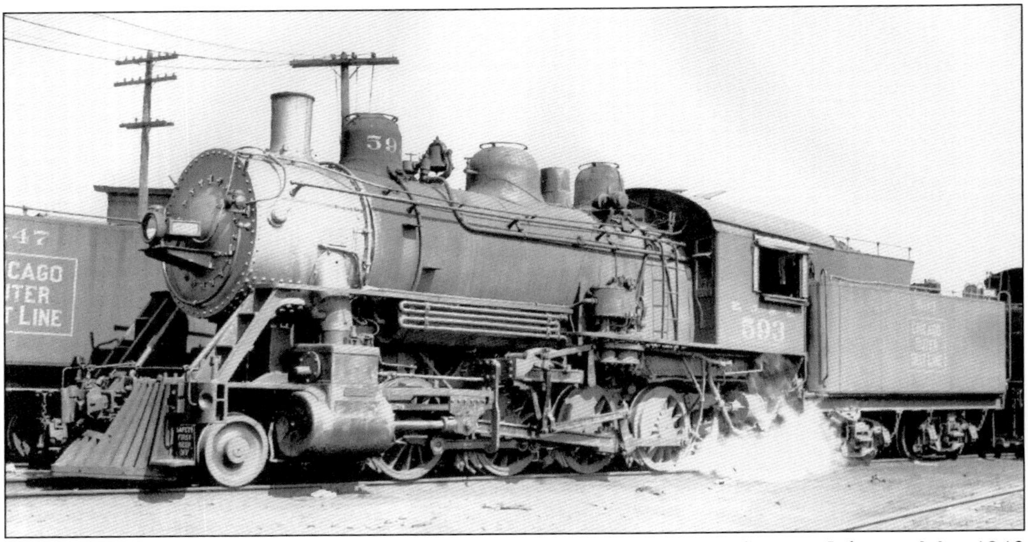

Engine No. 593 was a class A 2-8-0, built by Alco in 1910. It is seen here in Joliet in May 1940 and was scrapped in 1947. The engines could pull 1,750 gross tons uphill from East Joliet to Frankfort. (Bill Raia collection.)

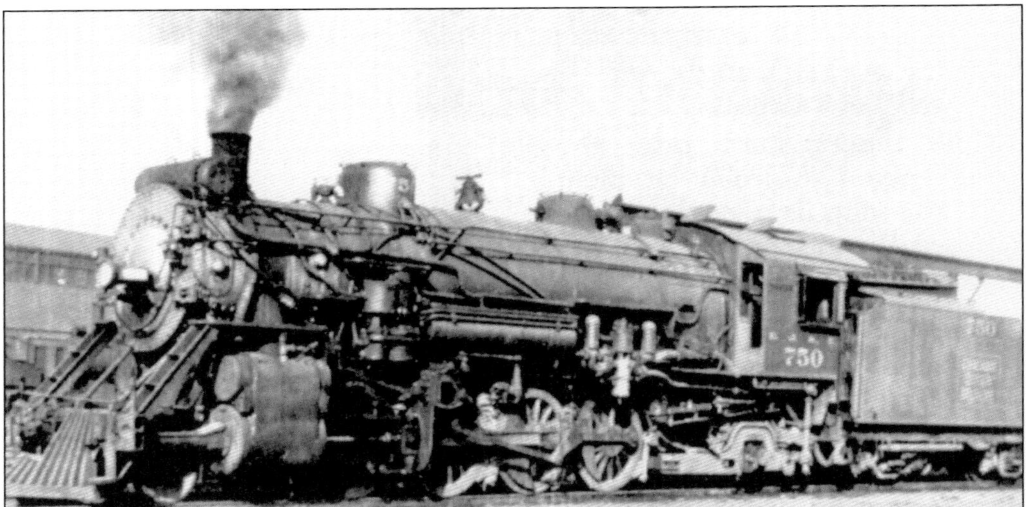

No. 750 was built by Alco Brooks in 1923. It was a 2-8-2, Mikado-type steam locomotive. It was equipped with Miller Train Control automatic train stop so it could operate on the C&EI line down to Rossville. It was rated to pull 4,150 tons from Rossville to Chicago Heights. The engine was sold to the DM&IR in 1948 and renumbered 1316.

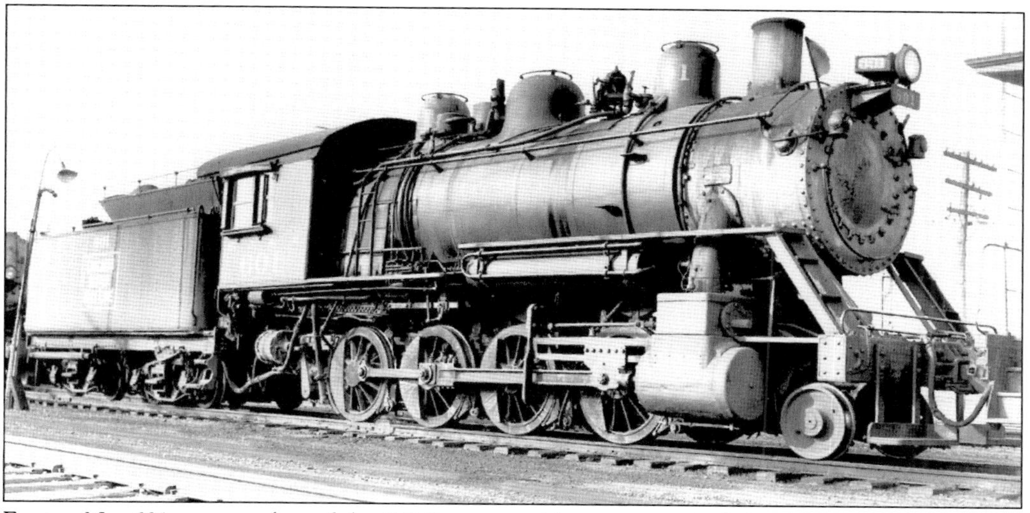

Engine No. 601 was another of the 2-8-0 type road locomotives built by Alco in 1910. It is seen in Dyer in October 1937. (Bill Raia collection.)

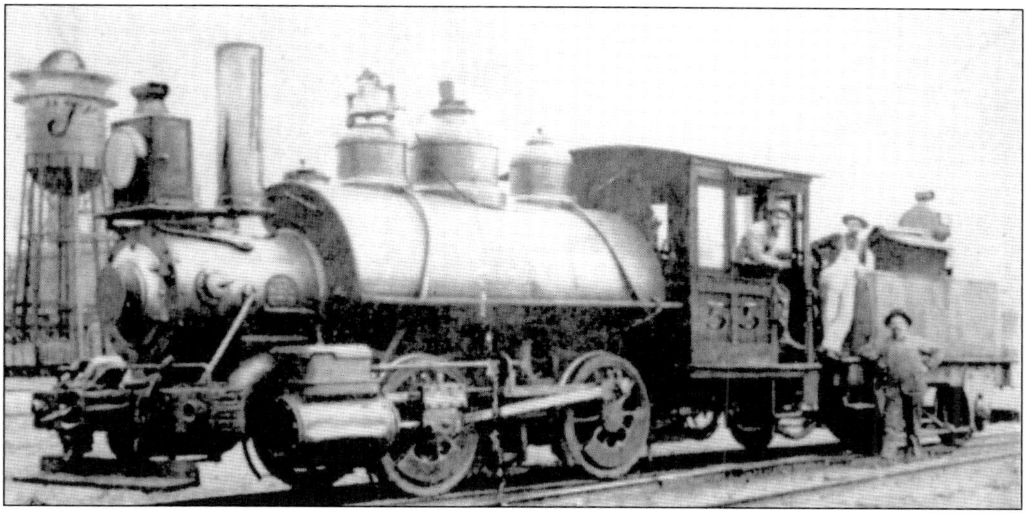

This rather strange looking 0-4-0 switcher was reportedly working at South Chicago around 1900. The crew was Jack Ferral, engineer; R. J. Dalbey, fireman; and Walt Trauler. The "J" on the water tower was drawn in and was not there in 1900.

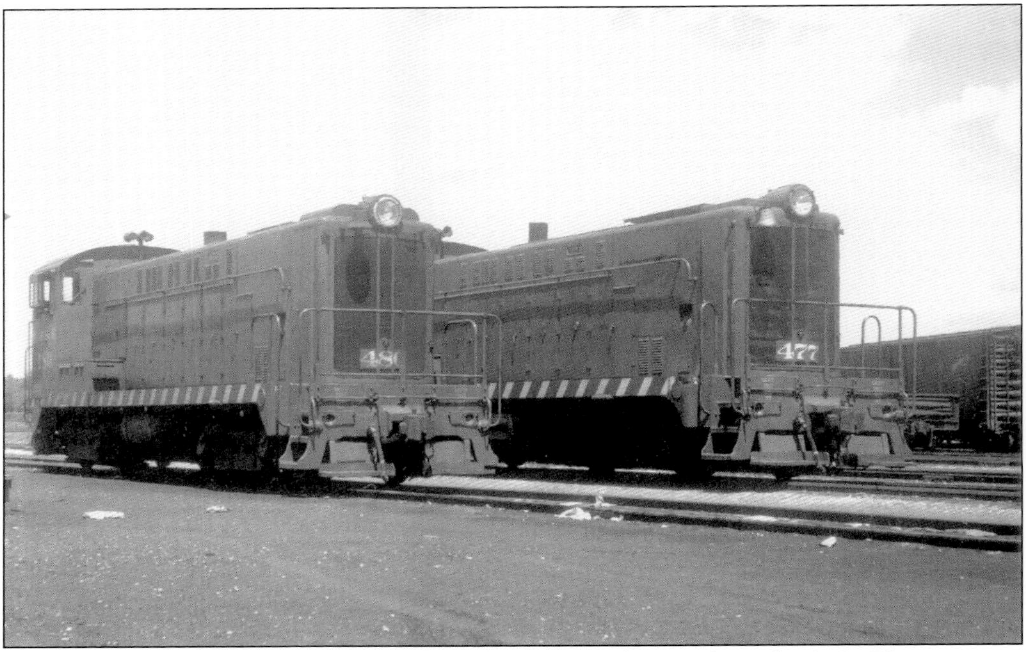

The EJ&E had ordered a total of 10 Baldwin VO1000 switchers in the early 1940s. These engines were repowered with new Baldwin engines in the late 1950s. In May 1963, No. 477 and No. 480 are seen in Joliet. Both units were in service for the EJ&E until the mid-1970s.

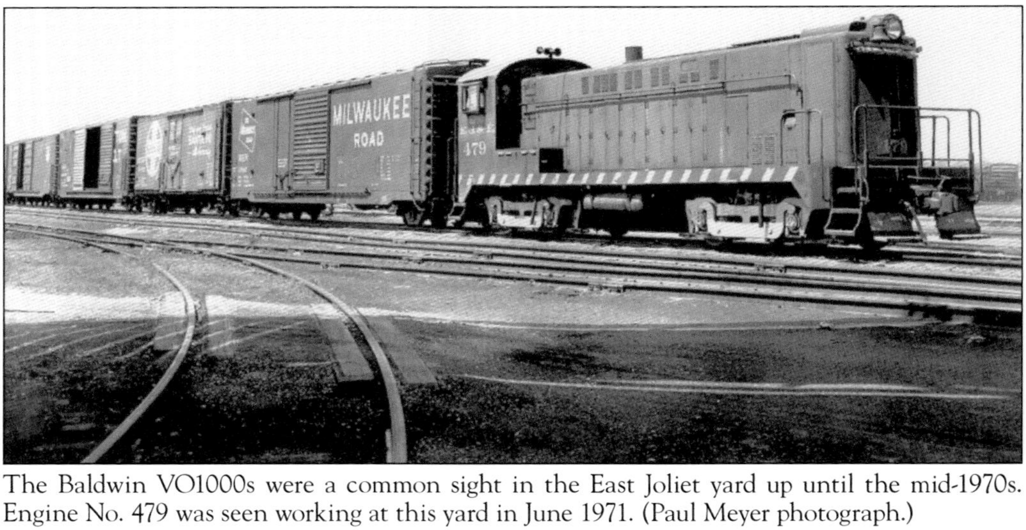

The Baldwin VO1000s were a common sight in the East Joliet yard up until the mid-1970s. Engine No. 479 was seen working at this yard in June 1971. (Paul Meyer photograph.)

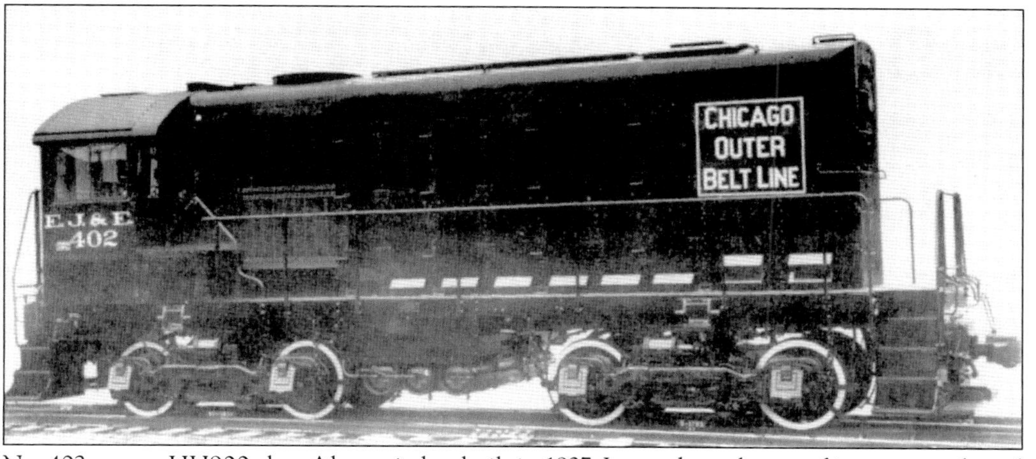

No. 402 was an HH900 class Alco switcher built in 1937. It was the only one of its type purchased by the railroad. The early diesels that were ordered were used to replace the 0-6-0 and 0-8-0 switchers that were used primarily in the yards. The EJ&E was an early customer of diesel locomotives, due to the amount of extensive switching it did at the steel plants it served.

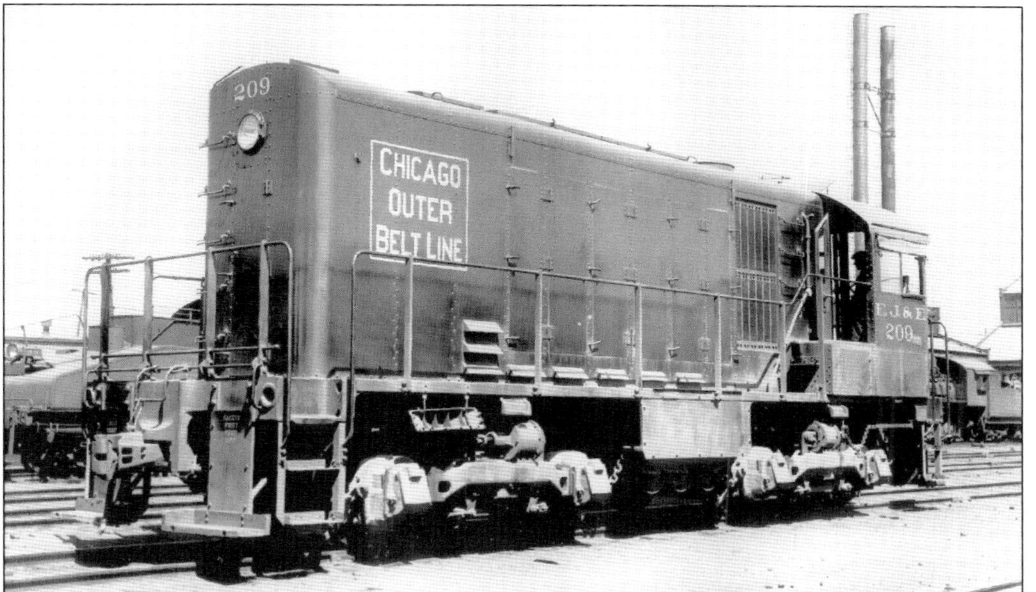

No. 209 was an HH600 class switcher built by Alco in 1937 and sold to Inland Steel in 1947. It is seen switching at Gary in May 1938. Four of these 600 horsepower types were purchased by the EJ&E. The EJ&E was one of the early purchasers of diesel locomotives in the railroad industry. (Bill Raia collection.)

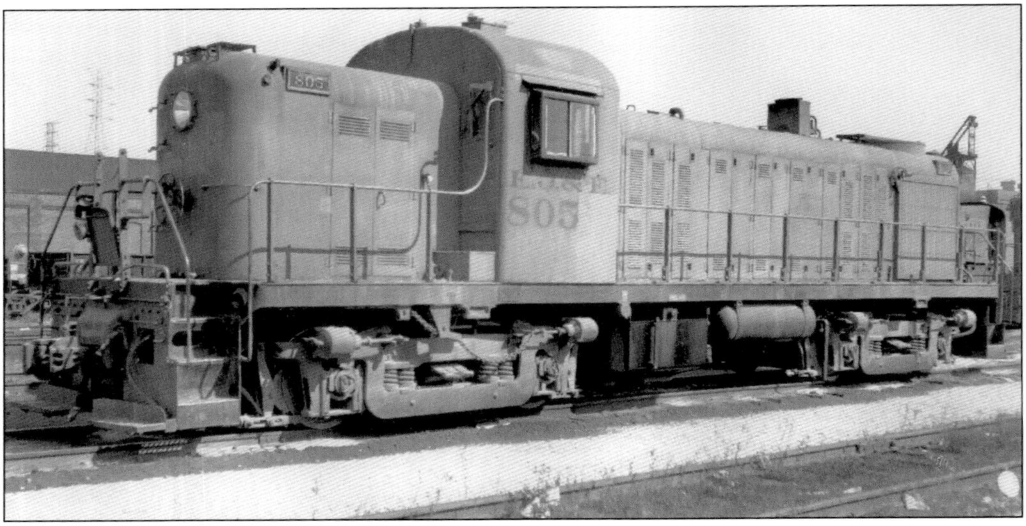

The EJ&E purchased 10 RS-2s in 1948–1949. No. 805 is seen here at Gary in October 1970. It was sold in 1973. (Bill Raia collection.)

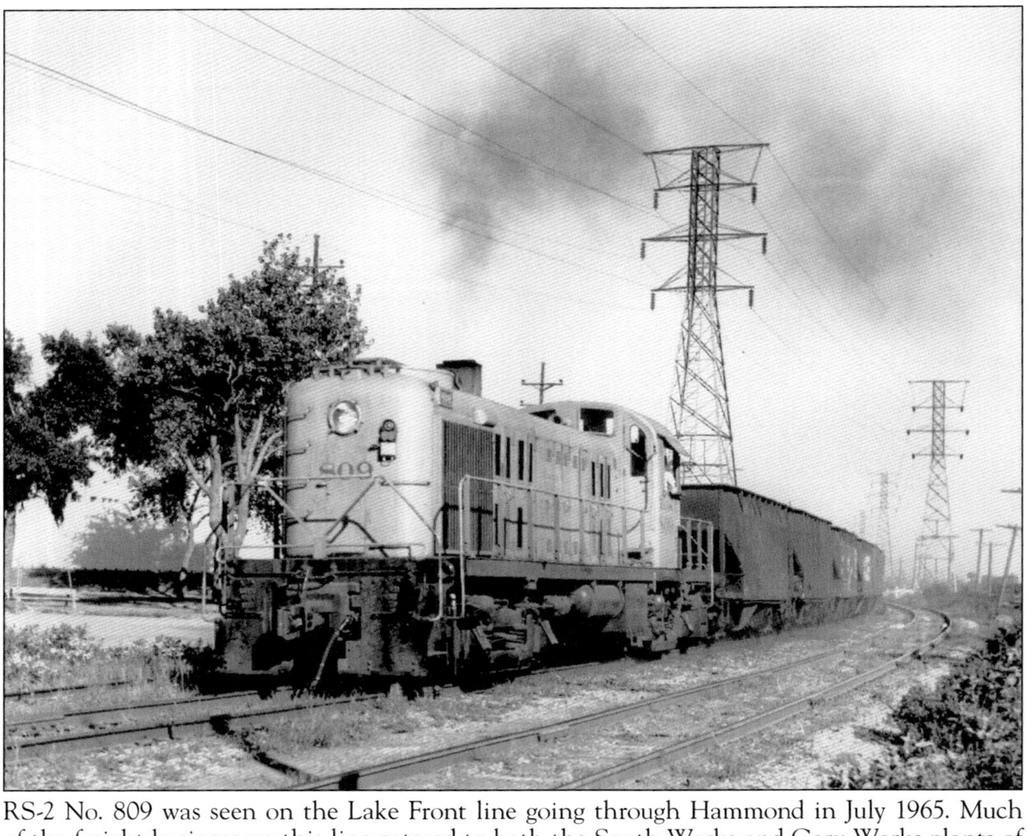

RS-2 No. 809 was seen on the Lake Front line going through Hammond in July 1965. Much of the freight business on this line catered to both the South Works and Gary Works plants of United States Steel Corporation, including unit coal trains. (Bill Raia collection.)

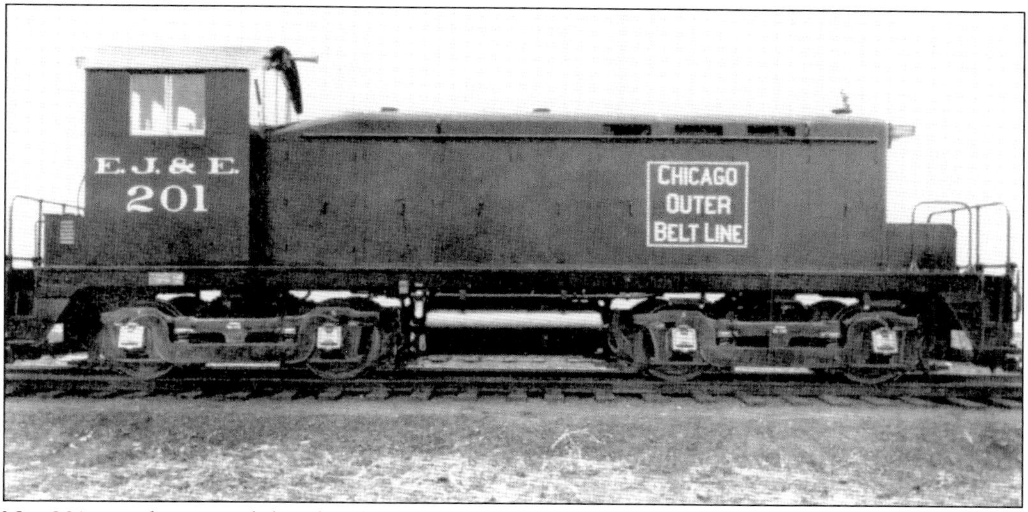

No. 201 was the second diesel to be purchased by the EJ&E. It was an EMC model SW built in 1936 with 600 horsepower. It was sold to Whistler Equipment in 1959.

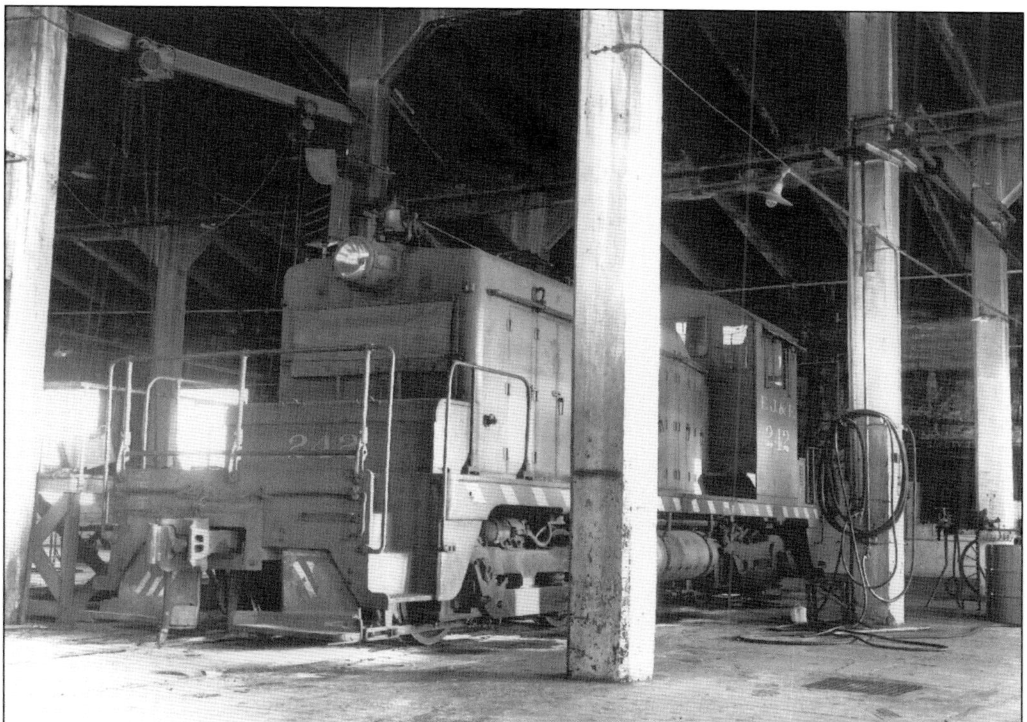

No. 242 was an SW1 built by EMD in 1941. It was seen in the roundhouse at Waukegan in January 1970. In 1985, the roundhouse was torn down. The EJ&E acquired 27 of these units. (Bill Raia collection.)

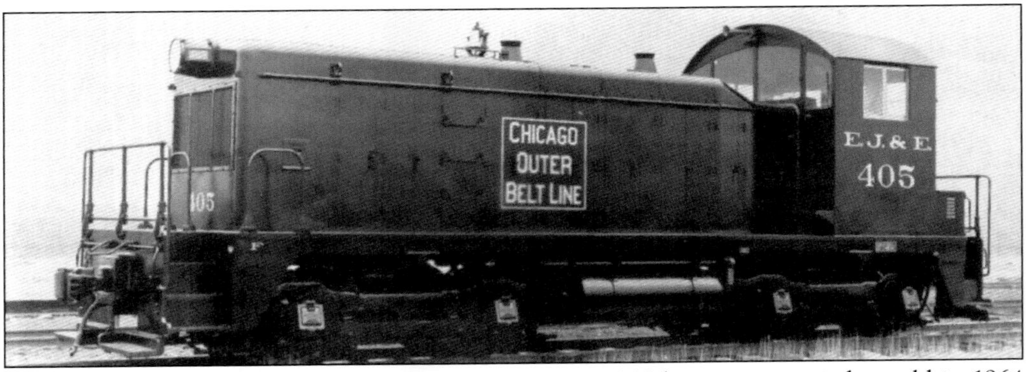

No. 405 was an NW2 built by EMD in 1941. It was a 1,000-horsepower switcher sold in 1964 along with four other EJ&E switchers to the Duluth and Northeastern Railroad to eliminate steam engines on this Minnesota lumber line.

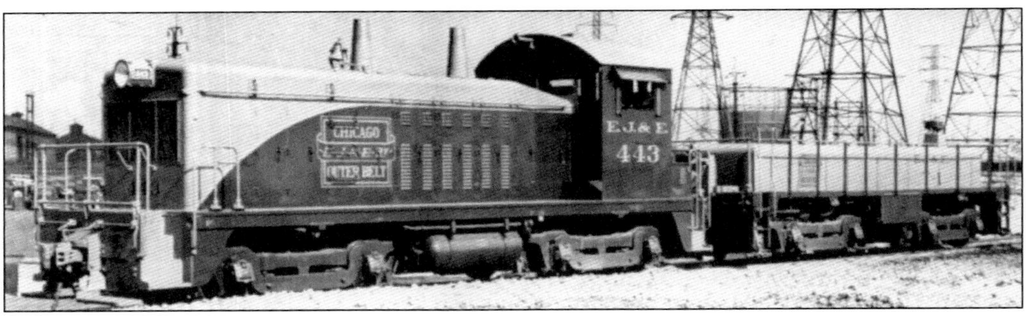

Engine No. 443 was an EMD NW2 switcher built in 1949. The trailer unit was given the number T-1. It was an ex–Illinois Central Railroad Alco HH600 that had its engine removed, with ballast placed over the locomotive frame. The two were mated in 1951 and saw service at the Gary Mill and South Works. There were a total of five of these cow-calf combinations that saw service on the EJ&E. This arrangement allowed the cow unit (No. 443) to run twice as many motors from only one generator.

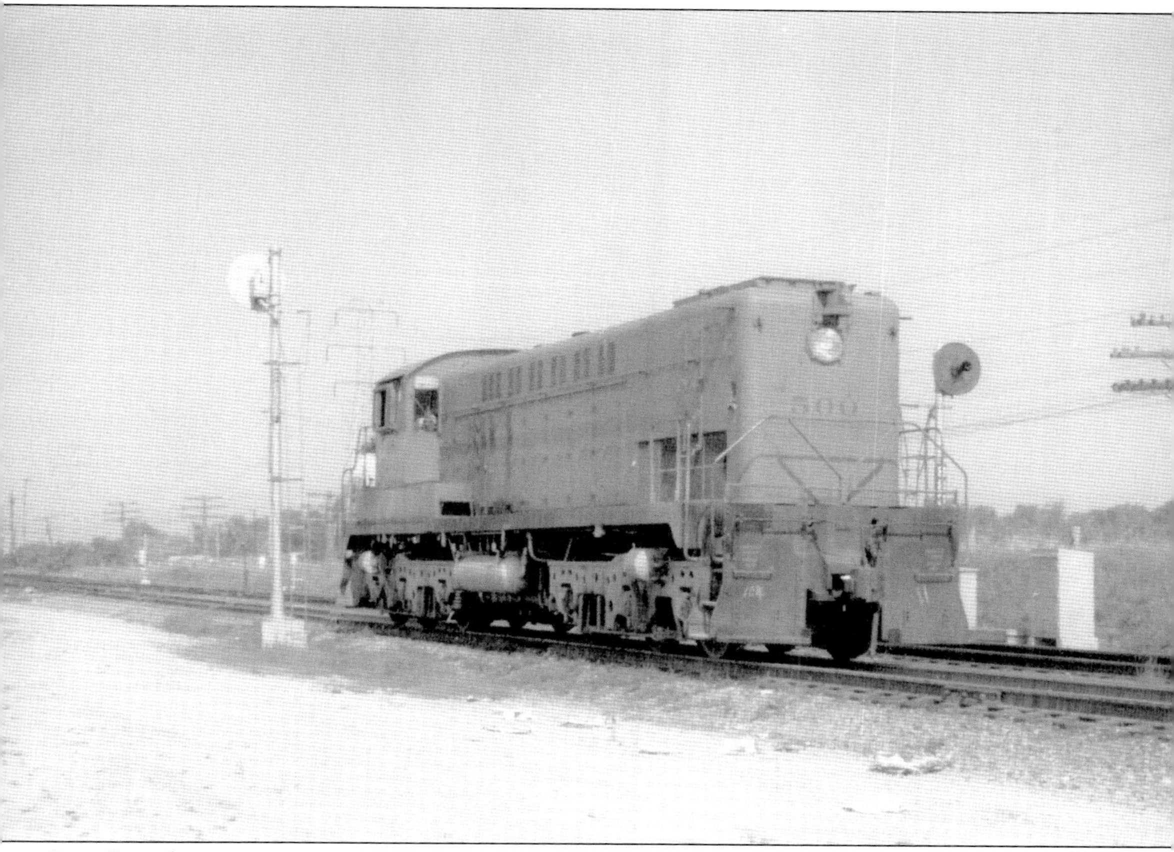

On a Saturday morning, engine No. 500 was switching the industries in Frankfort. It and its sister, No. 501, usually worked at East Joliet yard. On this day, however, probably due to a shortage of available engines, this one was put on a local train. Builder Baldwin designated the units DRS 6-6-1500, which stood for Diesel Road Switcher, six axles, six axle powered, and 1,500 horsepower. The units were originally Bessimer and Lake Erie (B&LE) No. 401 and No. 402. (R. A. Eisenbrandt.)

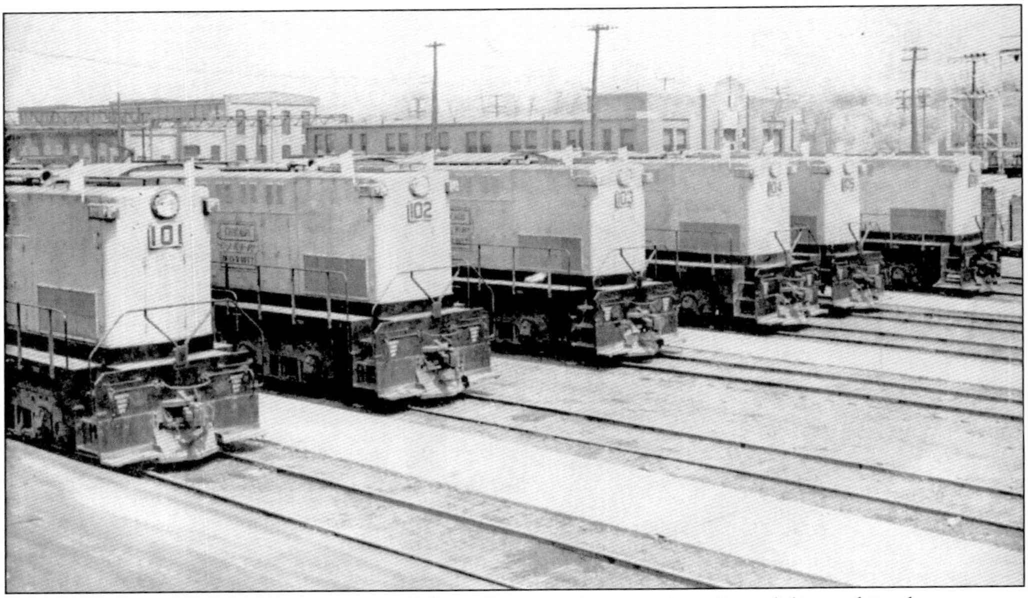

Six brand-new locomotives were posed for publicity photographs when delivered in the summer of 1948. They were model DT 6-6-2000s, which its builder, Baldwin, cataloged as a Diesel Transfer, six axles, six axle powered, and 2,000 horsepower. The EJ&E purchased a total of 27.

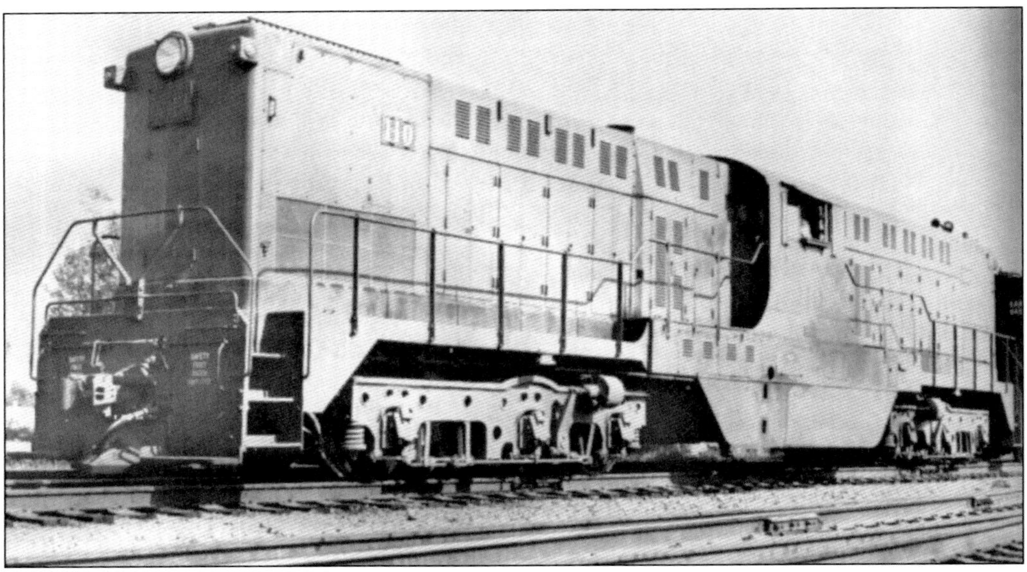

No. 110 was seen going through Spaulding in May 1951. A major selling point for Baldwin was its ability to build a locomotive to meet the needs of the individual railroad. The center cabs were bidirectional, built specifically for the EJ&E to accommodate its need for a unit that could be used for both heavy transfer work and road service. They could be reversed in direction without turning on a wye or turntable.

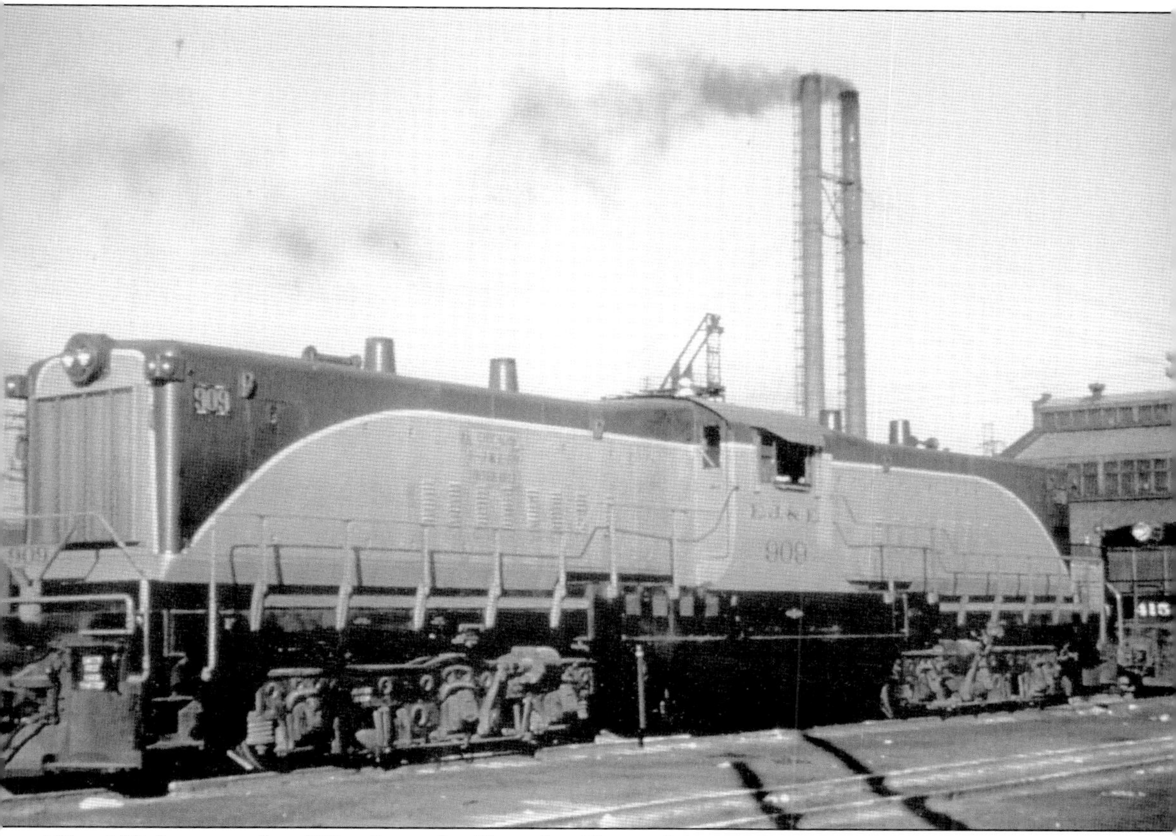

The 109 became the 909 after rebuilding by Electro-Motive Corporation in La Grange. The in-line, six-cylinder Baldwin diesel oil engines were replaced by EMD V-12 model 567 1,000-horsepower engines.

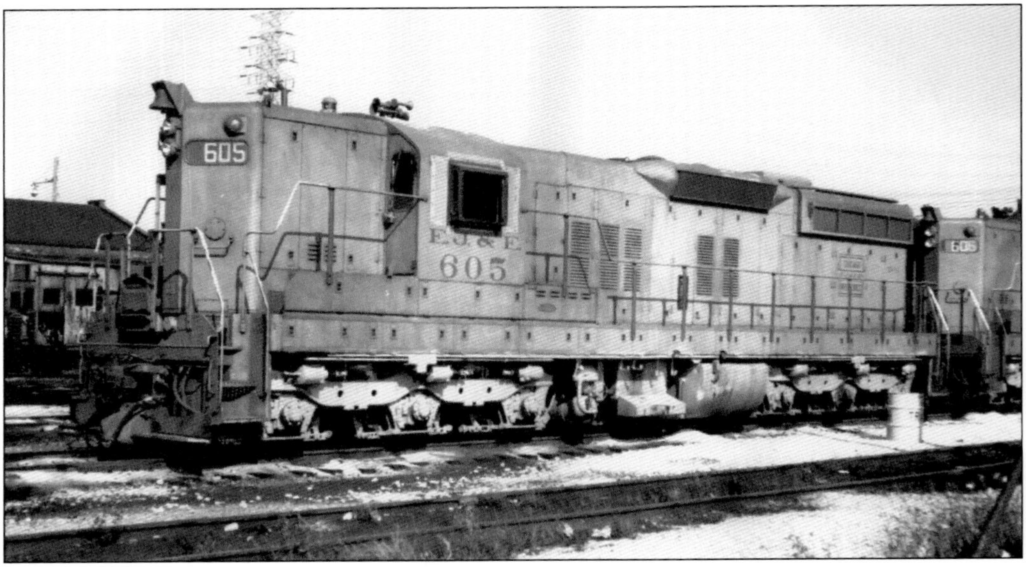

Newer motive power was needed to replace the aging Baldwin center cabs, which led the EJ&E in 1968 to acquire four SD9s, Nos. 603 to 606, from sister railroad DM&IR. No. 605 is pictured at Gary in September 1972. This unit eventually ended up seeing service on the Montana Rail Link. (Bill Raia collection.)

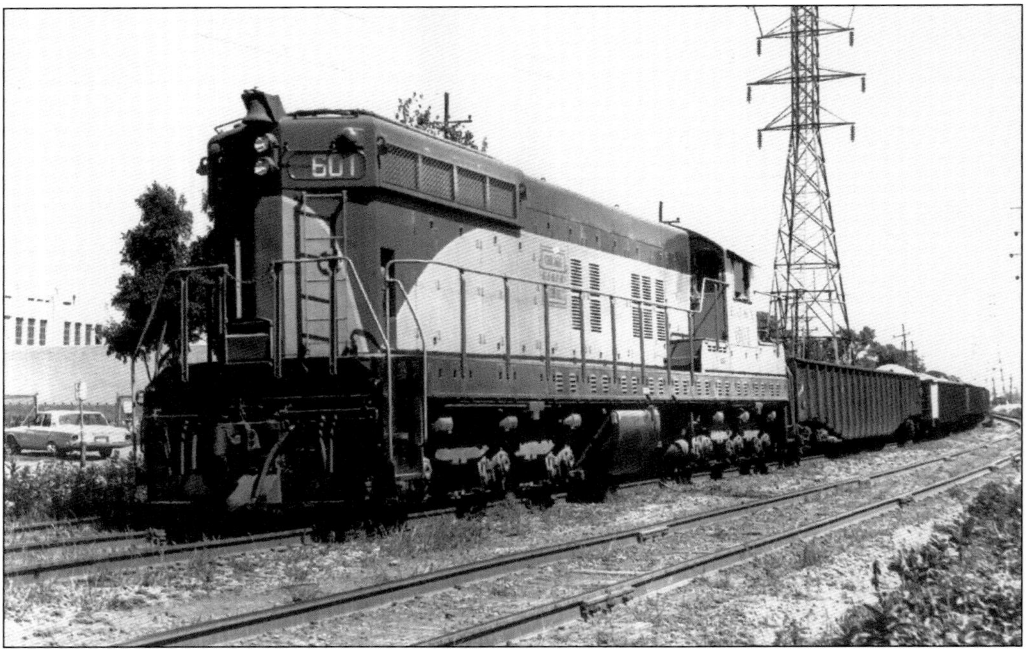

No. 601 was one of three original SD9s (Nos. 600–602) to be acquired by the EJ&E in 1957. It was seen on the Lake Front line going through Hammond in July 1965 pulling long end forward, which was the way it was intended to run. Eventually nine more of these units would be leased or acquired from the DM&IR. (Bill Raia collection.)

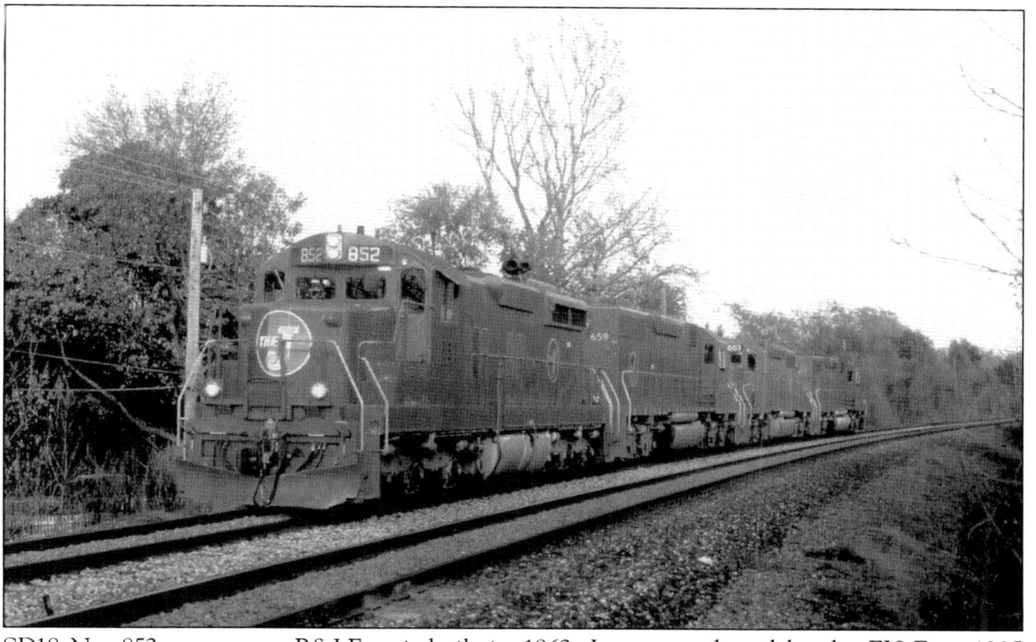

SD18 No. 852 was an ex–B&LE unit built in 1962. It was purchased by the EJ&E in 1995 and retained its old number. Four of these units were purchased from sister railroads B&LE and DM&IR. The engine is shown heading westbound at Matteson, with a trio of SD38-2s in October 2000.

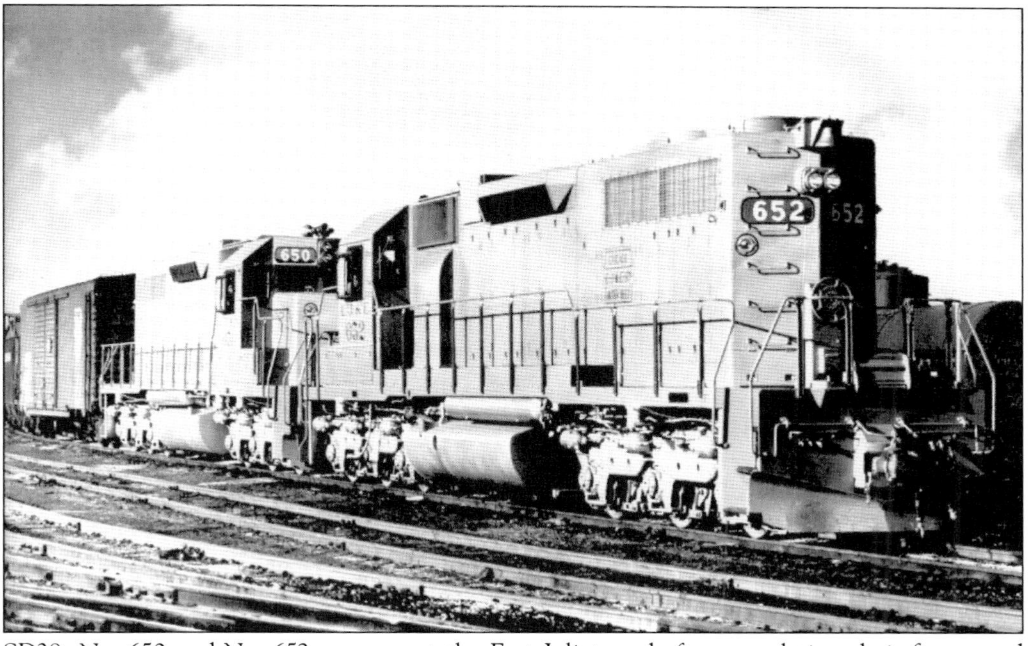

SD38s No. 650 and No. 652 are seen at the East Joliet yard after completing their first round trip to Waukegan with train No. 4 in February 1970. These diesels had a 16-cylinder engine and could develop 2,000 horsepower for traction. The six new locomotives that were delivered in this order had cost a total of $1.5 million.

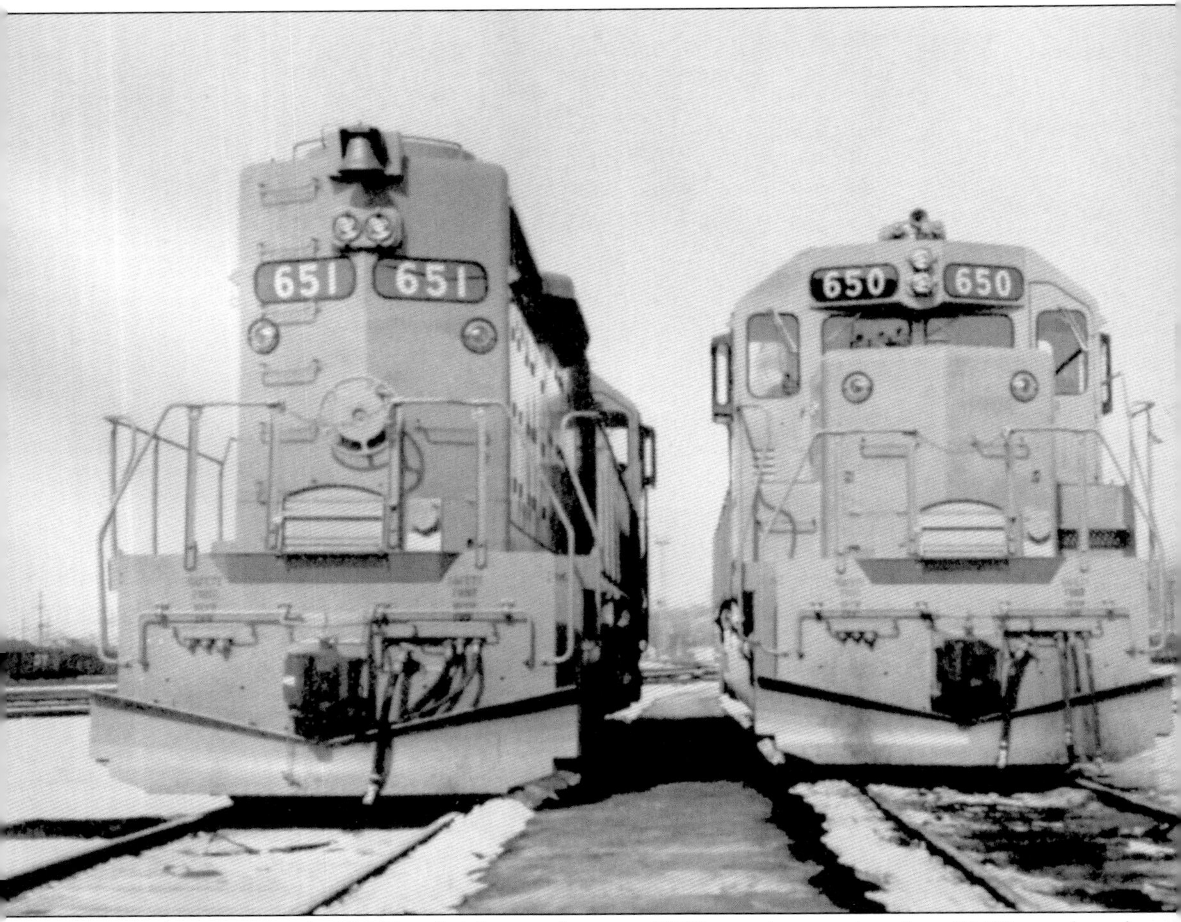

In February 1970, the EJ&E took delivery of six new SD38-type locomotives from EMD, numbered 650–655. They were the first new road power to be delivered since three SD9s were delivered in 1957. The new locomotives were bidirectional but usually were operated long hood end first, giving the engine crew 45 feet of protection in case of a collision with a motor vehicle.

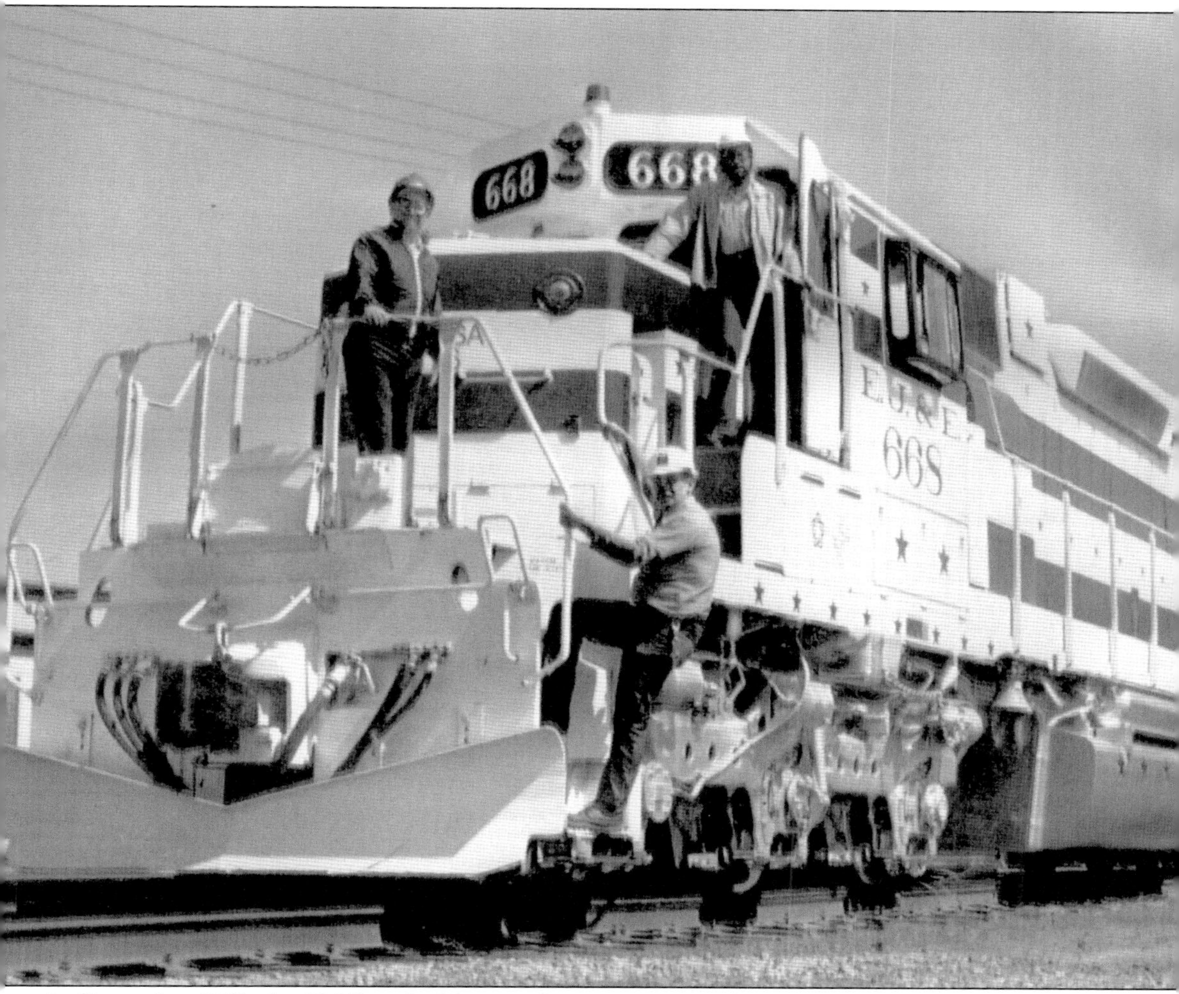

In December 1975, the EJ&E took delivery of engine No. 668 from EMD. It was painted solid white in preparation for its bicentennial paint scheme. The EJ&E shop forces applied the red and blue stripes, but it was eventually painted to the traditional solid orange in 1977.

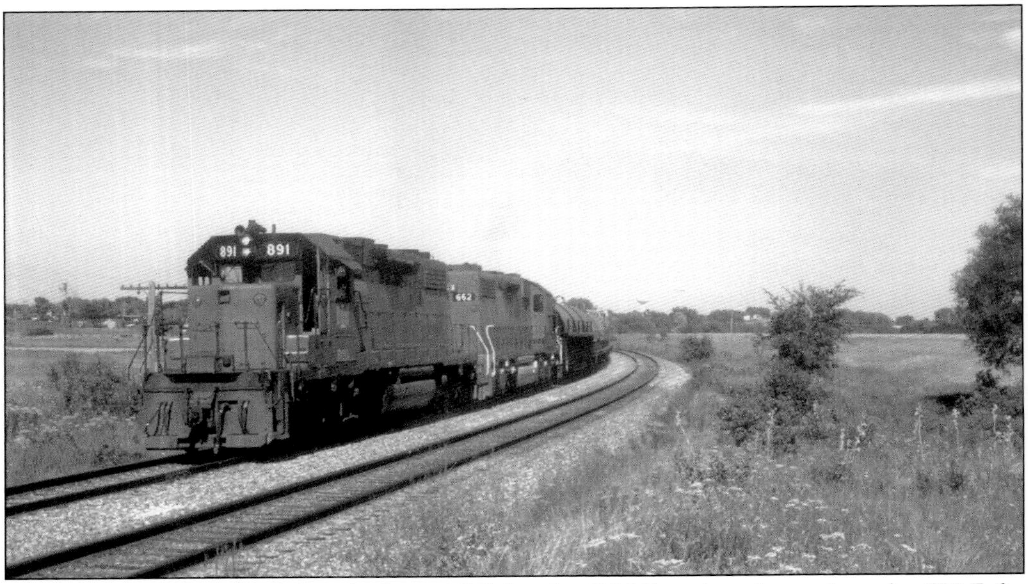

No. 891 was an EMD SD38-2 built in 1975 for the B&LE and exchanged to the EJ&E for SD38-2 No. 658 in March 1986. It was later renumbered 669. It was shown west of Matteson in the mid-1980s. Up until the early 1980s, scenes like this were typical along much of the EJ&E right-of-way but changed as the urban sprawl of the Chicago area grew outward and once rural towns became full-fledged suburbs.

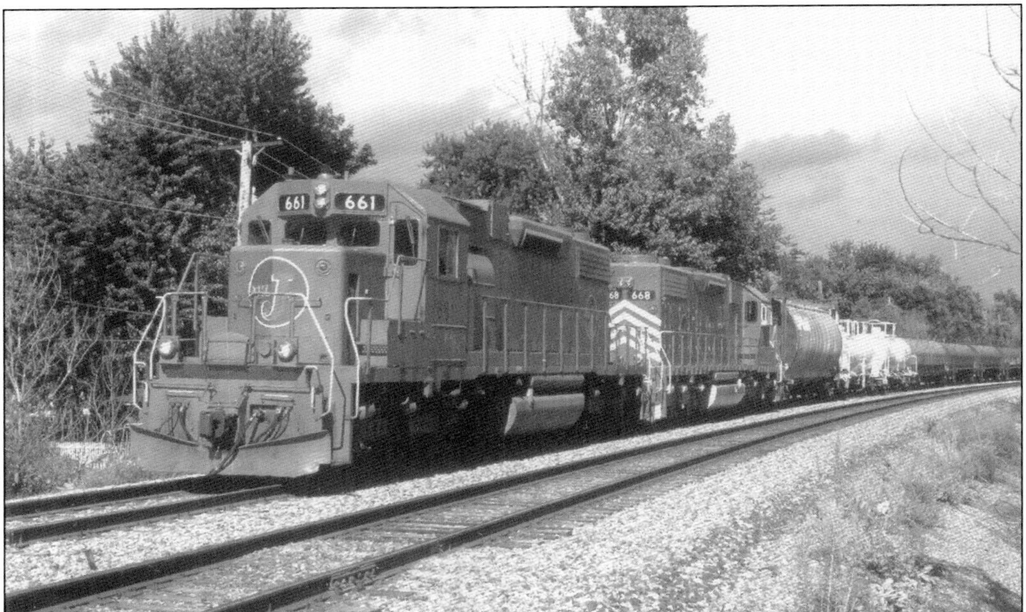

The SD38-2s are the backbone of the current EJ&E locomotive fleet, and some of them have gone through a rebuilding due to the many years of service. In August 2005, No. 661 was rebuilt at the Gary shops to Dash 3 specifications, which included an anti–wheel slip system and computerized control cabinet. It is seen heading westbound through Matteson in August 2001, with ex-bicentennial unit No. 668 trailing in a new chevron paint scheme adopted the same year.

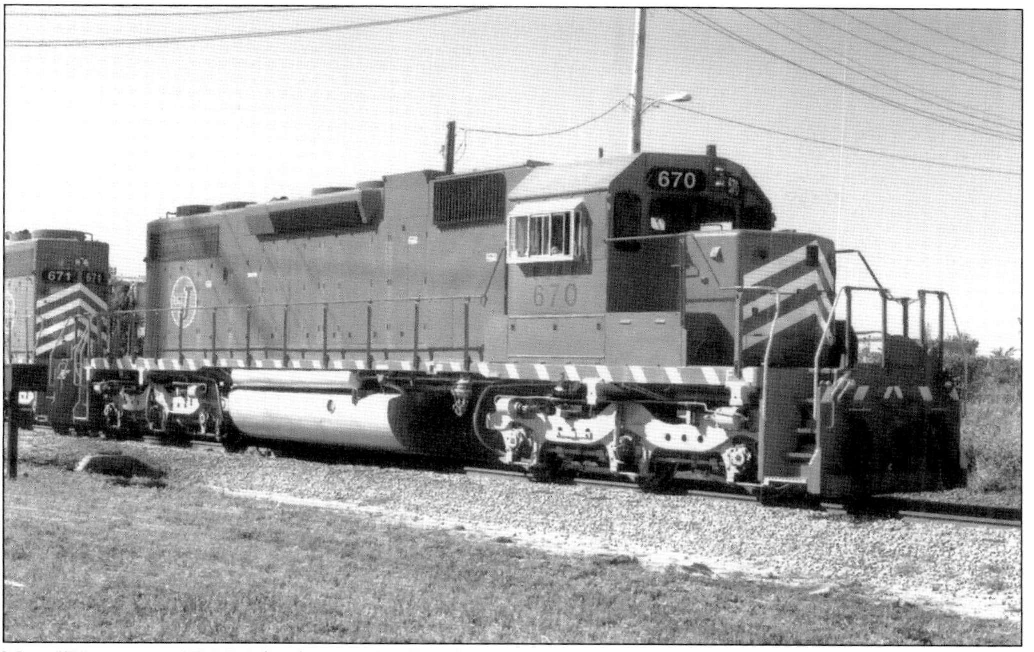

No. 670 was an SD38-2 built in 1973 for the B&LE. It was purchase by the EJ&E in 2001. It is seen here in September 2003 switching at the Quantum Chemical Company off the East Morris spur on the Illinois River line.

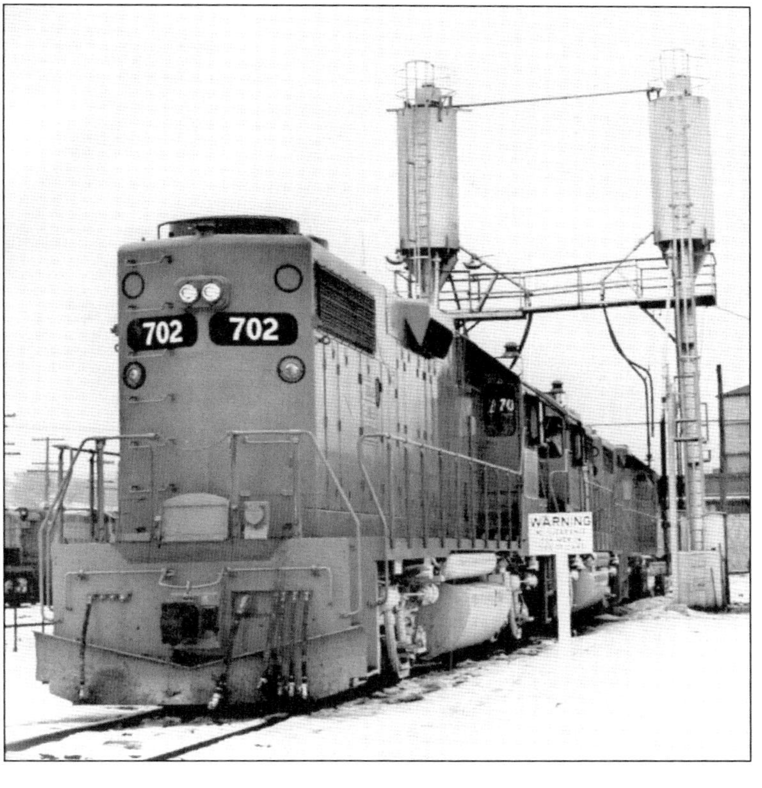

Four EMD GP38-2s, Nos. 700–703, were delivered in December 1972, with No. 704 following in October 1973. They were first used in local switching to accommodate the tight radiuses found on industrial track. These were the only GP38-2s purchased by the railroad. They were later sold to the Birmingham Southern Railroad in 1985. Engine No. 703 was repurchased by the EJ&E in 1996.

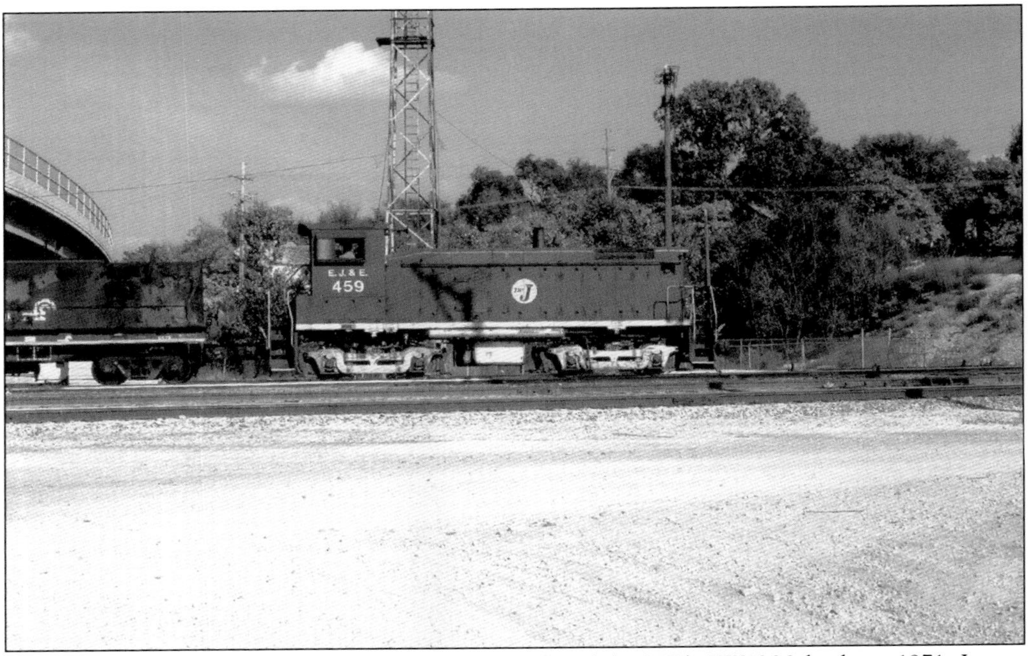

No. 459 was an ex–New Orleans Public Belt Railroad (NOPB) SW1000 built in 1971. It was purchased in 1989 from NOPB and sold in 2006 to Delray Connecting Railroad. It is seen here switching the East Joliet yard in November 2000.

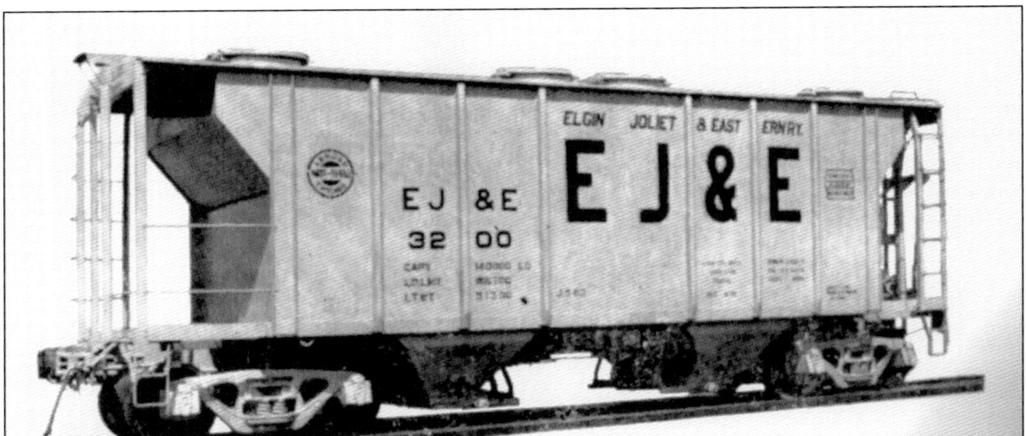

In the mid-1960s, the EJ&E had owned approximately 10,000 freight cars. Railroads use cars from other carriers to meet the demands of their customers and as a result the expense incurred is called a per diem charge, which is the Latin phrase meaning "by the day." The system of paying another railroad a daily rate for the use of their equipment started back in 1902. Cement hoppers are used to transport dry cement and other similar bulk materials.

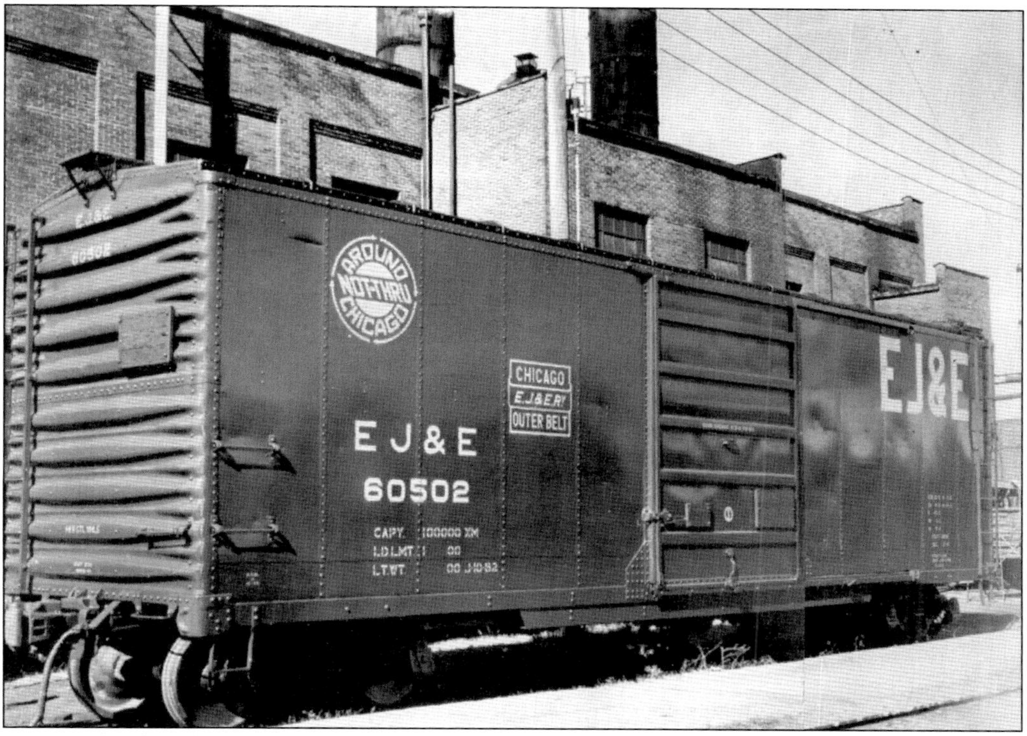

In 1962, the shop forces at East Joliet refurbished 150 of these 50-ton boxcars. They were fitted with new plywood lining and heavy-duty floors to accommodate heavier loads demanded by the shippers that were using the cars at the time. The boxcars were painted in green, which was a departure from the famous orange that most EJ&E boxcars were painted in.

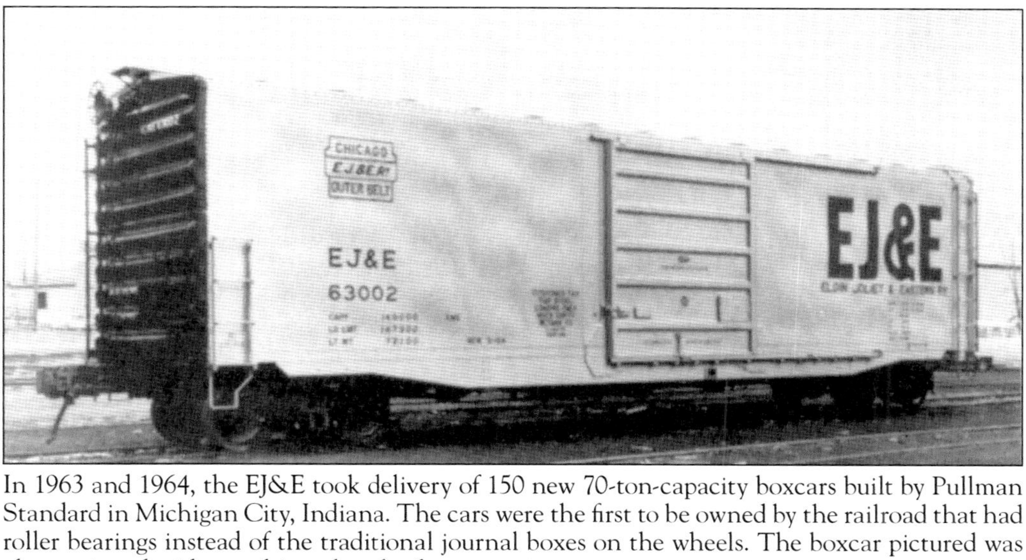

In 1963 and 1964, the EJ&E took delivery of 150 new 70-ton-capacity boxcars built by Pullman Standard in Michigan City, Indiana. The cars were the first to be owned by the railroad that had roller bearings instead of the traditional journal boxes on the wheels. The boxcar pictured was also equipped with a cushioned under frame.

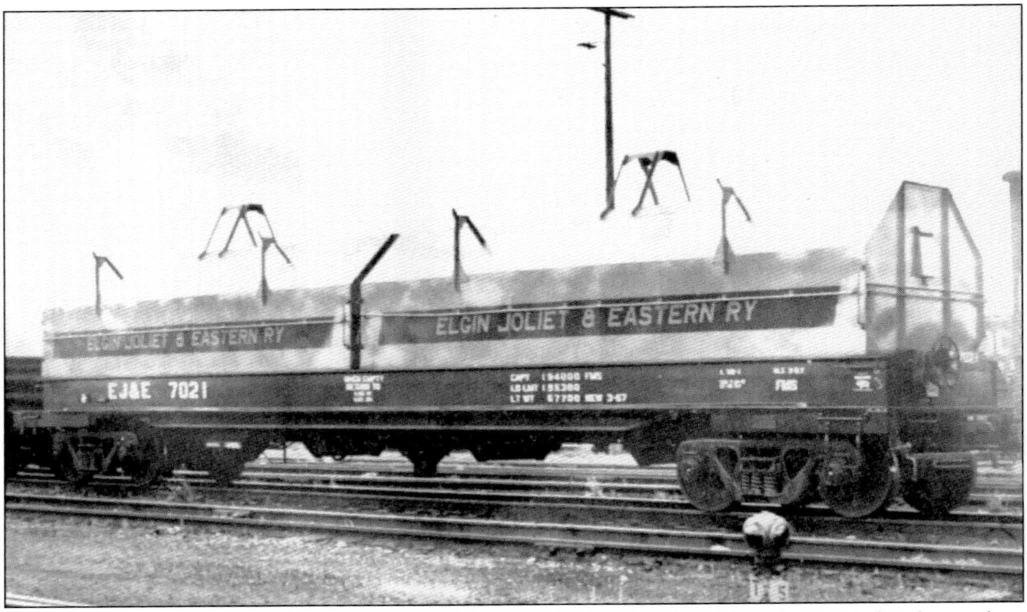

In 1967, the EJ&E had purchased 25 of these 100-ton covered steel coil cars to haul tin plate from the mills to customers nationwide. The hoods were easy to remove and offered maximum protection from the elements.

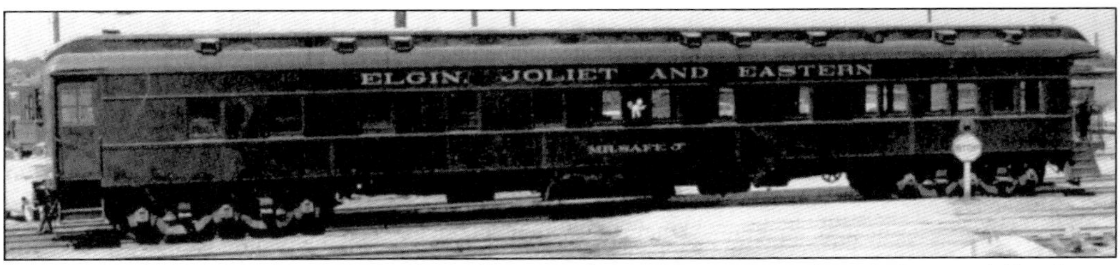

Mr. *Safe "J"* was the name applied to this car when it was assigned to Safety and Employee Activities under LaVerne C. Hahney. Train rules examiner F. O. "Sam" Morse also made frequent use of the car. Classes on safety, operating rules, air brake instruction, and eye tests were given inside. There was an office, plus seating for 40 employees.

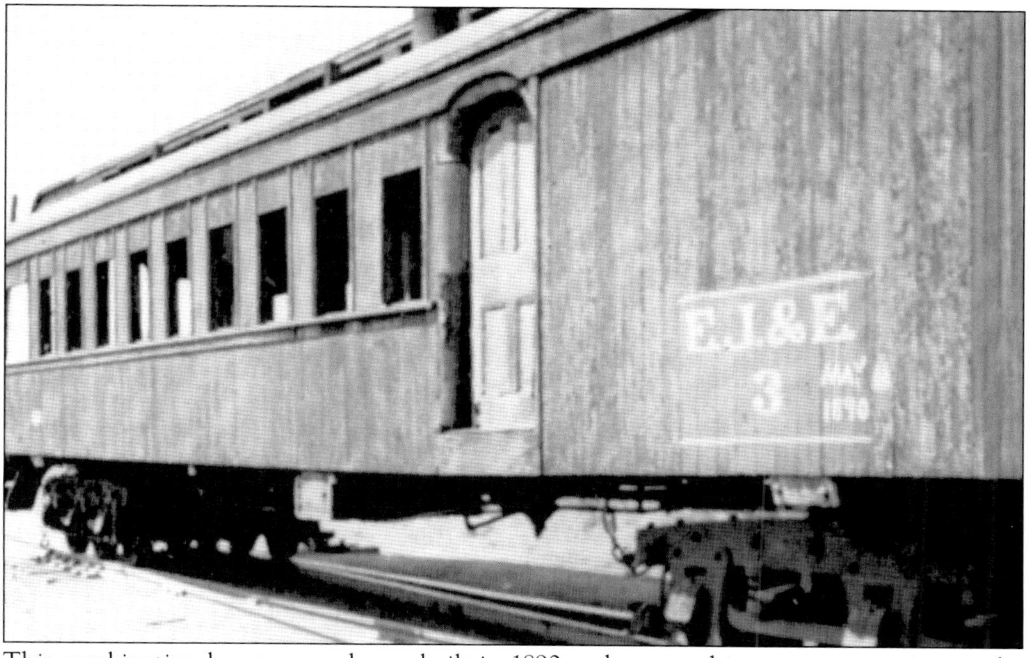

This combination baggage-coach was built in 1890 and was used in passenger service on the EJ&E. Around 1910, it became the safety examiner's car. In May 1949, it was scrapped at Gary.

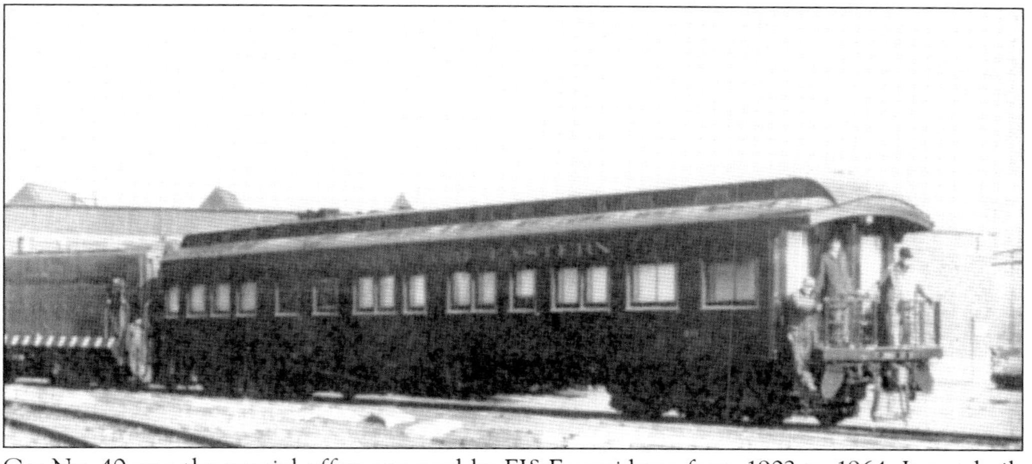

Car No. 40 was the special office car used by EJ&E presidents from 1902 to 1964. It was built by Pullman Car Company in 1902. Due the availability of more convenient ways of touring the right-of-way and rising maintenance costs, the car was sold to a private owner and was taken up to a location near the Wisconsin Dells. The car's interior was finished in mahogany and consisted of six bedrooms, a kitchen, and a lounge. Each bedroom had its own toilet and washstand.

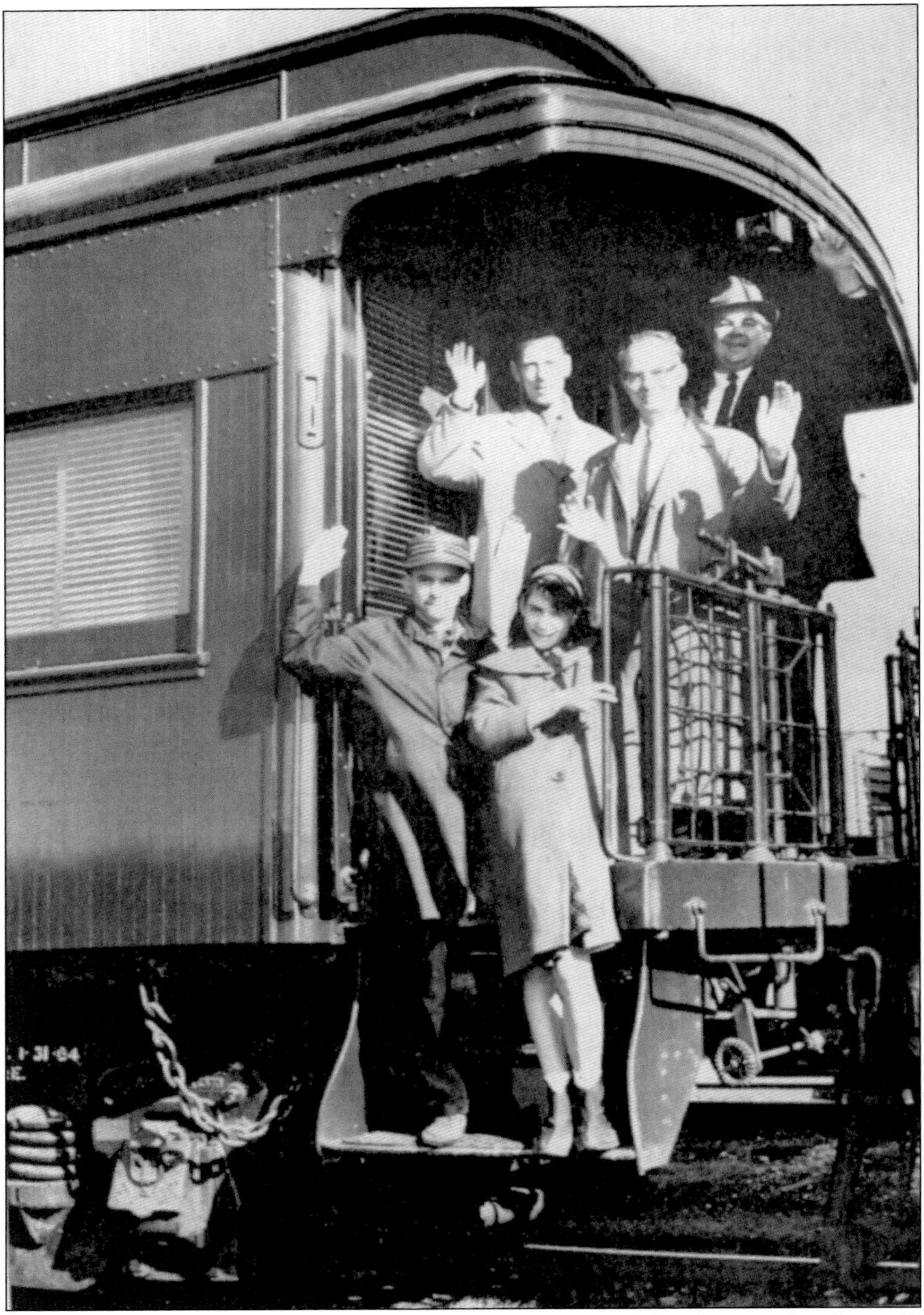

Russ Porter, the new owner of the No. 40, is seen in the center of the photograph, taken at East Joliet in 1964. His son, Robert, and daughter, Susan, are seen waving on the bottom step just before they left the yard. The car was routed to Rondout where the Milwaukee Road was used to reach its final destination.

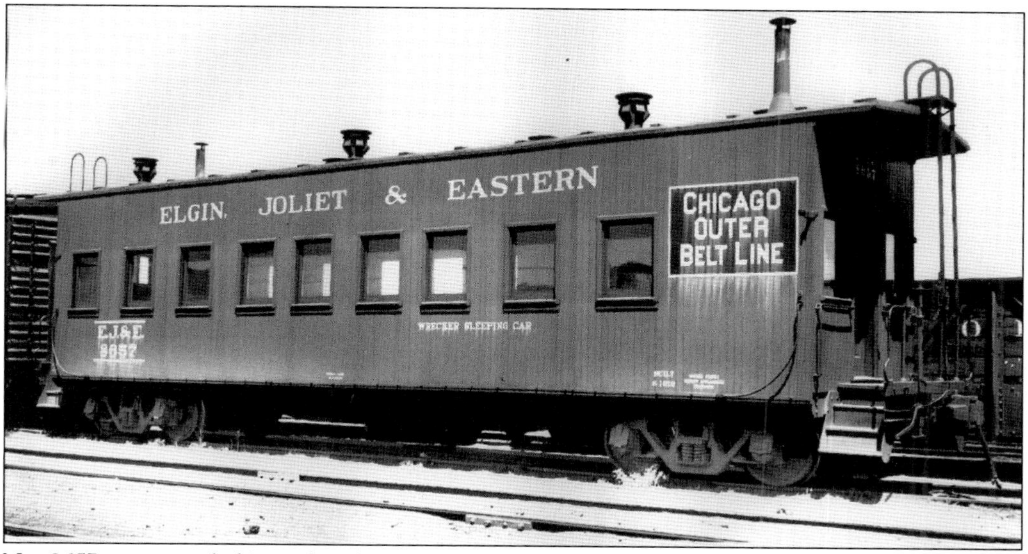

No. 8657 was stenciled "wrecker sleeping car." The EJ&E had several special-use cars, such as this one. A "wrecking train" would consist of the derrick, an idler car, a tool car or two, a dining car, and maybe a sleeping car. As for the wrecker and its train, one hoped it would see very little use. (Bill Raia collection.)

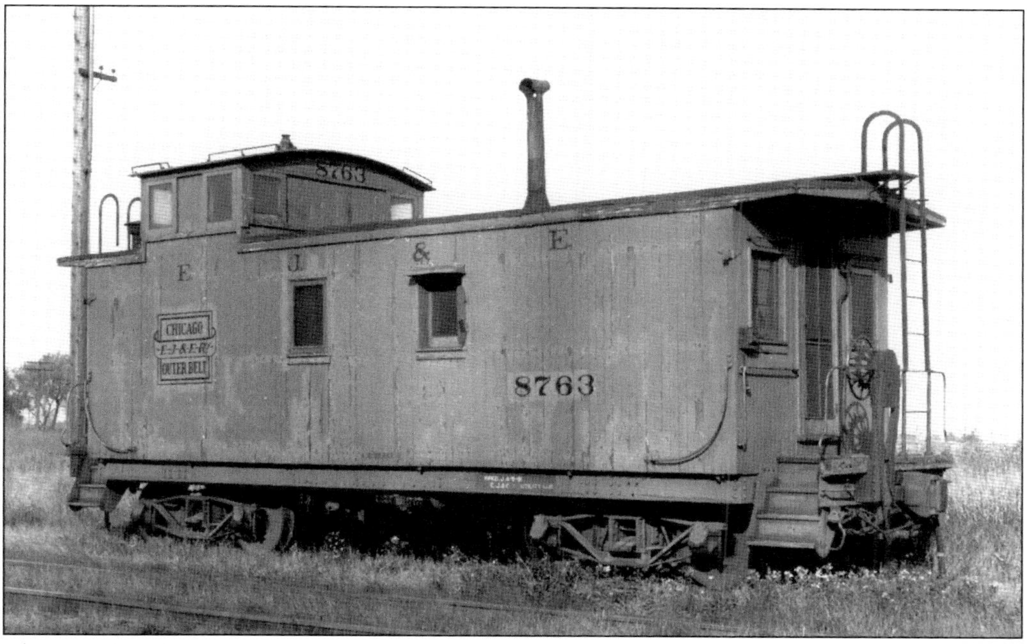

This wooden sheathed cupola caboose has evidently seen a lot of miles of travel on the EJ&E. There were once 128 cabooses on the equipment roster for the railroad. (Bill Raia collection.)

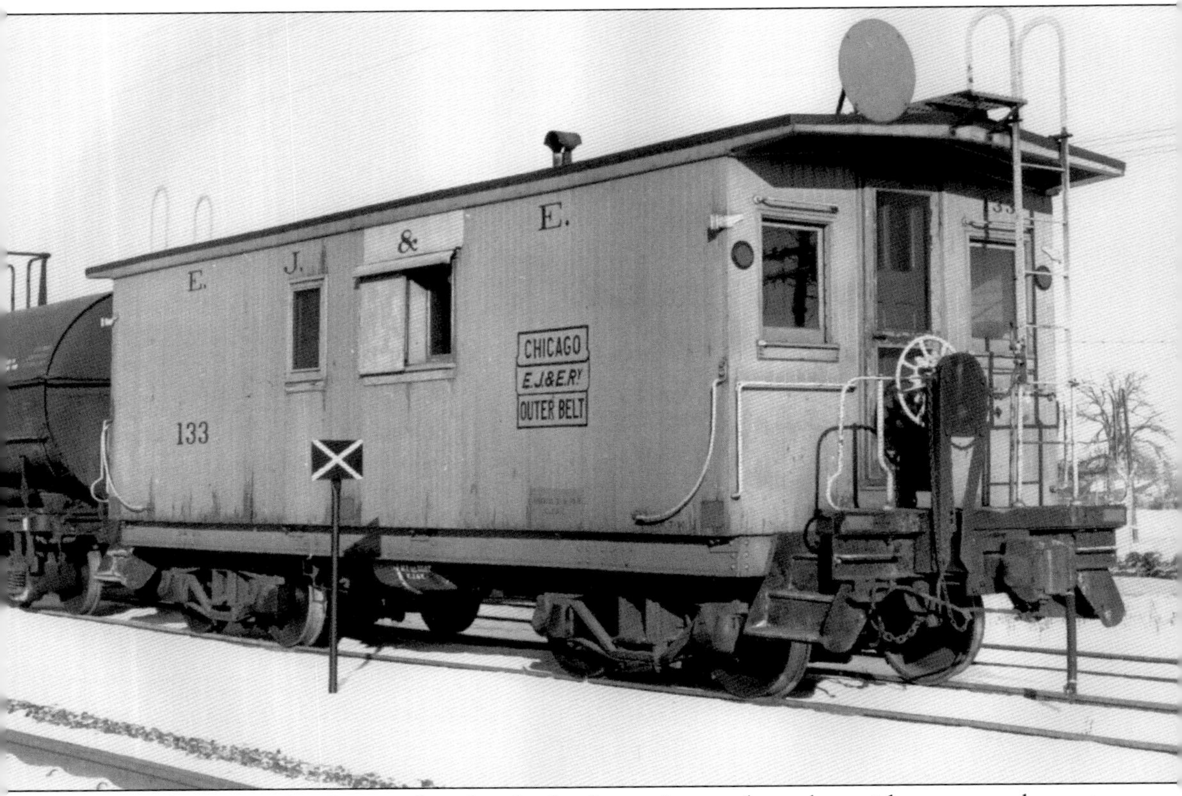

Another example of a wooden sheathed caboose is seen here, but without a cupola on top. Cabooses of this type were used on the industrial switching assignments. Note the round, reflective disk on top. Those were used after the late 1950s rather than the old, traditional, kerosene-lit lanterns.

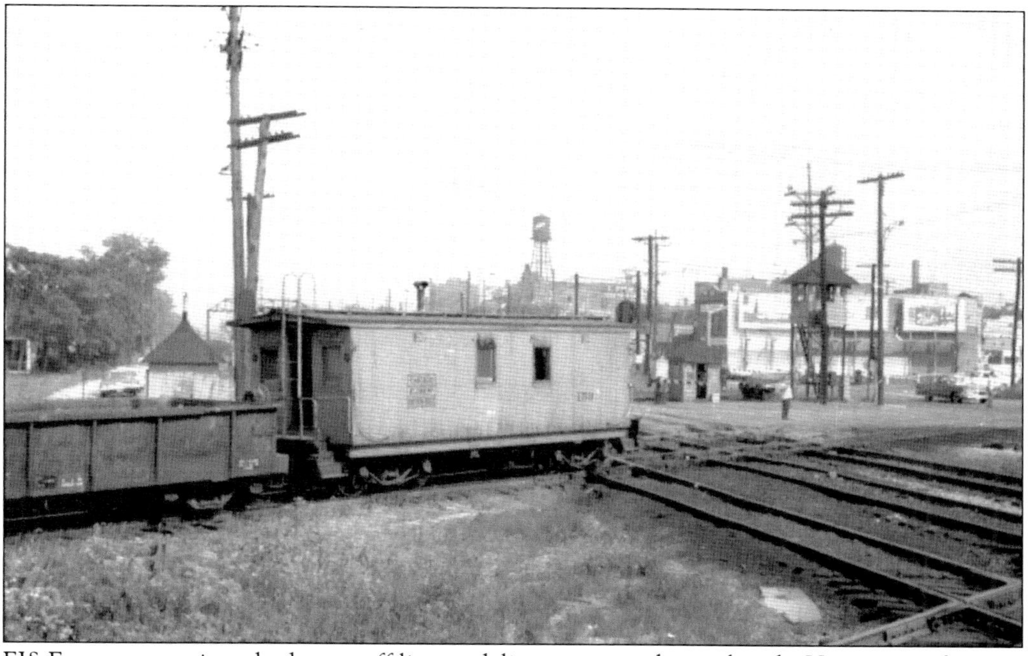

EJ&E crews sometimes had to go off-line to deliver cars to other railroads. Here a transfer crew is leaving the Erie-Lackawanna Yard in Hammond en route back to home rails at State Line. The exact location was Hammond Tower in downtown Hammond at Hohman Avenue and Willow Court. (R. A. Eisenbrandt.)

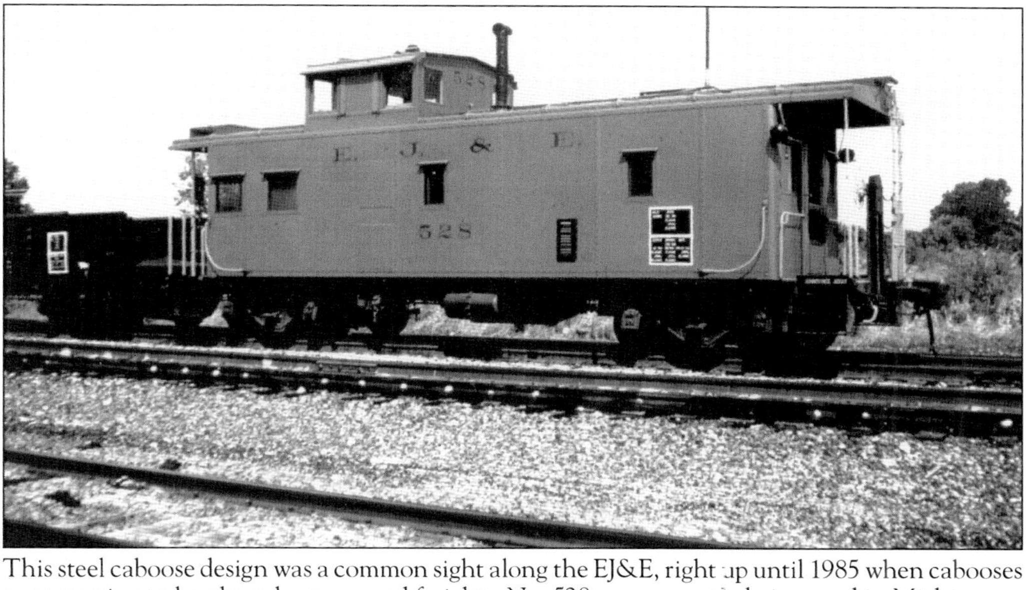

This steel caboose design was a common sight along the EJ&E, right up until 1985 when cabooses were starting to be phased out on road freights. No. 528 was currently being used in Michigan as an office for the Kal Haven Trail State Park.

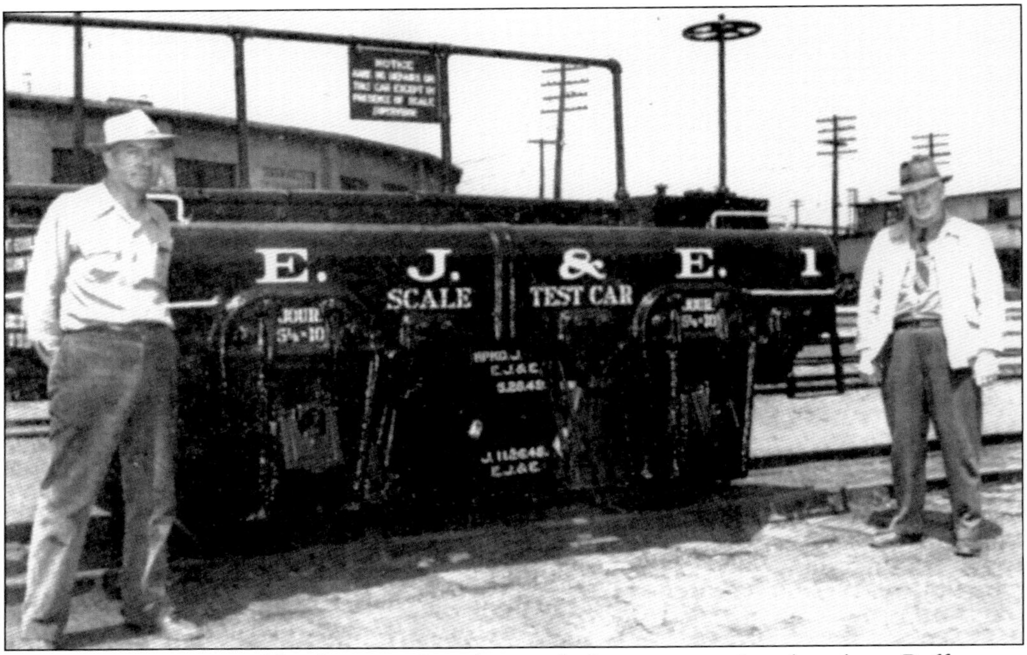

EJ&E No. 1 was a special "scale test car" used to verify the accuracy of track scales at Buffington, Gary, Joliet, Kirk Yard, South Chicago, and Waukegan. The car contained steel and/or concrete weights. The scale being tested then had to be set to correspond to that weight. (Bill Raia collection.)

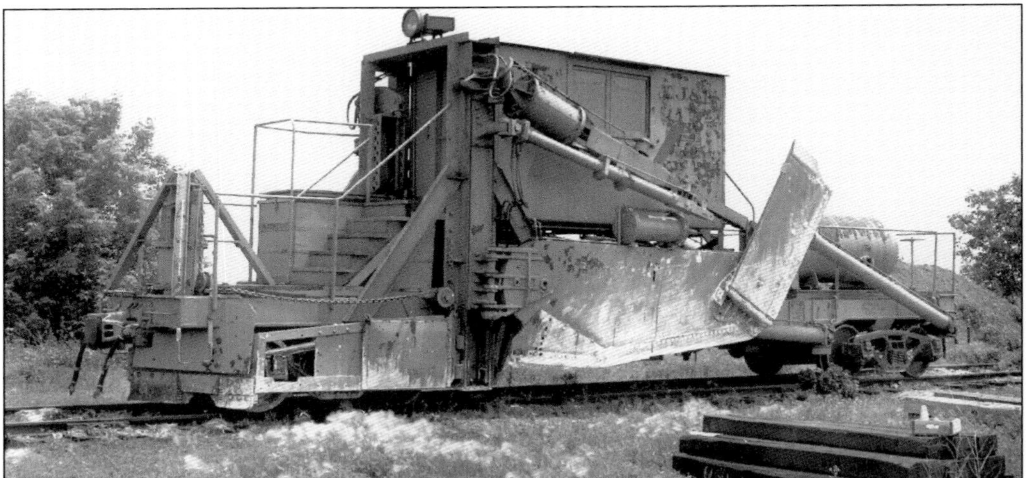

The Jordan spreader was invented by Oswald F. Jordan, who was the road master on Michigan Central's Canadian Southern Railroad. The first spreaders were believed to have been built under his supervision at the St. Thomas Shops in Ontario around 1900. They were originally used to spread stone and cinder ballast between ties, to dig wayside ditches, and to plow snow. This was one of the spreaders used by the EJ&E. The wings were moved out and back and up and down by the air cylinders. (Bill Raia collection.)

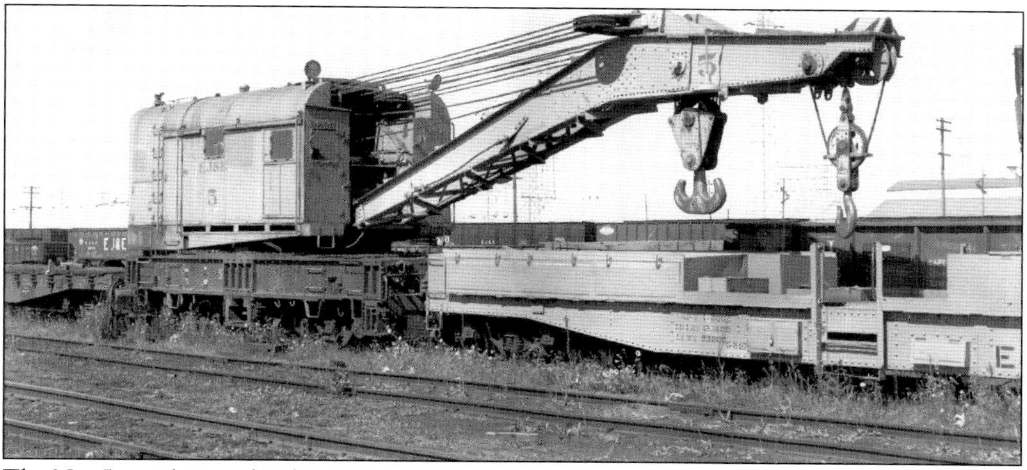

The No. 5 wrecker or "hook" appears here at Gary on September 1968. It was rated at 150 tons lifting capacity. Though designed for handling derailed and overturned cars, the hooks were sometimes used for other heavy jobs around the railroad. Older wreckers on many railroads were usually powered by an internal steam engine. The EJ&E powered its later derricks with a diesel motor. (Bill Raia collection.)

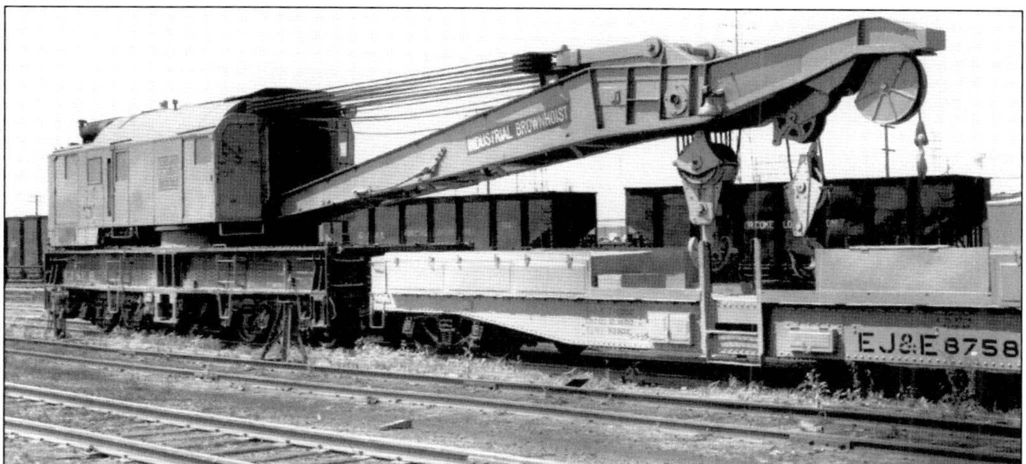

This was the one that railroaders referred to as the "Big!" hook. The Industrial Brownhoist Company in Bay City, Michigan, built it. No. 6 was rated at 250 tons capacity. A derrick of this size was powered by two diesel engines of 600 horsepower each. Because of its tremendous lifting capacity, other railroads often borrowed it and the work train that went with it. (Bill Raia collection.)

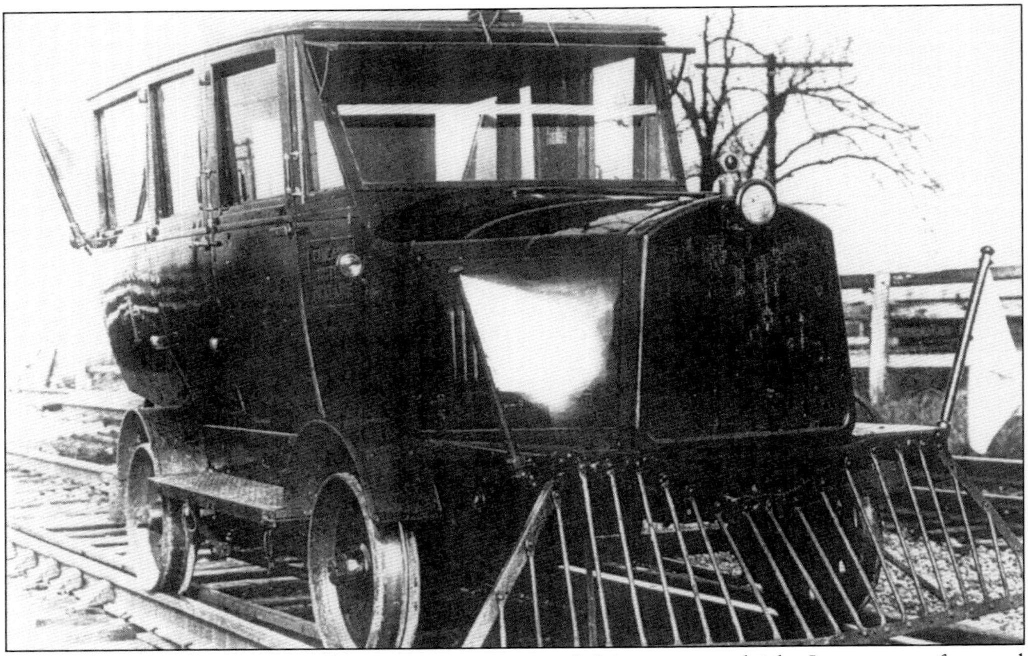

The EJ&E officials, for on-track inspection trips, used this strange vehicle. It was one of several motors used by the EJ&E over the years.

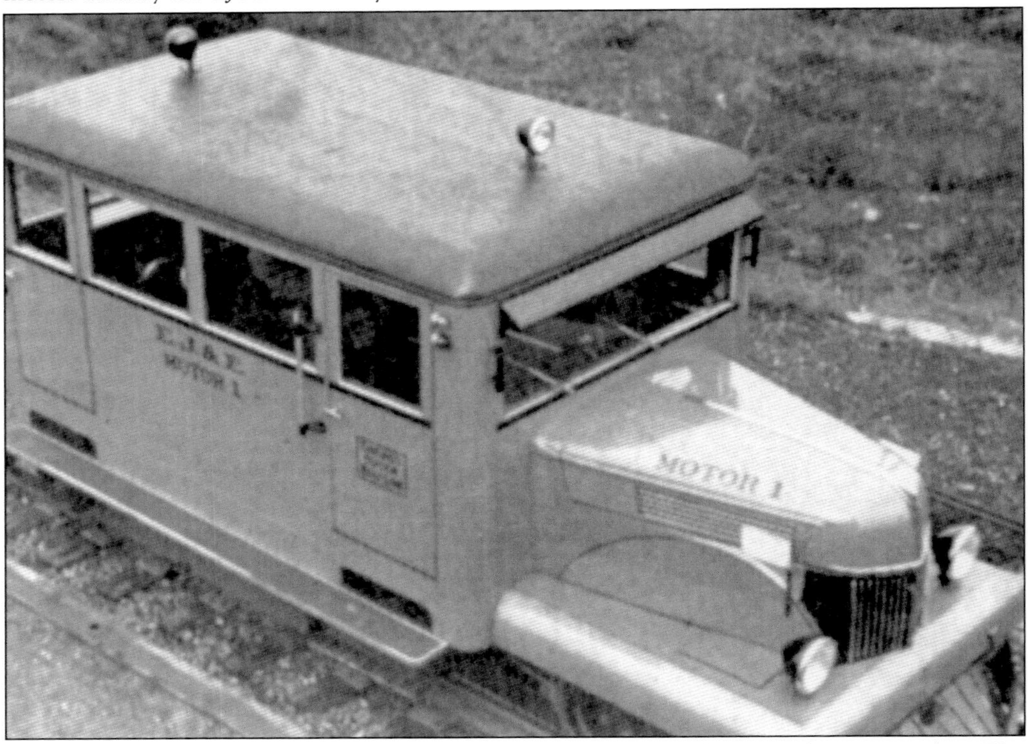

By the 1930s, officials could ride in comfort and were well shielded from inclement weather. The inspection cars were always designated with the number one.

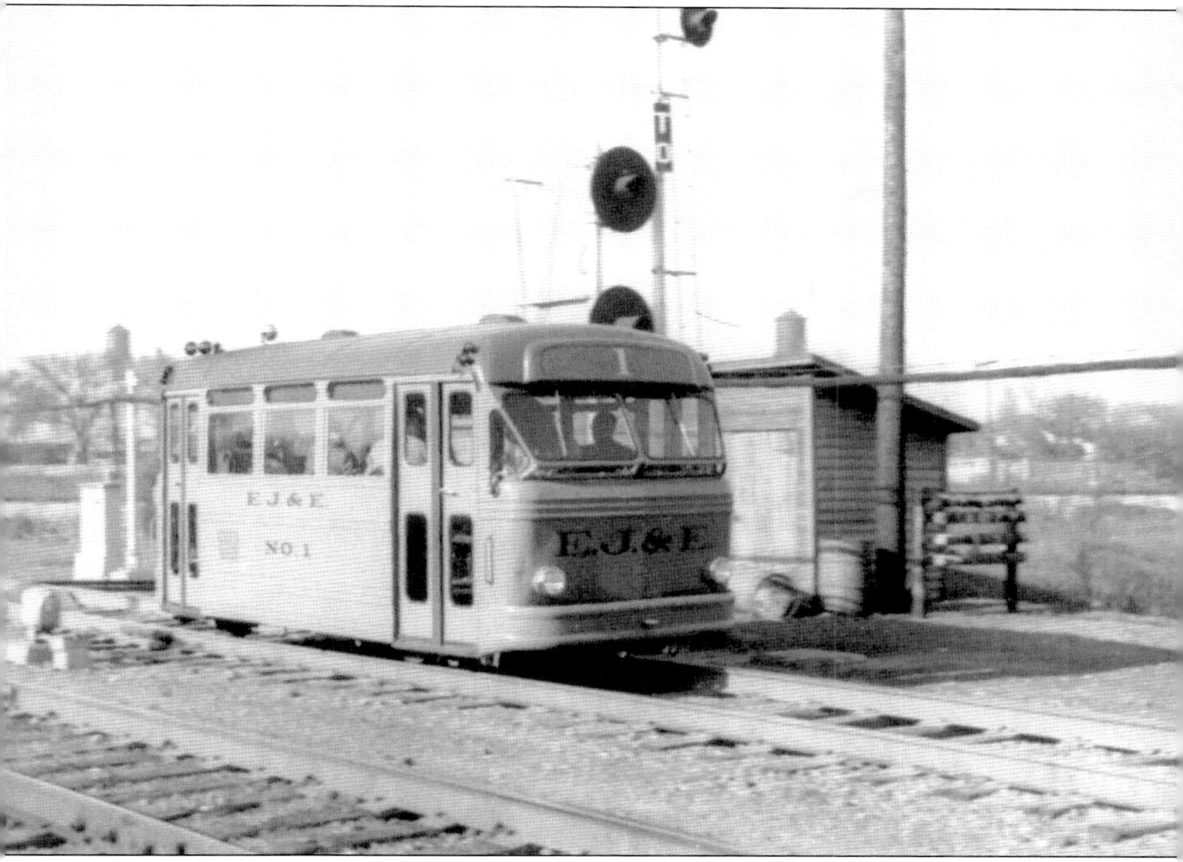

This "Motor 1" was obviously the nicest one. It is shown here at the Rock Island tower going east on a summer morning in 1958. Because the employees have always been conscious of working safely, the EJ&E has always, and still does, deliver dependable transportation services to its customers day after day, year after year. (R. A. Eisenbrandt.)